THE
MARATHON
MAKERS

FOREWORD BY SEBASTIAN COE

THE MARATHON MAKERS

JOHN BRYANT

A Century Ago Three Heroes
Changed the Course of the Olympics
This is Their Dramatic True Story

JOHN BLAKE

Published by John Blake Publishing Ltd,
3 Bramber Court, 2 Bramber Road,
London W14 9PB, England

www.blake.co.uk

First published in hardback in 2008

ISBN 978 1 84454 560 5

British Library Cataloguing-in-Publication Data:

A catalogue record for this book is available from the British Library.

Design by www.envydesign.co.uk

Printed and bound in Great Britain by William Clowes Ltd, Beccles, Suffolk

1 3 5 7 9 10 8 6 4 2

Papers used by John Blake Publishing are natural, recyclable products made
from wood grown in sustainable forests. The manufacturing processes
conform to the environmental regulations of the country of origin.

Every attempt has been made to contact the relevant copyright-holders,
but some were unobtainable. We would be grateful if the appropriate
people could contact us.

For Grace and Tess, and all those who
follow in their footsteps

FOREWORD

From its mythical military origins in the small Greek town of Marathon approximately 2,500 years ago, the act of running a marathon has become a universal symbol of achievement and inspiration, and organised marathons – especially at Olympic Games and in major cities around the world – have become a pinnacle of personal achievement recognized and respected in countries and cultures around the world.

While major mass participation marathons are landmark events for athletes of all standards, attracting global TV coverage and international attention for cities hosting them and their participants, the development of the marathon as one of sport's greatest attractions remains less well known – a situation which is skilfully addressed in this new book by former Fleet Street editor, author and sports enthusiast John Bryant.

In the finest traditions of *Chariots of Fire*, Bryant's book vividly recreates one of the most dramatic days and events in sport – the 1908 Olympic Games Marathon in London, an epic contest which, along with the intense rivalries, idealism, controversies and spectacle of the Games shaped the evolution of modern sporting culture.

Appropriately entitled *The Marathon Makers*, the book follows the fates of legendary runners Dorando Pietri from Italy and American Johnny Hayes, who took the emerging sport of competitive distance running to the extremes of human endurance, and so helped the marathon distance establish itself for ever in the popular imagination. They, along with the British sprinter Wyndham Halswelle, the embodiment of modern Olympic founder Pierre de Coubertins's vision for sport as central to creating a fair society, helped to establish the unique aura of the Olympic Games as the world's most important sporting, social and cultural event.

Bryant's book is a timely tribute to the early Olympic athletes whose performances captured the imagination of the world and laid the foundations for the Games to flourish, and provides a compelling reminder to all Olympic and Paralympic organisers of the power of the Games to inspire and change lives. This is the central focus of the London 2012 Games, which will build on the bravery, courage and efforts of the athletes and organisers of the 1908 London Olympic Games so well documented in the following pages in ways that will inspire future generations.

Seb Coe
Chairman, London 2012 Games

ACKNOWLEDGEMENTS

A book, like a marathon, can never make it to the finish without enormous help and support from an army of enthusiasts.

The friendship and support of Dave Bedford, the race director of the London Marathon, has been invaluable, and his tireless team and relentless pace setting has kept *The Marathon Makers* on course.

My lifelong running companion, Olympic Marathon runner Donald Macgregor, is an inspiring researcher and he and Stan Greenberg, one of the world's foremost track and field statisticians, have kept me firmly on track.

From Carpi, Italy, the birthplace of Dorando, my gratitude goes to Ivano Barbolini, the director of the Maratona d'Italia Memorial Enzo Ferrari and all his team, both for their research and permission to use their archive of pictures, along with Cristina Corradi, Luciana Nora, Augusto Frasca and Mirco Barbolini.

In the United States the efforts of Wayne Baker proved invaluable. My thanks also go to Walter MacGowan, Elliott Denman, Roger Robinson, Mary Wittenberg, Guy Morse, Gloria Ratti, George Hirsch, Ralph Cohn and Amby Burfoot.

Doug Gillon in Glasgow, Nancy Murphy in Tipperary, Ireland, and Nick Barrett, genealogist, helped me bring both Halswelle and Hayes to life. From the Flora London Marathon team there were invaluable contributions from John Disley, Nick Bitel, Brian Webber, Nicola Okey and many others.

Special thanks to Volker Kluge, a fine Olympic historian; Jan Paterson and Amy Terriere of the British Olympic Association; to Bob Wilcock, for permission to use his archive of 1908 postcards; to my agent Mark Lucas; Peter Lovesey, Steve Torrington, Dave Terry, Neil Allen, William Cockerel, Judith von Bradsky and Helen Elliott. And, of course, to Lamine Diack of the IAAF and Seb Coe for their generous words of endorsement.

I would like to express thanks for permission to quote from many newspapers. In Britain, *The Times*, the *Daily Mail*, the *Windsor Express*, the *Daily Telegraph*, the *Pall Mall Gazette* and *The Sportsman* proved invaluable. In the United States the *New York Times*, the *Boston Herald*, the *San Francisco Chronicle* and many others gave life and colour to the athletes of a century ago.

I am most grateful to all those fellow journalists and their newspapers who originally reported such vivid and compelling accounts of the races.

Thanks, too, to the skill and encouragement of John Blake and his team and my editor at John Blake Publishing, Clive Hebard.

Above all, for patience in the face of an obsession with running and writing that brought *The Marathon Makers* to the finishing tape, thanks to my wife Carol and my sons, Matthew and William.

PREFACE

It is with the greatest of pleasure that I write these few words of introduction to this wonderful narrative of the first Marathon run over what has now become the standard distance of 42,195 metres – the metric equivalent of the imperial 26 miles and 385 yards – which was established one hundred years ago at the 1908 London Olympics. That race also produced the legendary runs of Dorando Pietri and Johnny Hayes and added two more heroes to the annals of our sport.

The story of the Marathon Race is emblematic. Today, just the mention of the word Marathon evokes visions of thousands of runners competing in the big city marathons around the world. The Marathon has become one of the most visible manifestations of the sport of athletics and it is, along with road races run over lesser distances, the greatest participation sport in the world.

For millions of runners around the world this distance has also become magical, the symbol of personal challenge and a sign of individual achievement. Running the Marathon in the company of thousands of other runners, be they elite athletes or fun runners, is now a social phenomenon that is also a wonderful expression of athleticism. Over the years, it has also grown into a major source of funds for a huge range of charitable causes. The Marathon race has become a symbol of peace, of charity and of positive social change, providing the stimulus for hundreds of thousands of people to adopt a healthier lifestyle while creating a sense of community for runners around the world at all levels, irrespective of age or ethnicity, social class or ideologies. This is the same ethos that the whole sport of athletics embraces and which is a fundamental principle of the International Association of Athletics Federations.

The IAAF is extremely appreciative of this development and in 2007 created a dedicated Commission to examine ways in which we, as the world governing body of athletics and all areas of road running, can increase our participation in and support of this most dynamic branch of our sport, a sport that owes much of its success to the dedication and commitment of individual race organisers and the vision of the directors of the city marathons.

From the recognition of world records for road races to the introduction of the IAAF Road Race Label, endorsing the world's leading road races, and our ongoing work with AIMS (the Association of International Marathons and Distance Races) on the standardisation of the best measurement practices for road races, we will continue to give all our support to the future growth of road running around the world.

Lamine Diack
IAAF Presiden

CONTENTS

Introduction: The Great Dorando   xv

1   Once a Winner   1

2   A Taste of Defeat   7

3   Two Wheels to Happiness   13

4   Conan Doyle and the Mystery of the Dirty War   23

5   The Stamp of Love   31

6   Cheating for Boys   37

7   Digging and Dreaming   43

8   The Soldier Returns   53

9   In Love with a Legend   63

10   The Race that Saved the Games   69

11   Torn Apart by Passion   77

12   The Baron's Lost Vision   81

13   The Shambles of St Louis   89

14   The Great American Winning Machine   97

15   Humbled by Distance   103

16	Eruptions in Athens	109
17	Meet Mr Fair Play	117
18	I Will Win or I Will Die	125
19	A Ticket to London	131
20	Secrets of the Great White City	139
21	No Earthly King	149
22	The Tug-of-War Nations	159
23	Testing Positive for Profit	171
24	By Royal Command?	179
25	The Marathon Contenders	191
26	The Great Halswelle Affair	199
27	The Road From Windsor	209
28	The Man Who Lost and Won	221
29	A Fair Field and No Favour	227
30	The Morning After	235
31	The Lion in Chains	243
32	Marathon Mania	249
33	The Sweet Music of Fame	257
34	Running to Death	265
35	Victoria's Secrets	277
36	The Battle Is Over	289
	Afterword	297
	Appendix I *Entries for the 1908 Olympic Marathon*	301
	Appendix II *Result of the 1908 Olympic Marathon*	307
	Appendix III *Dorando Pietri's Marathon Career*	309
	Index	315

– INTRODUCTION –

THE GREAT
DORANDO

In the spring of 1948, in a London still recovering from the Blitz, a diminutive, middle- aged and slightly balding café owner from Birmingham turned up, and announced to the world: 'I am the Great Dorando.'

He stepped out of the shadows to haunt the Olympic Games, which were staged defiantly in this austere city that was still patching itself up from the ravages of war; he swanned his way around town, cashing in on the Olympic fever that was beginning to build up in the press, and would boast colourfully of the exploits of forty years before.

Dorando told the tale of how, on a scorching hot day in July 1908, he had staggered into the stadium at Shepherd's Bush looking near to death, and how he stole headlines around the world during one of those endless Edwardian summers before the war to end all wars ripped the world apart. He told how the famously evocative picture of him reeling and collapsing dramatically at the finish of London's first-ever Marathon had turned him, like Charlie Chaplin, into one of the first internationally recognised celebrities of the twentieth century.

In the London of 1948, he was invited for drinks here, a lunch there. For one crazy moment he was the hero men still spoke of whenever they told of the Marathon.

'I am,' he boldly asserted, 'the man who long ago launched the great marathon craze on both sides of the Atlantic Ocean. I am the man who thousands flocked to see when I conquered the finest runners in the Madison Square Garden in New York. I am the man who was given a special Golden Cup by the hands of the Queen of England herself for my pluck, my courage and for Italy.'

By the time he strutted around Britain's capital, two world wars had wiped the name and the memory of Dorando from the headlines. But here, as a battle-weary world once more turned their thoughts to the bloodless struggle of sport, the legend seemed to rise from the dead.

On 5 August 1948, as the day of the Games loomed closer, four Italians from Dorando Pietri's hometown of Carpi, near Modena in Italy, along with three reporters, turned up on his doorstep to meet him. The Italians began to talk to Dorando in the lilting strains of the local Carpigian dialect, and as the panic showed in the imposter's eyes, one of them told how he had seen the real Dorando lowered into his grave in 1942 and inspected the words on his tombstone, announcing that here lay the 'Champion Runner of the World – Gold Medallist'.

A few days after the hoaxer was unmasked, the *Evening News* in London printed an apology to the real Dorando's widow, Teresa Dondi, who lived on until 1979 in San Remo. The hoax

Pietri's real name was Pietro Palleschi. He was married to an English woman called Lucy Evans, born in Tuscany, and in 1948 he was 65 years old. Pictures in the London newspapers taken outside the Temperance Bar he ran in Barford Street, Birmingham, show him in a white coat.

It was an amazing story but such was the power of the man who, forty years before, had shaped the future of twentieth-century sport, that, like others from those same Games in 1908, the legend lived on. The Games were important because they defined sporting archetypes that were to endure for the better part of a century.

As the life of Queen Victoria drifted to a close, a new century was opening: the century of the Edwardians, which swept in an era that was to bring the most profound changes – industrialisation, worldwide conflict and changes on a scale never seen before – changes that would overturn the rules by which we wage wars, run races and live our lives.

As the twentieth century was born, the British were at war with the Boers in South Africa. The theatre of that war was visited by those great chroniclers of Empire and chivalry, Rudyard Kipling and Arthur Conan Doyle. It brought fame to Robert Baden-Powell and sowed the seeds of the Boy Scout ethos that was to influence generations, who would die in far fiercer conflicts to come. And it set the stage for the young Winston Churchill, who witnessed the very rules of war mutate as he galloped through the century from horse to Spitfire.

The real spirit of the age was the way in which so many questioned the patterns of Old World thinking. At the beginning of the twentieth century, Britain was the most powerful nation in the world. A quarter of the world's land mass, and a quarter of the world's population, owed allegiance to the Union Jack. Occasional setbacks such as the British defeat by the guerrilla tactics of an amateur army of Dutch settlers in the Boer War could be taken in their stride, but other nations were confident of taking up the challenge to British supremacy. Increasingly, Germany posed as the new strong man of Europe, and across the Atlantic America was confident that she would soon outstrip Britain as the most powerful nation on earth.

Sport, like every other aspect of life in the new century, was in a state of revolutionary change; already the hard edge of professionalism was cutting into the character of games codified by the Victorians to help civilise the gentleman amateur. Spectators who could pay their monies at the turnstiles were becoming central to the progress and conduct of team sports, and winning became more important than taking part. The spoils of victory could make you rich, or turn you into that strange new twentieth-century beast – the celebrity.

In 1896, Baron Pierre de Coubertin's dream of resurrecting the ancient Greek Olympics was realised. He had in mind conduct and rules for competitors that embraced fair play yet prepared them to be physically fit for the battlefields of the future. The objective of this French aristocrat was to promote a vision of sport uncorrupted by the real world. De Coubertin saw sport as pure, unsullied by professionalism, nationalism and the drive to win at all costs.

But these were never the values of the ancient Greek Olympics. Rather, they were the romantic and mythological values of the European middle classes, practised by the gentlemen amateurs who prided themselves on playing the game. Despite de Coubertin's idealism, however, the nations of the world refused to play the game on the Olympic track or in the trenches.

On the very eve of those 1908 Games, world leaders met at The Hague to lay down the laws of war. They thought they could civilise war, come to terms with the industrialisation of war machines – which now included weapons of mass destruction, bombs, balloons, the aeroplane and poison gas – and prescribe codes of conduct for struggles yet to come. Also there at The Hague in May 1907, the International Olympic Committee was eager to take on board British proposals for the future conduct of the Olympic movement, and following the Games in 1908, the British sporting authorities, appalled by the rows and rivalries that had nearly wrecked the Olympics, commissioned a sixty-page report to defend what the British regarded as the laws of sport.

Conan Doyle, who was knighted for writing a history of the Boer War, was fiercely critical of the way the Boer had used dirty tricks in South Africa. He believed soldiers should stand and battle cleanly in a fair fight and scorned the part-time guerrilla or the invisible sniper.

At the Olympics, which he attended as a reporter for the *Daily Mail*, he was equally critical of those who tried to cheat or bully their way to victory. But cheating and bullying, particularly by what the British knew as 'athletics' and the Americans as 'track and field', was to be so fierce that the London Olympic Games of 1908 were to be remembered as 'The Battle of Shepherd's Bush'. The fallout from those Games was to haunt sport for one hundred years and give us the sporting archetypes recognised today.

These were never quaint nostalgic Games. Instead, they brutally foreshadowed the path Olympic sport was to take in the future. The most immediate legacy from 1908 came from the Marathon course that gave birth to the standard marathon distance now accepted worldwide. But the most enduring legacy came in the way sport was to be defined throughout the twentieth century.

That hoaxer who turned up in London in 1948 was an embodiment of the myths and mysteries that surround the 1908 Games. Here was a man trading on somebody else's fame, somebody else's legend. He knew that those Games were still alive in folk memory and, in victory or defeat, what lives on is greatness; we thirst for legends. The Games of 1908 were packed with legends and the hoaxer realised that in Dorando he had the perfect example of one money-spinning legend – the sporting celebrity.

Baron de Coubertin fought in vain to keep the Olympics free from professionalism, nationalism and winning at all costs, but these Games were ferociously competitive and soon descended into international uproar. Too many, it seemed, believed in the great fallacy that sport is first and last about winning. It never is – it's about style and it's about glory. Some of the athletes who lined up for the gun in 1908 realised that truth.

The winners and losers might have caught an echo of that sentiment in the words of the American sports writer and poet Grantland Rice, penned while the scars of the 1908 Olympic Games were still painful and raw:

When the One Great Scorer comes
To write against your name,
He marks – not that you won or lost –
But how you played the Game.

– CHAPTER 1 –

ONCE A WINNER

Wyndham Halswelle peeled off his shirt and twisted it between powerful hands until the sweat splashed dark patches like blood on the parched, dusty track. He smiled at the man screwing his eyes up at a watch.

'I can win this, even here,' he said. 'About the only thing that can stop me is a bullet in the back – I can beat them all.'

'You can,' said the trooper, 'but it's not the Dutchmen you've got to worry about, it's the men who line up alongside you.'

Wyndham Halswelle, young, strong and a soldier, knew all about winning; it had filled his life for as long as he could remember. He searched for the smell of it, the secret of it everywhere. He saw the prospect of winning on the flags of armies, in the stride of an athlete, in the courage of a statesman and in the physical perfection of a warrior.

Halswelle was born on 30 May 1882, at No. 4 Albemarle

Street, Piccadilly, in the heart of the great British Empire. He was born into a city that seemed to rule the world, a city full of energy that could inspire great literature and a tumult of ideas. Here was the Westminster that laid down the laws that echoed around the world. But here too, just a few miles to the east, was Whitechapel, home of Jack the Ripper, where a man might tear your life and your dreams apart under the cover of darkness.

Halswelle's father was an artist and a prosperous one. His mother, Helen, came from a traditional army background. She was fiercely proud of her grandfather, Nathaniel Gordon, a major general in the Indian Army, who carried his scars and his medals with pride.

There was much talk of military tradition, of Scotland and of his father, Keeley Halswelle, who earned his living as a water-colourist and had exhibited in London and Edinburgh. Keeley travelled frequently to Paris and Italy, looking for the light and for inspiration. He was an associate of the Royal Academy and when he died in Paris in April 1891, his estate was valued at around £2 million in today's terms.

As a child, Wyndham looked up to his mother, that fierce upholder of the family military tradition. Mama always said he would be a soldier. Born in London, he wrapped himself in his Scottish heritage. Occasionally he would play with his older brother, Gordon – christened with the family name that his mother admired so much – but from the age of five, Wyndham lived in a world of his own. He was forever playing soldiers.

On the days when it rained, he would manoeuvre his armies of tin soldiers in the drawing room of the family home in Richmond. Then, whenever the sun shone, he would be out in the garden or the park, marching and drilling his brother and his imaginary troops on the well-kept lawn there. Sometimes he would sport the uniform that his mother had bought for him. He dreamed his dreams and nothing in or out of school so preoccupied him as tales of chivalry and knights fighting in single combat.

As a teenager, Wyndham was strikingly fluid. He moved with an animal grace and the languid, loose-limbed lilt of a cricketer. At school, the younger boys were mesmerised, hanging around him and hero-worshipping him a little, drawn by his magnetism and his athleticism. They would do anything for him and would quarrel over who would scrape the mud from his studded boots, who would massage the grease into the soft leather of his running spikes.

The mothers of other boys who visited the school would smile at his easy good looks and his cascading blond hair. By fifteen, he was winning all the foot races at school, but as his schooldays drew to a close, he was excited by the rumblings of the war to come in South Africa, a war that would test and harden the soldiers of the Queen in battle.

Young Wyndham longed to get out of Charterhouse School and into Sandhurst, Britain's Royal military academy, where he could train to be a real soldier. His greatest fear was that the war would be over by Christmas; he ached for the chance to fall in with the others tramping off to the troop ships to the haunting marching tune of 'Goodbye Dolly Gray'. When he signed up for Sandhurst at his mother's insistence, his father struggled with his own disappointment that his talented boy would cut himself off from his artistic side. But Keeley Halswelle understood that most young men were only interested in war, young girls and sport. For Wyndham, the world was just awakening and he was interested in all these things.

3

Photographs were rare enough at this time, but one captured the young Wyndham caught between school and the military academy, showing his youthful spirits, vaulting with a grin over his sister-in-law Ethel. Another caught him long jumping over a wheelbarrow on those well-trimmed lawns in Richmond.

Halswelle was determined to demonstrate to his father that he could achieve things in the world on his own account, that he too could be a winner. And to do so he did not have to prove himself, either in the artistic studio of his father or in the regiment of his mother. Sport was his canvas: he would win his races and he would remember with a smile the admiring knots of schoolboys cheering his victories and saluting his triumphs.

That summer, as the war in South Africa warmed up, he gave his father a glimpse of the different kind of artist that he himself could be – an artist on the track. At Sandhurst, the admiring schoolboys were now replaced by senior officers who recognised, however fleetingly, that they were being seduced by the magic of a man in motion. For Wyndham Halswelle really could run. Even among fine sprinters, men who fancied themselves as quick movers and who were so fancied by others, this was an exceptional man.

A boy like that, the officers would say, needs a trainer, someone to show him how to be a great champion. Such men existed, but mainly across the Atlantic, where the New World's first athletic coaches were already issuing orders to their well-drilled squads and where they reckoned that men like Halswelle lacked the killer instinct. In England, they would say, they churn out good losers but there's no such thing as a good loser – it's kill or be killed. In sport it is always the winning that matters. But for Halswelle running was about far more than just winning, it was an expression of the human body, of rhythm and grace, strength and belief. He loved to win, of course, but for him the satisfaction was to do it on a level playing field in an even contest.

Sometimes he would share his philosophy of winning with his friends at Sandhurst. They would smile over a drink and a cigar, and the soldiers would joke that all this talk of fair play would someday be the death of young Halswelle.

– CHAPTER 2 –

A TASTE OF DEFEAT

In spring 1902, Wyndham Halswelle's affair with the running track came to an abrupt end. He and his regiment were packed off to South Africa, where Lord Kitchener was mopping up the war. Here, he was to get his first taste of action.

Once again, Wyndham was a six-year-old drilling his tin soldiers on the lawn, taking on the enemy face to face in single combat as he had done in his playground fantasies. Life at the front, though, turned out to be very different. There were huge periods of inactivity while he would kick his heels waiting for the chance to be a hero, but there were other opportunities to play the hero on the playing field or on the running track.

When Halswelle landed in South Africa in 1902, he just caught the end of that strange business, the Boer War. The Boers, who were the off-cuts of Dutch colonialists, were keen to fight for their independence from Britain but they were not so keen to bring the benefits of democracy to those who had descended on this part of the world in search of gold and diamonds – the get-rich-quick merchants. Certainly, they were completely against any idea of extending the franchise to the black population, the indigenous people they found in the land in which they made their home.

As soon as Halswelle moved with his regiment, the Highland Light Infantry, towards the front, he found that the fighting had descended into a messy guerrilla conflict. He was keen to fulfil his dream of getting a taste of the action but his vision of himself was as a soldier, someone who would take on an opponent in a fair fight man to man, face to face. This war was baffling to the young soldier; it was a dirty war.

Wyndham Halswelle had been brought up with a code of chivalry that was remarkable for its lack of realism. Fellow troopers would talk of snipers and the guns that could deliver death without the giveaway trail of smoke emitting from their own British rifles. Given half a chance, they would say, these Dutchmen will shoot you in the back.

Life outside the city of Bloemfontein was a mixture of infrequent fighting and unbearable boredom. The troops would arrange spontaneous cricket and football matches, picnics, fêtes and parties. They weren't always peaceful either, for there was plenty of drink around. Fights would break out, and gambling, which could land you on a charge, was rife. There was no shortage of women or civilians around the block houses and tented camps. Plenty of men had wives and children back in Britain, but that never stopped them from picking up the women around the camp.

Halswelle shone at cricket and football, though rugby, his

chosen game, was not popular among the men. Almost every morning, he would be found running around the camp to keep in shape and a lot of his off-duty hours were spent complaining about the nature of the war and the conduct of the Boers.

His daydreams at Sandhurst invariably had him facing hordes of fanatical natives or the disciplined ranks of crack European troops. There was glory in that daydream. But Halswelle and his fellow officers shared their doubts and sometimes contempt for the Boers, who, though God-fearing, did not shape up as an acceptable enemy. They were scruffy and had no professional army as such; often they wore no uniform either.

Plenty of men in the regiment knew of Halswelle's reputation as a runner.

'Why don't you take a race here?' they would ask, but Wyndham seemed wary of racing far from the organised meetings he had known back in Britain. He would watch and shake his head at the sight of a few men toeing a line scratched in the dirt, then barging their way to the finish.

This was never quite the way it was at Sandhurst, where the track was marked out with painted white lines on firm grass, measurements were accurate and the starter controlled everything. You ran to orders there, but here the course was a roughly paced-out distance over hard, dusty, uneven ground. Close to the battlefront there was no finishing tape, no fancy running, and nowhere to dig decent holes for your spiked shoes on the starting line. But when the requests to run turned to taunts, Wyndham thought again. Perhaps he might race there, after all.

His appearance on the track was enough to stir groups of soldiers to watch him in action. They knew this tall, muscled, slightly tanned man, whose white vest contrasted with the reddening of his skin, had been a champion; his very appearance could cause a ripple of excitement. It was not that often you got the chance to see a runner of his calibre in action. You could only guess what was likely to happen when a man like this toed the line.

If there is one thing that excites spectators, it is the chance to witness a champion performing, asserting his dominance with power and authority. But they can be excited, perhaps even more so, by the prospect of seeing a champion, a certainty, toppled and humbled by a dark horse. The bookmakers love to see that too, and some of the officers remembered the time back at Sandhurst when even the mighty Halswelle tripped and fell hard on the track.

Gambling always seemed to be in evidence whenever such impromptu race meetings were organised by the regiment in South Africa. 'Evens on the field,' the bookies would murmur, and the murmur would breeze around the camp. Of course, they shouldn't have been there, for betting was strictly prohibited. But when it came to gambling or taking prisoners, you could always find an officer who seemed blind or deaf. It was difficult to stop a trooper from putting a handful of shillings on a runner they fancied, or a race where they seemed certain of the outcome.

Win or lose, this was the chance to see a gifted runner in action. Where, they wondered, did he get that extra ingredient that makes one athlete dominant? Sometimes technical differences make a champion – some wear spiked shoes, others dig starting holes, while cork grips may be strapped to the hands with elastic bands, for there was a theory that sprinters ran faster if they had something to grip onto.

But none of these techniques accounted for Halswelle's superiority. Whenever he lined up for races, he looked preoccupied, aloof almost; slowly and silently he moved to the start. But even here, so far from Sandhurst, one sensed the starter's orders would spark an explosion.

'Strip out, gentlemen, please!' came the booming command. The crowd would hush, waiting to catch a glimpse of the eight or nine figures crouching to strain for the first smoke of the gun that would pitch them forwards like shots from a sniper. For a moment, they would be frozen and the stomachs of the spectators would flutter as they held their breath, waiting to witness the young, fit men fighting to get the better of each other in this trial of strength, speed and will.

Then they'd be off, with some heavy-footed and making fierce noises as they moved, others staying too long in contact with the South African soil between strides. Their facial expressions were quite extraordinary too. Teeth were clenched in ferocious or agonised grimaces. Some looked as though they were snarling. Heads would be thrown back or jerked to one side; arms thrashed wildly instead of pumping in time with the legs. Energy would be spent recklessly as torsos rocked and twisted. It was like watching men trying to grab a lifeline just out of reach.

But when Halswelle came out of the holes he had scraped at the start, he was a revelation. You could see that he had a gift, that he ran with fire in his belly. Once he took off, he seemed to gain a yard or two just by starting.

It was hard to believe that a man could fly into action so quickly. There was no slow build-up, no hesitancy, no changing of gear. Ruthlessly, smoothly, the legs produced a stride that could cut through the opposition like a sword on the battlefield. The body was steady, the face showed no strain. Arms and legs moved forward with no sideways sway; the head looked as though it were floating, with no rise and no fall – it was all poise, pace and purpose.

Like an arrow snapped from a bowstring, he reached towards a finish that wasn't just a simple piece of rope between two posts but a declaration of his rightful place as a champion. For other runners a race was fun, a gamble, a game – maybe a way to a prize – but to Wyndham Halswelle it was a declaration of his identity.

'By God,' one of the troopers muttered, his eyes shining as he watched him run, 'he's got class!' But even as he ran, the gambling men, those who had taken the illicit bets, knew what was to come.

As Halswelle eased ahead, one man clawing his way down the track stretched forwards a hand and clipped his trailing leg. Suddenly, the beauty of the arrow that seemed to be heading straight for the target was thrown off-course. Halswelle tripped, one leg smacked against the other, then he lurched. It was his own speed, his own purity of motion, that brought him crashing down.

He fell heavily, his hands scraped red raw by the sand. His knees, from which the blood dripped, left stains where the blood met the dust of the veldt. Halswelle shook his head in anger: he had been way in front and the other runners knew it, but he had been robbed. It was enough to make him want to throw the whole thing in.

Looking down at him was a trooper shaking his own head in disbelief. The man who hauled Halswelle to his feet that day was a squat, tough-looking member of the regiment with an accent that reeked of the borders between England and Scotland. His name was Jimmy Curran.

'You need to learn a thing or two, sir,' he said, looking down at the fallen man. It was a meeting that was to change both their lives.

– CHAPTER 3 –

TWO WHEELS TO HAPPINESS

D orando Pietri took his first, wobbly steps in the sleepy
      village of Mandrio, a 20- minute jog-trot from the town
of Carpi, between Verona and Bologna in the north-east of Italy
– a maze of cobbled streets huddled around a grand piazza and
still, in the days when Pietri was young, half hidden behind the
city walls. His father, Desiderio, scraped a living where he could –
selling fruit, baking bread, renting a shop here, a market stall there.

Dorando was born on 16 October 1885, the third of four sons.
A small, wiry child, he was full of energy – strong as a bull, they
used to say – and always hungry. With three sons to feed and
another on the way, Desiderio would drag his wife, Maria, and
their family from village to village and from town to town,
desperately seeking work.

At one point, in search of pay, Desiderio took his family to
settle in Carpi, the traditional centre for the making of straw hats,

with grasses to plait and softening water flowing through its streams. It was here, in a new century of industrialisation and mass production, that men from Rome would tell you how a machine could make as many hats in a day as a family might fashion in a week. People poured into Carpi in the hope that the hat trade might bring them if not wealth then at least sufficient prosperity to fill the stomachs of their children.

Even then, there was a special, indefinable quality about Dorando. Somehow he sensed that the world ran far beyond the horizons of Carpi. He had learned from his restless older brothers that adventure and perhaps even fortune and fame were to be had out there beyond the town. To the south was Rome while to the north were London and Paris. He would hear snippets of news from there; sometimes strange words, unfamiliar accents, even foreign languages as travellers and businessmen passed through Carpi.

Sometimes, too, visitors would come to the piazza and Dorando would sit open-mouthed in wonder as the first flickering silent movies gave him glimpses of a world beyond even the wonders of Rome and Paris. Here was America, a new land of promise where any dream seemed possible. His father was a labourer while his mother looked after them all by scouring the markets for food, and although Desiderio and Maria had never learned to read without effort, they could add up well enough. They understood enough to know that this new century might offer the chance to make more lire by your wits than by your hands.

They had seen the frustration in the eyes of the two elder brothers, Antonio and Ulpiano. Carpi, it seemed, was always too small for them. The builders and developers were beginning to pull down the city walls, but for Antonio and Ulpiano, the place seemed like a prison and they couldn't wait to leave.

While Dorando's father sold apples and roasted chestnuts close to the market in Carpi, Antonio, who was six years older than Dorando, tried to make his way by working in the hat factory. But he hated it, for it was noisy and it reeked of sulphur, while the constant need to lift heavy parcels was too much like hard work.

'I feel trapped, it's like being a slave,' Antonio would complain restlessly.

Ulpiano, four years older than his brother Dorando, had no intention of being a slave. He was restless and ambitious. Even as a boy, those who knew him would say there was something shifty about him.

'He looked like a little fox,' said a boyhood friend, who'd spent a lifetime making shoes in Carpi. 'He had the face of someone full of cunning so he went to England – he'd do anything to get out of Italy. Ulpiano was on the make. He learned English, got to know what life was like out there in the world. He was always going to make a fortune, one way or the other.'

Dorando's mother and father had seen how their elder sons had felt about staying on in Carpi, and they didn't want Dorando to go the same way. They clung onto him.

'You'll never be hungry here at home,' his mother would say, while his father, also small and wiry, was forever pointing out to him the important men who ran the hotels, the hat factory, even the big sports club La Patria in Carpi.

'Look,' he'd say, 'you can make something of yourself here in Carpi. You don't have to spend your life selling fruit and bread like me. You're a little boy now, but you can be a big man. You don't have to leave. Show them you can do it, right here in Carpi.'

It was as if a torch had been passed into Dorando's hand, like a gift from father to son; it lit up his life. He looked at those people in Carpi with new eyes and saw the ones who represented something grander than others renting a shop here or a stall there. They were big men and he studied their every move, watched what they represented. As his father's words stiffened his ambition, Dorando toyed with the idea of perhaps getting an apprenticeship or at least something more ambitious than helping with the shop.

Ultimately, it was his father's idea. He knew a man called Ferrari, who did watch and clock repairs, and soon Dorando was signed up as his apprentice. But Dorando had seen his brother Antonio wither over a job that kept him imprisoned; now he too found himself hunched for endless hours doing repetitive work.

'I can't stand it,' he admitted, and he made a bid for freedom. Bur he still harboured the dream of making a mark there in Carpi, and when a wealthy new shop owner moved to the town, he seized his opportunity. The name was Pasquale Melli and he was well known locally as the manufacturer of the famous Nazzani sweets, a company renowned throughout the whole of the Emilia region for the quality of their chocolate.

Melli was a real gentleman with a distinguished and elegant wife. He set himself and his family up in a fine shop just on the edge of the piazza. It was decorated throughout with sumptuous red velvet and with white seats, and there they sold chocolates of a kind never before available in Carpi. One of the specialities was an exquisite chocolate drink, but of course the only people who could afford such delicacies were the gentry. They could pay for home delivery too, because when they ordered blocks of chocolate, sweets and pastries, they wanted the luxuries delivered to their doorstep.

Fourteen-year-old Dorando got a job with Melli, who needed a shop boy. There, he learned how to whisk *zabaglione* and he enjoyed putting the eggs and sugar into his mouth – now there would be no more crusts of bread for him. He busied himself delivering parcels and packages, wore a smart white overall and apron, and congratulated himself on finding his ideal job. He had the freedom to roam the city streets and he could eat as much as any boy might want.

His job would take him to the doors of the great villas that stood around Carpi, where he would meet the men and women who lived inside, smile at them and make the extra effort to try to deliver items on time. Nothing seemed too much for the energetic delivery boy and he took huge pleasure in what he was doing. Often, he had to deliver a package of luxury pastries to the station to be taken off the train for a customer further up the line.

On one occasion, so they say in Carpi, he got to the station to find that the train had already left for Reggio, which was nearly 15 miles away. Dorando actually saw the train slowly pulling out of the station and thought about running back to the shop to tell the owner what had happened, but then he changed his mind, whipped off his apron and set out to run the 15 miles, package in hand. When he arrived at the town centre, he took a handkerchief, dipped it into a horse trough and wiped away his sweat. He smoothed down his hair and presented himself at the door with the package of confectionery.

The door was answered by a maid, who told him to wait to see if there was a repeat order or a message for the shop. Then the master of the house arrived, intrigued by the hand delivery. He scribbled a note, pressed a tip into Dorando's hand and the boy set out for the return journey. Back in Carpi, the shopkeeper was at first amazed and annoyed, but when he heard what had happened, he was to dine out on the tale for years. Signor Melli realised, too, what Dorando's father had always known: this boy was very special.

The seasons changed and Dorando grew stronger. But he didn't grow any taller; he was always small, standing just 5 feet 3 inches tall. For him, the shop and the piazza – Victor Emmanuel Square – seemed to be the centre of all life in Carpi.

In 1903, there was a huge gathering in the piazza. A statue was to be erected to a general, Manfredo Fanti, and to celebrate the event thousands of gymnasts came from all corners of Italy to give a display. Dorando was dazzled by their appearance, their agility and their strength. With all the sudden enthusiasm of a 17-year-old, he decided that sport was the thing: here was a way that he might make his mark.

His brother Ulpiano had already joined the local sports club. He found that waving Indian clubs, the fashionable aerobic exercise, went down well with the girls. Also at that time, Italy, like the rest of Europe, was in the embrace of a huge cycling boom. Dorando and his friends would read about cycle races and talk to each other about their heroes; he was excited by the thought of bike racing, and so, like Ulpiano, he joined La Patria. He was young and strong, so perhaps he too could make a name for himself in Carpi as a cycle racer. Why not?

Some of the more well-to-do boys had bicycles of their own. Dorando would stand and stare at these machines; he would see the sparkling spokes and catch the smell of India rubber and freshly polished paint. He would run his fingers along the enamel of the tubing. Sometimes Signor Melli would give him a few sweets, and instead of eating them himself or sharing them with his younger brother Armando, Dorando would use them to bribe one of the boys who had a bike to let him try to cycle.

Even on the rough cobbled streets of Carpi, he learned to ride and he knew that somehow he had to get his hands on a bike. By saving his tips from deliveries, he found that he could hire a bike and take part in the races organised by La Patria in Modena, 20 miles or so from Carpi. It was here that Dorando had his first races and he loved them. His legs were already strong from his work as a messenger boy and he discovered that he was competitive at the sport.

Of course, the roads were rough, the tumbles were frequent and Dorando found that his small and lightweight body meant he was never going to beat some of the more powerful, bigger boys. Nevertheless, he did well enough, even though the bikes were crude and heavy. In one race, his chain broke, but he was not a boy to give up easily; he heaved the bike onto his shoulders and ran his way to the finish.

One afternoon, at the beginning of the autumn of 1904, Dorando stood at the door of the café looking out onto the square and watched as a crowd gathered to see a tall skinny man and his helpers walk around the piazza putting chalk marks on the cobbles. The man was Pericle Pagliani, a champion runner from Rome, he was told. 'Here,' the men said, 'is the mighty Pagliani. He's come to give a demonstration of running. He is the champion of all Italy – he can run like the wind.'

Dorando peered through the crowd. All the town had turned out and formed a huge circle, jostling for the best view, while allowing Pagliani enough room to run around his chalk marks. The word went round that he was going to run 10,000 metres.

Pagliani had circled the piazza for the second time when

several of the boys thought it would be fun to join in, and within another couple of laps he had a little trail of them puffing, blowing, laughing and jostling, trying to keep up with him. Four laps later, most of the boys, red in the face and gasping for breath, found the pace far tougher than anything they had known during their games on the streets.

But Dorando was running easily. Away from the cumbersome bike he found his legs felt very light. He knew every cobble of this square and as he floated behind Pagliani, the crowd first of all started to laugh, but then the laughter turned to cheering.

As the run went on, Dorando drew up alongside Pagliani and grinned. But the champion gave him little more than a glance, his eyes fixed on his task. Then, as Pagliani's friends yelled that there were only two laps to go, Dorando was still there running. As they passed the cheering, excited crowd, he eased smoothly and easily ahead and crossed the finishing line just before Pagliani.

The champion didn't say a word; he refused to acknowledge Dorando's existence and the errand boy stepped out of the square and went back to the shop. But others smiled at him and slapped him on the back.

'Hey, Dorando,' they shouted, 'you can be a champion too!'

The crowd clapped and cheered for a few moments but already most of them were melting away. They had taken time out from their jobs – from the bars, the factories and the fields – and they seemed to disappear very quickly. Their disappearance may perhaps have had something to do with the fact that Pagliani's helpers were roaming about the square with a bowl and a bucket asking for contributions to his training expenses. It was a deep and sobering shock for Dorando. Here was a man they'd applauded and cheered as the champion of all Italy – and now he was begging for money.

Dorando's father had always drummed into him, 'Never see yourself as a beggar. There's always work even here in Carpi, but never, ever be a beggar.' But here was Pagliani begging for money.

Dorando wished he had money with him so that he could put something in the bowl. Running with Pagliani had been fun and inspiring, and he had tingled with excitement when he heard the cheering of the crowd. The clank of the coins hitting the bottom of the near-empty bucket was to haunt Dorando for the rest of his life.

– CHAPTER 4 –

CONAN DOYLE AND THE MYSTERY OF THE DIRTY WAR

Sometimes it would take six weeks for the letters from Mama to reach the hands of Wyndham Halswelle, but when they eventually came they were long and well worth waiting for. The evocative letters reminded him of England and London itself. Mama's words would bring back the smell of cut grass on the lawn, the gentle rain that kept the great park in Richmond so very green, and strolls beside the River Thames, along the waterfront towards the gardens at Kew. But she would also write to him of serious matters, of war and politics.

The letters would remind Halswelle, too, of what made him a soldier – a word here or a phrase there would transport him right back to playing with those tin soldiers in Richmond or marching proudly in his playroom uniform. Mama would also bring him London's news of the war. She wrote so vividly of the relief of the siege of Mafeking in South Africa and the heroism and example of Robert Baden-Powell in Afghanistan.

'Never forget,' she wrote, 'that you and he were at the same school. You played in the same grounds. He's a great hero and a great soldier.'

By the time Halswelle arrived in South Africa in the spring of 1902, the great Boer War had been won, but was not yet finally over. The tide had turned with the arrival of two of Britain's most respected Generals: Lord Roberts and Lord Kitchener. Field Marshall Frederick Sleigh Roberts, Baron Roberts of Kandahar (known throughout the army as 'Little Bobs'), was virtually hauled out of retirement to turn the course of the difficult war. A tiny man, just over 5 feet tall – 2 inches below the minimum height for enlisted soldiers – with a large, drooping white moustache, he was legendary for marching his army 300 miles across the wastelands of Northern India from Kabul to relieve the besieged garrison at Kandahar. It was the sort of legend to inspire Halswelle – that and the Victoria Cross Little Bobs wore for his bravery during the Indian Mutiny of 1857. Roberts returned to Britain at the beginning of 1901 in triumph. He was met by the Prince of Wales, later to be Edward VII, and paraded through the crowds on the streets of London, cheered as the war's great hero.

His command was taken over by Kitchener – a fine, if ruthless soldier, who had the task of mopping up the guerrilla war being waged by the Boers. There was still plenty of skirmishing, and a smouldering resentment fired up the Boers against the imperialism of Britain. Destined to last for another eighteen months, the war was to lay the British open to charges of rape and torture and to bring about the establishment of concentration camps.

By the time Halswelle arrived, Kitchener was ordering farms

to be burned and food destroyed to reduce the Boers' infrastructure. Barbed wire and blockhouses further limited their manoeuvrability, and the raids steadily became less frequent.

With time on their hands, the principal enemy for officers like Halswelle was boredom, and there was an immense amount of debate in the regiment about the charges laid against the British, both by the Boers and by their sympathisers around the world, who wanted to grab every opportunity to attack the British armed forces. Nothing angered Halswelle more than these charges of dirty tricks.

The British army had taken some heavy defeats before its leaders realised that their tactics were outdated, for the Boers were a fast and highly mobile guerrilla force, using the new smokeless cartridges in their German rifles, which hid their positions. They employed hit-and-run tactics that not only caused losses the British could ill afford, but thoroughly frustrated the Empire's view of a fair fight.

It was a letter from his mother that brought Halswelle the news that Arthur Conan Doyle, the creator of Sherlock Holmes, was about to leap to the defence of the Empire and fair play. Charges of war crimes, Conan Doyle believed, could not go unchallenged. Always a man who loved a cause, he was angry. 'In view of the persistent slanders to which our politicians and our soldiers have been equally exposed, it becomes a duty which we owe to our national honour to lay the facts before the world,' he said.

Conan Doyle was certainly familiar with the subject of warfare and the Boer War in particular. Just before Christmas 1899, in what was known as the 'Black Week', the British military suffered three staggering defeats at the hands of this army of rag-tag South African farmers. In Britain, there was concern together with an upsurge of patriotism, and on Christmas Eve, Conan Doyle declared to his horrified family that he was going to volunteer for the war.

Although his great reputation came from his Sherlock Holmes stories, Conan Doyle's real love was writing historical fiction: he loved tales of war and heroism, and wrote stories about the Napoleonic wars too. He was in love with the tales of chivalry learned at his mother's knee. Having written about many battles in his historical works, he felt it was his duty to try his own skills as a soldier. However, the army had little use for a forty-year-old, somewhat overweight recruit and rejected him, so when the chance came for him to go to the front as a doctor, he jumped at it.

A friend of his, John Langman, was sending out to South Africa at his own expense a hospital of 50 beds, and he suggested that Conan Doyle should help him choose the team and should supervise the entire operation. The Langman hospital sailed in February 1900, reaching Cape Town on 21 March, and Conan Doyle was to spend his next few months in a wartime hospital devoted to the treatment of typhoid, fevers and other assaults on the intestines.

As soon as he arrived in South Africa, Conan Doyle started to assemble notes for a history of the campaign. The charges that the British had committed atrocities enraged him, and in just one week he wrote a 60,000-word pamphlet rebutting them. Published in January 1902, *The War in South Africa: Its Cause and Conduct* sold for six pence per copy in Britain. Thousands of translations were given away in France, Russia, Germany and other countries, and all the profits from the sale of the book were donated to charity.

There was not a trooper in the whole of South Africa who had not read Conan Doyle's sixpenny pamphlet, and for Halswelle, the writer became more than a hero: he was a role model. 'Here is a man,' he would say to his fellow officers, 'who's passionate about fair play in war, sport and life.' It was true that Conan Doyle had always taken pride in being a sportsman – he was an expert in cricket, golf, body-building and even baseball. He made a century at Lords, once took the wicket there of W. G. Grace and was inspired to write a poem about it; he was even invited to referee the first world heavyweight boxing contest between a white and black boxer in America, the so-called 'Fight of the Century' of Independence Day 1910, between Jack Johnson and Jim Jefferies in Reno, Nevada. Following this, he wrote an extravagant West End play about prize fighting and the gambling and dirty tricks surrounding it, entitled *The House of Temperley*.

For Halswelle, Conan Doyle's sixpenny pamphlet gave him all the ammunition he needed in his battle for fair play. Sometimes he would ride back to camp with a bunch of troopers still breathless from a raid on a Boer farmhouse. On one such raid, they had come across snipers picking off the troopers. The Boers had put up a white flag but the British had been warned constantly about this tactic, for all too often the farmers would feign surrender before opening fire again. There had been a skirmish, and several Boers were killed or ran away; there were two dead children and three dead adults – one a pregnant woman. But several troopers had been wounded and one killed the day before, and in their anger, the British troopers burned down the farmhouse and chased the survivors. A man and a woman tried to run away but were shot. Those were Kitchener's orders.

Back at the camp, Halswelle watched the soldiers unwind; their mission achieved, they would drink – but still they were uneasy.

'Kitchener knows what he's doing,' they said, 'this thing could drag on forever if we don't clear it up now.'

'That bloody white flag,' said another, 'why do they do it? And all these stories they put out – the bayoneting, what we do to their women... I read it in the papers. My father wrote to me from London – it's all in the French and German papers; they tell these lies. Conan Doyle, he's right, he's been out here. Have you seen what he's writing? That's a man who knows the truth.'

The lies that so angered Conan Doyle were certainly getting worldwide coverage. Typical was a report in January 1902 from the Boer General, Jan Smuts, later Prime Minister of the Union of South Africa:

> Lord Kitchener has begun to carry out a policy in both the Boer republics of unbelievable barbarism and gruesomeness which violates the most elementary principles of the international rules of war. Almost all farmsteads and villages in both republics have been burned down and destroyed. All crops have been destroyed. All livestock which has fallen into the hands of the enemy has been killed or slaughtered. The basic principle behind Lord Kitchener's tactics had been to win, not so much by direct operations against fighting commandos, but rather indirectly by bringing the pressure of war against defenceless women and children.

The truth was that even in Britain, prominent voices were speaking out against the slaughter. David Lloyd George, who later served as the British Prime Minister during World War I, vehemently denounced the carnage during a speech in Parliament on 18 February 1901. He quoted from a letter by a British Officer:

'We move from valley to valley lifting cattle and sheep, burning and looting and turning out women and children to weep in despair beside the ruin of their once beautiful homesteads.'

One Irish Nationalist MP, John Dillon, spoke out angrily against the British policy of shooting Boer prisoners of war. On 26 February 1901, he made public a letter by a British Officer: 'The orders in this district from Lord Kitchener are to burn and destroy all provisions, forage etc. and seize cattle, horses and stock of all sorts wherever found and to leave no food in the houses of the inhabitants, and the word has been passed around privately that no prisoners are to be taken.'

Dillon produced other letters from soldiers in the *Liverpool Courier* and the *Wolverhampton Express and Star* alleging that wounded Boers and prisoners would be shot. His denunciation of the war carried special significance: while British troops robbed the Boers of their national freedom in South Africa, Dillon was implying that the British government also held the people of Southern Ireland under colonial rule against their will.

One crusading English woman, Emily Hobhouse, alerted the world to the horrors of the prisoners' camps. 'In some camps,' she reported, 'two and sometimes three different families live in one tent. Most have to sleep on the ground. These people will never, ever forget what has happened. The children have been the hardest hit. They wither in the terrible heat and as a result of insufficient and improper nourishment. To maintain this kind of camp means nothing less than murdering children.'

To men like Conan Doyle and Halswelle, such charges were outrageous: they were fighting for King and Empire, a cause they believed in, against an enemy who used dubious tactics. 'It's the Boers that started this,' the men would say to Halswelle. 'We take too many prisoners. The trouble with you, Halswelle, is that you want to fight like you play cricket. There aren't any bloody umpires out here! They'll get you, if you don't watch it. We don't mind a scrap, but these Boers have got to learn to stand and fight, not cower behind their women and children.'

The men who shared the barracks with Halswelle were merely echoing the views of their leader. 'The Boers would never stand up to a fair fight,' complained Lord Kitchener, and it was this view that angered so many in the British ranks.

For the success of his sixpenny pamphlet rebutting the charges of war crimes, Arthur Conan Doyle was knighted on 9 August 1902. Intriguingly, he considered refusing the offer because he said he wrote the work out of conviction and not to gain a title. Conan Doyle wrote to his mother, explaining that he was reluctant to take it up, but friends and relatives, and above all his mother, persuaded him that he should accept the knighthood and that it was a suitable way to honour his patriotism.

Back in London, the gossipmongers took a more cynical view, however. They said that the King was an avid Sherlock Holmes' fan and that he'd put Conan Doyle's name on the honours list to encourage him to write more stories. Whatever the reason for the knighthood, His Majesty and many thousands of his subjects must have been delighted when, in 1903, the *Strand Magazine* started serialising *The Return of Sherlock Holmes*.

Back in London, Halswelle's mother was equally delighted. 'There's no finer writer in the land,' she wrote to her son, 'than Sir Arthur Conan Doyle.'

– CHAPTER 5 –

THE STAMP OF LOVE

Dorando Pietri's sporting career was almost over before it
began. Always a boy of sudden enthusiasms, and ever eager
to follow the latest fashion, he had simply fallen in love with
cycling. He had seized on bike racing as a way to make his mark
and be somebody, as a route to success and standing in Carpi. The
seductiveness of the machines, the scent of the oil, the bright
clothing, the cut of the racing jerseys, the way his heart beat when
lining up for the start – he loved it all. He also enjoyed talking
about the sport and reading about it in the papers after a race.

The members of La Patria were enthusiastic supporters of this
infant sport. They pointed out that it was healthy as it got you
outdoors and just about anyone could do it. Newspapers such as
Luce gave plenty of space to cycling too. Their editors reckoned
the bicycle was a way of emancipating the working classes in
northern Italy, where the poor had been forced to spend hours

trudging their way to work from their homes and hamlets outside the cities. Now, because of the bicycle, they could reach their places of work quickly and cheaply. For Dorando, the bike was far more than just a cheap way to travel: it gave him speed and a way to prove that he too could be a champion.

A particularly dangerous form of cycle racing, especially in the early years of the twentieth century, was a ride paced by motorbikes, as neither they nor the bicycles were up to much mechanically. But Dorando was certainly keen on the sport – it all seemed so wonderful at the time. He savoured the moments at the start of the race when he was held motionless in the saddle, his head dipped deep over the handlebars, while the motorbikes coughed and spluttered their way into life.

'They'll pace you, they'll shelter you,' his friends shouted at him. 'All you have to do is ride till you drop – you'll move faster than anyone could dream.'

In mid-August 1904, Dorando found himself in a two-man race behind men perched on two 2.5 horsepower Peugeots. Once he got going, the feeling of speed was sensational, as if men had never gone this fast but now you could do it all under your own power. The closer you could get to the motorbike in front, the more you would benefit from the shelter and the faster you might go.

Inevitably, with the crude machines of the time, trouble was waiting around every corner, and on the fifth lap of this 25km race, Dorando clipped the back of the pacing motorbike. Both riders were sent sprawling and he was taken to hospital. Luckily, although he was covered in blood and scrapes and was bruised through to the bone, nothing was broken. Even so, he was a painful mess and remained in a hospital bed in Modena for eight days.

The experience gave him plenty of time to think. Maybe his

friend Tullio was right after all and he should give up cycling. Perhaps he should see if he couldn't make his mark as a runner. They had been saying he was in the wrong event, so maybe the bruises were telling him something.

There were other reasons, too, that made him uneasy about bicycle racing. He had read about men who could push their body way beyond all human endurance – a thought that excited him, but he had also heard about some of the methods they used to tap these powers. After all, the great cycling boom was already sweeping Europe and a man might win fame and a sizeable fortune because of his powers on a bike. Why waste your life labouring or down the mines if you could earn far more this way? And already there were trainers haunting the racing circuits to show how it might be done.

One such man was Choppy Warburton, an English impresario and trainer who operated like a Svengali whenever there were big prizes to be won. His men would sometimes finish glassy-eyed and semi-conscious, almost living corpses, but still somehow they would find the strength to win. Warburton would goad them to even greater efforts and, as some sharp-eyed spectators noted, he would sometimes pull a mysterious bottle from his greatcoat pocket and encourage them to drink from it.

His face half-hidden beneath a Derby hat, and always wrapped in a huge black overcoat, Warburton exuded a great air of mystery. Many spectators reckoned his methods were all hocus-pocus, a crude form of psychology, but others thought the little bottles contained some of the most powerful drugs known to man at that time – a mixture of strychnine to stimulate the body and morphine to kill pain. For these cyclists, taking the stuff was a matter of life and death because so much money was at stake.

There were many deaths from cycling in the two decades from 1890 to 1910, some cyclists dying in the saddle and others shortly afterwards, and eventually Choppy Warburton was warned off every cycling track in Europe. But he was not the only such trainer and the life expectancy of racing cyclists at the turn of the century was terrifyingly low. The cyclists were said to have died from exhaustion and fatigue, but in fact, they mostly died from abuse to their bodies.

Dorando had no wish to kill himself and he believed that there was no stimulant that could match his own burning desire to win applause and acclaim for his races. So, after his accident and, weeks later, the incident when he matched strides with Pagliani in the piazza, he switched his passion from cycling to foot racing.

Within three weeks of that exhibition in Carpi, he was lining up for a 3,000-metre race in Bologna. There, on 2 October 1904, in his first official race, he came second to Aduo Fava, and in the weeks that followed he would take on races and distances wherever he could find them. A week later, in fact, he got his name in the record books when he captured the Italian record for covering almost 9,000 metres in half an hour.

More races followed. He would take on anything between 5 and 15 miles, and during October and November, Dorando found that he was winning most of his races. *Luce*, which had given over so much space to cycling coverage, suddenly started to allow a few more column inches to the exploits of the runner Dorando Pietri.

Dorando would make sure that his father saw the press reports, pointing them out with excitement. 'You see,' said Desiderio, 'you might not be so keen to leave this place after all.' Besides, there was now another reason for his son to stay in Carpi.

Teresa Dondi was a shy, delicate girl with large eyes, who looked younger than her years. There was something still and contemplative about her face, though her movements were quick and impatient. She was, in fact, just a few months younger than Dorando. Her father was a share cropper, a tenant farmer of sorts, and certainly not wealthy but still a few notches up the social scale from the Pietri family. She had caught the eye of Dorando's boss, Pasquale Melli, who saw that she was bright as well as pretty. He had offered her some work, to act sometimes as a maid at his home and occasionally to help out if she were needed in the shop.

Dorando first ran into her at the confectioner's and he couldn't take his eyes off her. Teresa was nervous and coltish; she moved quickly, almost jerkily, and whenever she reached up to pluck a box of chocolates from a shelf, the glimpse of lace beneath her overskirt produced a feeling in his legs and stomach that he had only ever known before the start of a big race.

He fluttered uncontrollably and was tongue-tied, but although neither of the pair could find the words, both knew there was much to be said between them. They were inseparable – the girl next door, so shy and so young, and Dorando, the boy who was winning a reputation to be proud of because of his other passion, for running. For as long as they could, they kept their friendship secret. But others could see, from the looks that lingered too long, what was going on.

Teresa's mother would squint through the shutters, looking out for the messenger boy.

'Look at his clothes,' she would say to Teresa. 'Why do you bother talking to someone like that? He's poor and he'll always be poor.'

Teresa's eyes would swell with hot tears, and she bit her lip when her father told Dorando to stay away from her.

But Melli's family, the owners of the shop, liked the girl. 'Where's the harm?' said Melli, and so the lovers would snatch forbidden time together, keeping their secrets. Teresa was so proud of Dorando – she loved to see his name printed in *Luce* and she could see how happy that made him. She let him touch her and kiss her, and only the blushes would make him pull back, and he ached whenever he was away from her.

'If I can be a champion, maybe it will help me to a fine job,' Dorando would dream. 'They know all about me at the hat factory – perhaps there's something there for me.' Teresa let him dream on.

Dorando certainly made sure that his dream of Teresa didn't die. One morning, when he was away in Turin doing his national service, Teresa received a picture postcard. It was addressed in a neat copperplate hand to *Gentil Signorina Dondi Teresina, Via S. Giovanni, Carpi*. On the front was printed, 'A thought from Turin', and it carried a picture of a flower against the background of the city's main railway station. There was no message, no greeting and no signature. Teresa looked at the card with a blush and a shrug. Twenty minutes later, she was at the Melli home, alone in the kitchen with the kettle steaming and trembling on the hob. As the steam softened the paste on the stamp, she gently peeled it off.

There, written in a tiny hand for her eyes only, was a message: 'This is Dorando writing to remind you that he loves you, please forgive me for what happened when we were last together.'

Teresa read it again and again, and kept the card beside her until her dying day.

– CHAPTER 6 –

CHEATING FOR BOYS

There is a copse behind the solid Victorian buildings of Charterhouse School, near Godalming in rural Surrey. It's where generations of boys from the school, free from the shackles of classroom rules, could run a little wild and indulge their dreams and fantasies. It was here, as Wyndham Halswelle's mother constantly reminded him, that you could find the first playground of a boy who went to the same school: the soldier, hero and role model of every schoolboy in the Empire – Robert Baden-Powell. They were, as she so often mentioned in her letters, old boys from Charterhouse.

The acts of ingenuity, courage and resourcefulness of Baden-Powell during the seven-month siege of Mafeking during the Boer War were followed in every detail throughout Britain and the Empire, and made a deep impression on Halswelle. Beyond that, the philosophy and ethos that Baden-Powell carried over into the Boy Scout Movement captured the imagination of generations of schoolboys to come.

Baden-Powell never really shone much at school subjects but he thrived at Charterhouse, where the public school ethos of cheerful courage under pressure, loyalty to the team and playing the game, which was already fuelling the armies of the Empire, suited this energetic sportsman, artist and actor.

'The whole secret of success in life is to play the game of life in the same spirit as that played on the football field,' he was fond of telling his audience of boys.

When war was declared in South Africa, Colonel Baden-Powell and 1,000 men were left to defend the town of Mafeking, which was the supply centre for the British. The town's success in surviving the longest siege in that war, from October 1899 until May 1900, without any real loss of life, would in any case have elevated the name of Baden-Powell to the status of an imperial symbol, the hero of an empire under threat. But it wasn't just his ability to succeed, it was his capacity to do so with nonchalance and a taste for fun and adventure, using a combination of fake barbed-wire defences and Sunday baby competitions, that in the eyes of the British public turned him into the very epitome of pluck and team spirit. A master of bluff, Baden-Powell thought up all sorts of schemes to make it seem as if the town of Mafeking was heavily defended.

When ordered to South Africa, his task was to raise two regiments of mounted rifles and to use them to hold the Western frontier of the Transvaal, drawing Boer forces away from the British landings on the coast. With his men, he became trapped in Mafeking, 250 miles away from the nearest reinforcements.

Almost immediately, he was faced with a Boer force four or five times greater than his own and while they must have expected a quick and easy victory, they were to be disappointed.

As well as digging a strong set of defensive earthworks, Baden-Powell missed no opportunity to trick his opponents about his strength and intentions. Imitation forts were built, complete with a prominent flag and flagstaff to draw the fire of the enemy. Not only this, but he issued orders for non-existent assault troops attacking at night. He used a tin megaphone to make sure enemy sentries heard him and he managed to rouse the Boer camp while his own men got some sleep. He also improvised a searchlight and managed to con the Boers into thinking that all his forts were equipped with a searchlight.

One of his best schemes was to have a lasting significance. He recruited a bunch of boys to act as messengers and orderlies in order to release men to fight on the front line. This corps of boys was to provide the blueprint for the original Boy Scouts.

The Boers were sufficiently discouraged to abandon any hope of taking the town by assault, and settled down for a long siege. As the trench lines drew closer, a battle of snipers, as bitter as anything to be found on the Western front a decade and a half later, followed. But the siege was also a quite civilised affair: a ceasefire was observed every Sunday and the garrison amused themselves with concerts and cricket matches.

One day, a Boer gunner fired a letter into the town of Mafeking in an empty shell case, wishing that he had something with which to drink the health of the garrison. Baden-Powell immediately sent him a bottle of whisky under a flag of truce. Later, the Boer commander sent Baden-Powell a note that he and his friends were proposing to come into town and take them on at a game of cricket. Baden-Powell replied with panache: under the flag of truce he sent a letter that read:

Sir, I beg to thank you for your letter of yesterday. I should like nothing better after the match in which we are at present engaged is over. But just now we are having our innings and have so far scored 200 days not out against the bowling of Cronje, Snijman and Botha and we are having a very enjoyable game.

I remain, yours truly,

RSS Baden-Powell

But the tide of war was slowly turning against the Boers and eventually it was all over. The long-awaited relief column arrived on 17 May 1900 and helped Baden-Powell's ragged defenders drive out the Boer forces. It was the end of a siege that had lasted 216 days at the cost of 212 killed and wounded. But Baden-Powell was a national hero and endowed with a celebrity he was later to build on as founder of the Boy Scout Movement.

Prompted by fears of imperial decline and fall raised by the Boer War, Robert Baden-Powell became increasingly concerned about the wellbeing of the nation, in particular that of young people. One report, published in 1904, claimed that out of every nine who volunteered to fight, only two were fit enough to do so. Physical deterioration and moral degeneracy became themes in many of the talks and speeches that Baden-Powell gave in the years that followed.

Soon he was exploring a ragbag of different schemes, mixing his experience of camping, woodcraft, military tactics and educational theories, and overlaying it all with his own vision of chivalry and empire. In August 1907, 11 months before the Olympics at Shepherd's Bush in London, Baden-Powell conducted the famous Brownsea Island experimental camp. He wanted to test out the ideas he had been developing for his scheme of work for the Boy Scouts.

Modelled on his idiosyncratic vision of the hardy colonial frontiersmen, the ideal Boy Scout, disciplined and self-sacrificing, appeared as the culmination of a mythical lineage in British national history. He would embody the virtue and honour of the medieval knight and the stout-hearted courage of an Elizabethan explorer. The amount of energy that Baden-Powell expended in *Scouting for Boys* to encourage boys and men to hold the Empire together gives an indication of the level of British anxiety at this time, about both the state of the Empire and the state of the nation.

By 1900, Germany, the USA and Japan had started to challenge Britain's leadership in terms of industrial production, and there were other threats to stability from within the British Isles, particularly from the newly organised Labour movement and the rise of the Women's movement and demands for self-representation. Many chapters of Baden-Powell's *Scouting for Boys* lay huge emphasis on the dangers of deterioration of the British race and the physical breakdown of the rising generation; he expressed contempt for the working-class 'loafer'.

One area of British life seemed to embody many of Baden-Powell's values – the public school playing field. The games ethic perfected by public schoolboys and their teachers seemed to mesh fluidly with the ideals of imperial service. To show loyalty to the group, to practise honour, to smile even in the face of defeat, this was the ethic that seemed to guarantee success in the colonies as well as embody the qualities of true masculinity.

Baden-Powell regarded the public school playing field very much as the cradle of so many of these qualities, and drummed home the message that to do one's best for the country was the way to succeed.

'Get the lads away from spectator sports,' he urged. 'Teach them to be manly, to play the game whatever it may be and not be merely onlookers and loafers.'

In *Scouting for Boys* he adapted Henry Newbold's resonant poem '*Vitai Lampada*' ('They Pass On The Torch of Life', published during the war in 1897) into a Scout tableau retitled 'Play the Game'.

> The Gatling's jammed and the Colonel dead,
> And the regiment blind with dust and smoke.
> The river of death has brimmed his banks,
> And England's far, and Honour a name,
> But the voice of a schoolboy rallies the ranks:
> 'Play up! play up! and play the game!'

Playing the game seemed to encapsulate the popular imperialism of the time and it was no wonder that it appealed to the young Wyndham Halswelle.

Baden-Powell certainly knew about winning. He was up for every trick of war, and was the first to pour scorn on the concept of fighting in bright, visible uniforms or to encourage using the cover of darkness, but always he managed to somehow combine this attitude with his own brand of British chivalry towards women, children and even the enemy.

'As in sport, so in war,' he said. 'There is always room for chivalry when men fight fair.'

– CHAPTER 7 –

DIGGING AND DREAMING

There was not a lot of time or room for chivalry in the rough, tough world of the Irish immigrant in New York at the turn of the century.

John Joseph Hayes was born in 1886 in Manhattan, New York. He was the son of Michael Hayes, born in September 1859, from Silver Street, Nenagh, County Tipperary. His mother was Ellen (or Nellie) O'Rourke, who was born in America but whose origins were in County Roscommon. The newly wed Hayes couple, Michael and Ellen, finally arrived on New York's East Side to join the seemingly neverending procession of immigrants, with Michael hoping to find work as a baker.

The East Side of New York was Italy, Germany, Jewish Russia and Ireland in miniature. This was a melting pot and all the ingredients were there: those who daily fought poverty but still shared in the wealth of family support, enjoying the favours and help they could give each other, with each apartment building its own community, every block a village, every street a reflection of the country they had left behind.

It was not unusual for newly arrived immigrant families in Manhattan to occupy every inch of their cramped and run-down dwellings. Families of six or seven might live in one small room, then take on a boarder or two to help meet living expenses. Some lived in hallways, in basements or in alleyways – anywhere they could squeeze themselves in – and all too often the rents they paid were extortionate. Living and working quarters were often the same. A family would cook and eat in the overcrowded room where they made their living, and from the oldest to the youngest, everyone took whatever work they could find and did their part. Wages usually tottered at the brink of subsistence.

There was no margin for any error in the family budget, for survival could ride on a few cents. Day after day, the people of the lower East Side would grind out a living, working, saving and trying to move slowly ahead, and in so doing they would create a niche for themselves in the complex economic and cultural world of New York City.

It was in those circumstances, there in the railroad flats that once existed on the site of Tudor City, the site of slums and slaughterhouses, that Johnny Hayes grew up. There, local gangs thrived and could be powerful, but the local politicians could be even tougher too. The men from Tammany Hall, the Democratic Party's bastion of corruption and power, knew that the Irish-American immigrants were like unformed clay and happy to be moulded in the ways of New York. And so they helped them to be a little more American, to feel a little more at home in their new world, and before long they were American citizens – and most of all, American voters.

The children of peasants – the shoemakers, bakers and so on who had been brave enough to cross the Atlantic – were not content to sit back and waste their lives amid the debris. What got them out of the slums and away from the clutches of the corruption that thrived during the 1890s was the determination to haul themselves up by their boot straps and to get out. To be an American was to climb into that great melting pot and to be poured out ready to take on the world as an American winner.

Johnny Hayes grew to be a small boy, but he was strong – strong enough to work while still a child, and he didn't stay the baby of the family for too long. He was the firstborn, but was soon joined by another baby and then another. They were hungry mouths to feed, and Michael Hayes grabbed every hour to slave as a baker in the cauldron of the bakery at Cushman's in New York. Soon even his 14-hour days were not enough and often he would bed down at the bakery, sleeping at the back in order to be up and ready for yet more overtime. Sometimes Johnny would join his father, earning a few more badly needed quarters long before he left his lost childhood behind him. 'Heat never bothered me,' he used to say, years later. 'My grandfather and father were bakers and I worked in the bakery as a boy – I was used to heat.'

Next after Johnny, and within the year, his brother Willie was born. Then two sisters came along: Harriet and Alice, who were six and eight years younger than Johnny. Finally, baby Dan joined the family when Johnny was already 11 years old. There might have been more but when the next baby, Philip, died in his mother's arms, Ellen knew she would need all her energies to keep her family alive.

Life was hungry and tough, but in Manhattan you could always feed on dreams and no little boy could walk along the quayside in the New York of the 1890s without being mesmerised by all he saw and heard. Sometimes, Johnny would walk past ships being docked, watch cargoes being unloaded and study the faces of the seamen as they swung down the gangplank. For a moment, he would be a sailor, voyaging out to take on the world. He would weave these men into his adventures, playing out the hero, drinking in their excitement.

Ambition was a fire inside him, and Michael and Ellen Hayes, both exhausted long before their time, took some comfort in realising that their eldest son shrugged aside this poverty and still burned with the unquenchable energy of the young. Exactly what he wanted to do they couldn't be sure, but still they admired the way he was not scared of hard work. They smiled with fondness at the effort and the hours he would put in and at his happy-go-lucky self-confidence.

But that confidence and thirst for hard work were about to be tested to destruction. Michael and Ellen, old long before they had reached middle age and wrung threadbare by the effort of surviving in New York, both died within weeks of each other in 1902. There was no money for a tombstone.

At the age of sixteen, Johnny Hayes found himself head of the family with two brothers and two sisters to support, the youngest of them just five years old. The children were taken into a Catholic orphanage and Johnny did what he had to to support them all there. He took the toughest, most dangerous job he could find, but a job that paid well for your sweat. It was working underground, digging tunnels for the New York subway, and shovelling sand until you dropped. They called the labourers 'sandhogs' and the work of the sandhogs was tedious, not to mention perilous and claustrophobic.

Johnny, and sometimes his brother Willie, worked shoulder to shoulder, straining to earn as much in a day as other labourers might bring home in a week. They needed the money now they had a family to keep. Each morning, the two boys would marvel at the tangle of derricks and scaffolding. There would be gangs of 60 or more men gulping hot coffee. Following a roll call, they would walk single file to the mouth of the shaft. Most of the men wore nothing but their shirts and trousers with waterproof boots reaching above the knees.

Just entering the tunnel took a long time. Crews would go into airlocks, one at a time, after which the doors at each end were sealed. An air pipe would start hissing and the men's ears popped as the air pressure climbed until it was the same as in the adjoining locks which took them underground. Then the workers were able to open the connecting door and crush into the next chamber, where the entire ordeal would start all over again. Once they got to the far end of the tunnel the men had to work quickly because they could only handle the pressure for a short while.

'Pinch your noses, keep your mouth shut and blow!' the foreman would yell. 'It helps your ears.' Sometimes eardrums would rupture and bleed, and the two Hayes boys soon learned the dangers of working too fast in these conditions.

'You need to pace yourself,' Johnny would say to his brother. 'Don't go so fast at the beginning.' Above all, the job was wet, and the dampness seemed to seep into their very bones. Half-remembered warnings from his now-dead Irish mother niggled away at Hayes' weariness. 'Keep yourself dry, Johnny boy,' he could still hear her saying, 'the rheumatism is a terrible thing – it's the ruining of the joints.'

When he wasn't working, Hayes would catch up on his sleep and fool around with the other Irish lads, sharing stories of sports heroes, throwing a ball, swinging a bat and sometimes for fun taking part in an impromptu foot race.

When Johnny was just ten years old, he experienced the ballyhoo that surrounded the return of the Americans from the first Olympic Games in Athens. No boy could forget the excitement of the crowds and bands, the flag-waving and the cheering, as New York saluted their conquering heroes. And among those heroes was the very first winner in those 1896 Games, an Irish-American boy like Johnny himself and a fine all-round athlete called Jim Connolly.

Connolly had won the hop, step and jump, and a year later he went on to become a prolific writer on sport, an author of sea sagas and a newspaper man for the *Boston Globe* and the *Boston Post*. But the ten-year-old Johnny Hayes never forgot the sight of him draped in the Irish tricolour on his way through Manhattan. Connolly made a huge impression on Hayes and all the other Irish-American boys in New York.

Aggressively proud, not only of his Olympic victory but of his Irish roots and sporting heritage, Connolly had been raised in the predominantly Irish-Catholic neighbourhood of South Boston. 'We were a hot-blooded fighting lot, but also clean living, sane and healthy,' he wrote. 'The children grew up rugged and just naturally had a taste for athletics. Among the boys I knew as a boy it was the exception to find one who could not run or jump or swim, or play a good game of ball.'

Local sporting heroes figured prominently in the young Jim Connolly's life. Among them was John L. Sullivan, the 'Boston Strongboy' and a world heavyweight boxing champion from 1882 to 1892. Another was a neighbour by the name of Gallohue, who enjoyed fame as a circus acrobat, and it was to him that Connolly attributed his earliest interest in track and field athletics.

'Our curious jumper of whom we were all very proud,' he wrote, 'was a true picture of an athlete six feet in height and weighing 190 lbs stripped.' On one occasion, Gallohue came home dressed in a superb new suit, which Connolly estimated had cost at least $60 – 'a lot of money for a suit of clothes then'. It turned out that the suit was a pay-off for a bet made by the circus manager and that to win it, Gallohue had to jump over a baby elephant.

'It was the professional athletes who were our role models,' said Connolly. 'In those days the Scotch and Irish societies used to run great festivals in the summer and the big drawing cards were the professional athletics games. We had schools of professional running then, not one but many. Every shoe town, every other mill town, had its champion. Towns would go broke backing their man.'

In May 1896, Johnny Hayes had seen his hero Jim Connolly wave his way across New York through a double line of policemen with crowds from kerb to kerb. Red, blue and green ribbons were everywhere and skyrockets flared from drug stores, homes and bar rooms, while a band beat out 'See the Conquering Hero Comes'. Hayes cut out a newspaper picture of the scene and kept it in his pocket until it fell to pieces.

In the years that followed, Connolly would hand out training advice to any young Irish-American who dreamed of emulating his deeds in track and field.

'Practise easily, but regularly,' he would say. 'Over-training is worse than under-training. After exercise, take a cold, quick sponge bath and rough towel rubbing. Eat any plain food you like, drink as little liquid as you can during the day of a race outside of your usual allowance of tea or coffee. Do not run the day before a race. From four to five in the afternoon is the best time to exercise and about five times a week usually gives the best results.' It was good advice and not wasted on boys like Hayes.

Connolly was convinced that his Irish lineage was in large part responsible for his sporting successes, but he was also proudly Catholic. 'It is in the blood and training of our Catholic boys to be not merely American,' he wrote, adding, 'These Catholic youths, patriots and athletes out of all proportion to their numbers are mostly such because of good Catholic motherhood and a wholesome childhood.' He thrived on hero worship and he got plenty of that; he was even the subject of Theodore Roosevelt's admiration when, in 1908, the President of the United States said, 'There's a great all-round man, Jim Connolly, mentally and physically vigorous and straight as a whip. I would like my boys to grow up like Jim Connolly.'

Growing up like Jim Connolly, with his fierce pride in sport and Ireland, captivated the young Hayes. The job as a sandhog had toughened up Johnny and Willie a lot. They learned how to pace their young bodies over the long, exhausting hours spent underground. There, they learned it was fatal to start shovelling too fast and they learned to build up their stamina slowly, for you still had to be on your feet at the end of the day.

Their work did not leave them a lot of time for relaxing, but when the priests at the orphanage organised ball games and foot races, the two boys, toughened by their underground work, showed their strength. Hard physical work was making Hayes fitter by the week. When he had a few pennies in his pocket, Johnny still had energy to burn, and with his friends he would go dancing at the Manhattan Casino in Harlem. They would happily jog all the way home at two in the morning.

These boys could run and the priests noticed it. 'Look at young Jack Hayes,' they would say, 'he could be a champion, a fine Irish boy like that. Get him out of shovelling sand all day and you'll see him run like a racehorse.'

No one would question the pull that the Irish-Americans had in New York at the turn of the century. If an immigrant needed naturalisation papers, a Tammany Hall man was there to pull the right strings; if a poor Irish boy got himself arrested, a Tammany lawyer bailed him out. Whenever an old widow couldn't pay the rent, Tammany money would come to the rescue. It was a simple enough deal – it was tit for tat. And all the Irish had to do to meet their end of the bargain was to vote the right way. With a word here and a word there, it was simple enough to get a promising young athlete onto a payroll, where the duties would be minimal or even non-existent.

Johnny Hayes, they decided, needed time to train, to rest, to race and to be coached. They had a word with the man who was president of the Irish-American Athletic Club, Patrick J. Conway. A close friend of the mayor, he joked about the Irish-American lad working every day in water up to his knees, saying how rheumatism might ruin a fine athletic career.

'We'll find him a dry job,' declared Pat Conway, and before he knew it, the young Hayes was on the payroll of a New York store then called Bloomingdale Brothers. When he showed up for work, the store said Mr Conway had suggested that he work in the dry-goods department. For Johnny, anything had to be better than ruining his health as a sandhog, and while at Bloomingdale's, his duties were variously described as a messenger, an odd job boy, an assistant in the caretaker's office or even a shipping clerk.

But his real job was to collect his money. Later, when he had found success and fame as an athlete, the store collected on their investment, plastered the place with pictures of him and put out stories of how he had trained on a quarter-mile track on the roof. In fact, Hayes rarely got to work in Bloomingdales, much less train on the roof. His so-called job was one of convenience arranged for him by the Irish-Americans and Pat Conway. The truth was that from the moment Johnny stopped being a sandhog, he became a full-time athlete. He drew a steady salary, reported to be $20 per week, but instead of working he spent his time training for long-distance running in the parks and roads beyond Manhattan.

Already, John Joseph Hayes had stepped way beyond Baron de Coubertin's romantic dream of strict amateurism; already he enjoyed unlimited hours to train and professional coaches to train with. But he was not the only one...

Even in faraway Britain, they hadn't managed to kill off the professionals.

– CHAPTER 8 –

THE SOLDIER
RETURNS

The swirling rain stopped just long enough for Wyndham Halswelle to get out of his coat and test his spiked shoes on the porridge-like track of Powderhall. Ever since he had returned to Edinburgh, Jimmy Curran had been out there with the stopwatch, growling at him about his style and pushing him like a sergeant major.

It was a strange set-up: Curran, huddled in his great coat, the collar turned up against the winds that whipped over from Leith, barking orders at the young officer, who was already sweating in his vest and shorts. But it seemed to work. Ever since the regiment had returned, Halswelle had felt his strength grow with every week that they pencilled the training details into his diary. He was getting faster and it excited him.

Like many of the people weaned in the tough border country where Scotland and England meet, Jimmy Curran, born at

Galashiels, some 40 miles south of Edinburgh, was wiry, tough and grew up hungry. He had formed a partnership, a friendship almost, with Halswelle when they were both soldiers, stuck in a messy war and cursing the heat of the South African sun. The unlikely double act of athlete and trainer had survived not just the sweltering heat of the veldt and the bone-stiffening chill of Scotland, but the even icier disapproval of Halswelle's fellow officers.

The problem for them, and indeed for Halswelle, was that Jimmy Curran, who had fought his way all through the Boer War but left the army two years after the fighting ended, was a professional. He had chosen to forsake the ranks of the amateurs to turn his abilities as an athlete into a living. In an athletic world that worshipped the gentleman amateur, here was Halswelle, an officer and a gentleman, being put through his paces by a man who rubbed shoulders with the professionals and knew all the tricks of the trade at Powderhall.

When Curran had run alongside Halswelle at the 1902 Caledonian meeting in Port Elizabeth, at the close of the war, both had been amateurs, but Curran was older and more experienced than the young lieutenant and he knew how to spot potential. Back in the Borders on leave in 1903, Curran encouraged Halswelle to make the most of his talents. He introduced him to the officials who ran the Edinburgh Harriers and was happy to share the secrets of training and racing.

Jimmy Curran had seen it all. He knew all about side bets, about rigging handicaps and about beating the gun, but he also knew about winning. In the dying days of the nineteenth century, Scotland and the north-east of England were strongholds of athletics, places where men gave the finest performances in the world. They might have picked up rumours of privileged and pampered athletes from the south heading off to de Coubertin's Olympic festival in faraway Athens, but if you wanted to witness men run really fast or vault, throw or leap like giants, you headed for Powderhall or Morpeth, where they didn't bother too much about seeing flags hoisted or bands playing anthems.

A sprinter might travel halfway round the world to Greece in the hope of winning a token gold-plated medal, but the victor in the 110-yard foot handicap at Powderhall could count on winning £100 and whatever his backers might gain from their successful bets. Curran knew he could be a good earner; he could take on anybody at the half- and the one-mile races – he had already shown that as an amateur, racing as captain of the Gala Harriers. But he knew that the life of an athlete was a short one, and that was why, when he saw the chance to cash in at the Hawick Common-Riding Sports in 1905, he seized his chance and joined the professionals. He knew there was good money to be made at Powderhall and he dreamed of rich pickings in America.

Like many of his contemporaries known to the press and the chroniclers of the sport as pedestrians, Curran ran under an assumed name, 'G. Gordon'. These professional winners would adopt a *nom de piste* sometimes to fool the bookmakers or to hide a more respectable identity, so they could shelter beneath a cloak of anonymity. One of the greatest professional runners of the time, G. B. Tincler, turned up in 1894 claiming to be a 'J. Craig of Inverness'. In the days of handicap racing, when competitors could be spread out down the track, giving the slowest a chance to finish with the best, this would have ensured that the runner got a better place on the starting grid.

At New Year 1907, at the Royal Gymnasium grounds, Curran won the half-mile, running off a 15-yard handicap. He was there again in the half-mile in 1906, 1907 and 1908. Although he had left to try his luck as an athlete in America in October 1907, he frequently came back to race and to pass on his advice to Halswelle. It wasn't until 1910, by which time he had settled to work in America as a coach, that he returned to Scotland to run under his own name of J. Curran of Philadelphia.

At the turn of the century, Powderhall had a fine 440-yard cinder track, with a straight of 180 yards on the south side and a roofed grandstand that could seat over 1,400 people. The events attracted big crowds and big profits. There were 10,000 to watch the first day of the New Year sprint in 1904, and 24,000 turned up over two days in 1907.

A century ago, athletic training was as clandestine as a visit to a brothel. You simply wouldn't talk about it and you made sure no one caught you at it. The biggest problem was betting, which, despite all the efforts of amateur rule makers, still haunted the sport. Another was the image – often an illusion – that most gentlemen amateurs, particularly the British, liked to project about their abilities. No one wanted it to be known that he was too serious about his sport – effortless superiority was the impression to convey.

Nevertheless, many an athlete, wishing to be the best, might seek advice from a bevy of ex-professional runners, who claimed to know the secrets of massage and took payment for the lore they had picked up when their livelihoods depended on their speed or their cunning. But in the Victorian social order, such wily old trainers, who would dispense their wisdom with a whiff of liniment, ranked rather lower than most servants, and even the best of the old-time trainers were being left far behind by a new breed of coaches across the Atlantic.

The Americans unashamedly studied and improved training methods and techniques, and it showed. One of the best-known Victorian trainers in Britain was an ex-professional runner called Jack White, known to the sporting press as the 'Gateshead Clipper'. In 1895, the Gateshead Clipper was trainer to the London Athletic Club, who visited America to compete against the New York Athletic Club.

This match was virtually a full-blown international contest between England and the USA. The result was humiliation for the English, who lost by eleven events to nil in a match where the Americans set five world records. The New York team had been trained by Mike Murphy, an Irish-American and the Yale University coach, who was to go as chief trainer to the American team at the 1908 Olympic Games. It took decades for the lessons of American coaching to filter through to the British athletics establishment, but they were not lost on Halswelle or, indeed, Jimmy Curran.

Curran had a restless mind, always seeking the edge that would turn him or one of his protégés into a winner. He would have known from childhood about Edinburgh's royal patent gymnasium, described by the press after its opening in 1865 as 'the new wonder of Edinburgh'. Often, he himself ran at the gymnasium grounds. Right from the start, the gymnasium was successful and for the entrance fee of sixpence the visitor was offered a wide selection of 'ingenious contraptions affording amusement and healthful bodily exercise'.

One of the main attractions was the patent rotary boat or Great Sea Serpent. This remarkable device involved a large circular pond with a post mounted in the middle. Long metal spokes radiated from the post to the wooden structure of the boat, which was 470 feet round and could take 600 people. Passengers sat at the end of the spokes and propelled the 'boat serpent' in fixed circles. Fully manned, the whole thing could hit speeds 'equal to that of a small steamboat'. In another part of the park was a wooden circular catwalk, above which moved an endless chain of 144 leather saddles. Here, Edinburgh fitness fanatics sat and propelled themselves around the catwalk with their feet.

More conventional pastimes at the gymnasium included vaulting, climbing poles, stilts, quoits, springboards and swimming baths. Or you could always hire a bone shaker and share in the great bicycle craze sweeping even Scotland at the turn of the century.

Curran would scour press reports and bookshops seeking any scrap of information that might help him in his quest to enhance human performance. In 1901, there was a book on sale in Edinburgh bookshops that was translated from the German. It was by F. A. Schmidt and Eustace H. Miles, and was entitled *The Training of the Body*. Here, a keen student of sport might read an analysis of such activities as running, walking, jumping, throwing, climbing, swimming and cycling. There was even a section on a revolutionary new style called bent-legged running.

But Curran was not the only professional athlete to help the gentleman amateurs. Already, in London, the legendary coach Scipio Africanus Mussabini from Lewisham, known throughout the sport as 'Sam', was earning a good living as an athlete, coach, referee, columnist, author and publisher. Mussabini was a frequent visitor to Edinburgh to watch the professional New Year's Day Powderhall sprint.

When he turned his efforts to training amateur athletes, he took on Reggie Walker of South Africa, later to become the 1908

Olympic 100-Metre champion. Coaches like 'Sam' Mussabini and Jimmy Curran were from the same stable. They knew the closely guarded secrets of the professionals and both started to apply these methods to their own training routines.

Given Curran's approach to both the practicalities and the theories of human performance, it was little wonder that he wanted to apply his knowledge and experience to the gifted Halswelle, but this team of professional and amateur was bound to lead to tensions.

'It's no use learning how to run like a deer if you let others make you a target and cut you down with cunning,' Curran would warn. 'There is no justice in sport,' he would growl. 'If you think you will win because you were better or because you did everything right, or that you will lose because the other man deserves it, then you are a loser. You win by outwitting your opponent with luck or because of his mistakes. If they give you half a chance to win, then beat them!'

With his experience as a professional, Curran could explore that fine line between out-and-out cheating and being cagey. In some cases, he realised these were part of the game, and even a big part – sharpening the buckle of a belt and using it to scuff a cricket ball, or keeping your mouth shut when a referee fails to notice that you have beaten the starter's gun. 'These things go on,' Curran would say. 'Sometimes if you want to win and you think you can put one past them, you've got to try.'

Halswelle would hear these views and he didn't always agree with them or the philosophy they carried, but one thing he was sure of was that his visits to the track could teach him much. Curran taught him the secrets of the punchball for speed, of distance work for stride length and dumbbells for strength.

'Keep your body fresh,' he would advise, sharing that nineteenth-century preoccupation with how the human body might react to being pushed to the extreme. The very expression 'spent force' bore witness to the fear that a person's essence could be drained from them in the process of a superhuman effort, a fear that was to persist well into the twentieth century when the greatest concern of many an athlete in training was that they might 'go stale'.

In the 1906 amateur championships at Powderhall, Halswelle won a clean sweep of 100, 220, 440 and 880 yards, all in the course of a single day, due to this sort of training. That year, the quality of the opposition was formidable. As well as facing the defending champion in both the short sprints, Halswelle beat Olympic finalist W. D. Anderson in the 440 yards and the Olympic 1,500-Metre silver medallist John McGough in the 880 yards.

Halswelle's 440-yards best performance of 48.4 seconds survived as the UK record until 1934, when it was beaten by Godfrey Rampling, a 1936 Olympic relay gold medallist in Berlin and the father of the actress Charlotte Rampling. As a Scottish record, it defied attacks by Eric Liddell and was finally beaten by John McIsaac in 1958. In 1906, Halswelle set a Scottish 600-yard record that was to remain unbroken until 1968. Two years later, he established the Scottish 300-yard record, then the world's second-fastest time, which survived until 1961. This record was finally beaten by a Glasgow University student who was later to go into politics; he was the future Liberal Democrat leader and his name was Menzies Campbell.

Curran realised that once Halswelle got out in front in a race he was unbeatable, but he still had to learn to fight in a tight corner.

'Your job is to win, right?' said Curran. 'So concentrate and do what's necessary now. If you are thinking, I failed in the past and I'm going to get beaten now, then go home and don't bother to compete! I'm not saying it's bad to lose, but it is bad to give up when you still have a chance.'

'Courage,' Curran would tell him, 'is a form of stubbornness. It's a refusal to quit when you want to quit because you are tired or broken. You need it in everyday life, and often everyday courage is more important than the great deeds sort of courage.

'You need it in the barracks just as much as you need it on the battlefield,' he continued, 'and you really need it on the track. I can help you there, sir – it's my trade.'

– Chapter 9 –

In Love with a Legend

Johnny Hayes never wasted much time agonising over the problems of employing a professional coach. For him, there were no such dilemmas. The so-called job at Bloomingdale's gave him all the time he wanted to train and he was going to grab the best and most professional training advice wherever he could find it.

By 1903, when Hayes was 17, the American papers were full of colourful reports on Baron Pierre de Coubertin's Olympic movement. Even the priests at the orphanage were excited by the coverage and they would boast to Johnny and his brother Willie that the Irish were the best athletes in the world.

The Olympics were coming out of Europe for the first time and were bound for America, so there was almost daily mention of stories linked to the Games in the press. There had been bitter squabbles between Chicago and St Louis over who should host the Games, which whipped up plenty of interest. American newspapers were full of colourful accounts of how de Coubertin had modelled his modern-day Olympics on the myths and fables of ancient Greece, and in Manhattan, Johnny Hayes devoured all he could read about the Games. The teachers and priests at the orphanage, too, couldn't escape the endless stream of often lurid stories about the Olympics and were happy enough to pour a little culture and history down the throats of their inmates.

The origins of the ancient Greek Games, as everyone knew, were lost in the mists of pre-history, and archaeologists are convinced that Olympia was a religious centre long before the first historical mention of the Games there in 776 BC. There are theories that prayers, accompanied by sacrifices – some of them human – were offered at Olympia for centuries before the birth of the Games, and that the sports were introduced as a substitute for sacrifices, or as part of the ceremony running alongside the sacrifices.

There, in the valley of Olympia, on the south-western coast of the Greek peninsula, existed one of the oldest shrines in Greece: the altar to the great mother of the gods – Rhea, Goddess of the Earth. Sacrifices were made to this goddess and some of them were human sacrifices.

According to tradition, at the climax of Rhea's feast day, a priest would stand before the altar with a blazing torch, poised to perform a human sacrifice. Young men would line up about 200 yards from the altar (known to the Greeks as *stade*). Following a blast from a horn, they would sprint to the altar and the first to get there would grab the torch from the hand of the priest. The victorious runner would hold it high above his head for a moment and then light the sacrificial fire – the first match to a somewhat sinister barbecue.

What we do know for sure is that in 776 BC , a young cook called Coroebus of Elis won a race over the same distance at Olympia. This is the date from which the ancient Greeks dated their calendar, and where formal records of the Games began.

All the legends of the ancient Games were reported in the American press in 1903, and thousands of young men like Hayes lapped up the highly sensationalised stories. There were plenty of lessons, too, for the teachers to pass on. During the month of the Olympic Games, they told the boys, no one was allowed to carry arms in ancient Greece; there would be an honourable truce throughout the country. Celebrities would turn up at the Games, and not just sportsmen. Poets like Pindar, philosophers such as Socrates, and the finest artists and sculptors all hoped to lend their glamour to celebrate the exploits of the winners.

A man didn't have to be rich to compete in the ancient Games, the boys were told, but wealth certainly helped. Each athlete had to devote himself exclusively to training for eleven full months in advance. He would spend ten months practising at home and then reported to the Olympic judges for the final touches to his training. Each competitor, at least for the first few centuries of the Games, had to swear that he was a freeborn native Greek.

He had to make pledges to the Greek gods, too, for the Olympic festival was essentially a religious ceremony and all the games and rituals were contrived to please the gods. For almost a month, under the strict supervision of the judges, who beat athletes with canes to impose discipline, the competitors trained full time, bathing to relax and massaging their bodies with oil to keep their muscles supple.

No women were allowed to compete in these ancient Olympics, and this was a philosophy that de Coubertin seemed happy to go along with for his resurrected Games. Any woman discovered at the ancient Games faced punishment by death: she was to be thrown from a nearby cliff. According to legend, this edict was disregarded only once when Pherenice of Rhodes accompanied her son Pisidores to the Games. She disguised herself as an athlete, but when her son won the boxing competition, she rushed up to him and threw her arms around him so eagerly that her robe slipped and everyone could see she was a woman. But because her father and her brothers had been Olympic champions, she was spared.

It was said that from then on, to avoid deception, all athletes in all events had to compete naked, but a less romantic view was that this rule was brought in to avoid cheating. The idea certainly appealed to Johnny Hayes, who had seen plenty of shirt-tugging during boisterous football games and rough tactics when boys were sprinting for a tape.

Legends of incredible heroes, part-fact and more than half-fancy, were trotted out to lend their history to de Coubertin's Olympic movement. None was more formidable than the wrestler Milo of Croton. His typical diet was reported to include seven pounds of meat, seven pounds of bread and four or five quarts of wine each day. Legend had it that in one day at Olympia, he ate an entire four-year-old bull!

Milo won the wrestling competition six times, but it was the tale of his party tricks that set young New York boys alight. He was said to have been able to tie a piece of string around his forehead and, by swelling his veins, to snap the cord. When they built a life-size statue of him, he carried it single-handed into the stadium. He would also stand on a disc covered in oil and fight off all-comers without ever losing his footing.

There were chariot races in these Games too – wild affairs, full of dirty tricks. And for a victory in the Olympics, each champion received an olive wreath. De Coubertin, with his ideas of amateurism, would have liked the awards to have stopped there, but of course that was only the start. An ancient Olympic victor became an idol when he returned home and his fellow citizens would shower him with gifts. The victor was often rewarded with a free house, meals for life and large sums of money. Statues would be erected and sometimes a street in his city renamed after him.

As the New York press pointed out, at these classical Games, losers earned only scorn – a point not lost on young Americans. For the Greeks, cheating was considered an even greater sin than losing. Athletes who violated the Olympic code had to erect their statues at the foot of Mount Kronius. Written on a loser's statue would be the name of the guilty athlete and his offence.

Above all, Hayes and the other New York boys learned that the Games were for champions, for professionals at their peak of their sport. They brought big rewards and contests were strictly about winning. These were the legends and the legacies the American press rammed home.

There was one further legend that captured the imagination of the young Johnny Hayes. When de Coubertin had his vision of resurrecting the Olympic Games, a colleague suggested a long-distance foot race based on the legend of the soldier said to have run carrying an historic message from Marathon to Athens.

The suggestion fired the imagination of the Greeks in 1896, and for them it proved to be the highlight of those first modern Olympics. Americans returning from the revived Games brought the idea back home with them and staged a 25-mile marathon of their own, on 20 September, from Stamford, Connecticut, to the Columbia Oval in New York. Their race was staged by the gloriously named New York City Knickerbocker Athletic Club.

In the spring of the following year, the Boston Athletic Association planned yet another marathon, this time to be held on Patriot's Day, 19 April, and to honour the story of Paul Revere, carrying yet another historic message, with his night-time ride to bring news of the American Revolution in 1775.

Even by 1903, the Boston Marathon, destined to become a great annual event, was establishing a legend of its own, and of all the legends of the ancient Games, this was the one to which Johnny Hayes constantly returned. On his daily runs, he daydreamed of the story of the Marathon, and he knew that, thanks to Boston, this was one part of the Olympic legend that he might hope to touch for himself.

– CHAPTER 10 –

THE RACE THAT SAVED THE GAMES

It was an advert in a travel agent's window in London, in the autumn of 1895, that caught the eye of a young Oxford student, George Stuart Robertson: the offer of a trip to the newly resurrected Olympic Games in Athens, not just as a spectator but as a competitor.

'The Greek classics were my proper academic field, so I could hardly resist a go at the Olympics, could I?' he said.

Robertson was a hammer-thrower at Oxford but there was no such event at Athens, so he entered the shot-put and the discus events, finishing fourth and sixth respectively. He also won a wreath of olive leaves for composing an ode in ancient Greek. Robertson found the whole Olympic experience: 'Most amusing. There wasn't any prancing about with banners and nonsense like that. I suppose we had some kind of Olympic fire but I don't remember it if we did. It was all a splendid lark.'

While there, he was presented to King George of Greece – 'nice chap, good sense of humour' as well as Baron de Coubertin – 'funny little man, the Baron'.

This 'funny little man', barely 5 feet 3 inches tall, was to change the course of sporting history. He attended St-Cyr, the famous French military academy, and decided soon in his career that military life was not for him. He quit before he graduated, turned to the study of political science and eventually devoted his life and wealth to the field of public education.

De Coubertin believed that mental and physical development were inseparable, a belief that caused him a lot of trouble with the French educational tradition. In French schools, he complained, 'physical inertia was considered an indispensable assistant to the perfecting of intellectual powers.' De Coubertin toured Europe and North America studying physical education systems, and during his travels he was excited by the ruins of the temples and stadium at Olympia, excavated between 1875 and 1881 by a German archaeological team.

The Baron was greatly disturbed by an international trend towards commercialism in sport and he gradually began to dream that a revival of the ancient Greek Olympic Games might return it to some idealised vision of purity. His proposal was simple: amateur athletes from all nations would gather every four years and compete in a variety of sports, but for no material reward and without a hint of commercial gain.

Everywhere he went, de Coubertin outlined and preached his idea. In June 1894, an International Olympic Congress was convened to look at the proposal and one of its leading figures, Michel Bréal, a French Jewish linguist and historian from the Sorbonne, wrote to de Coubertin saying: 'If the organising committee of the Athens Olympics would be willing to revive the famous run of the Marathon soldier as part of the Games, I would be glad to offer a prize for the new Marathon race.' The prize, he proposed, should be a fine silver cup.

De Coubertin delivered the letter to the Greeks, who seized on the idea with patriotic fervour. The official programme for those 1896 Games said that the Marathon was 'evidence of the Greek dedication to freedom as a nation and the sacrifice of the individual to maintain that freedom'.

There was some tradition of distance running in ancient Greece and, indeed, the ancient Greeks used long-distance foot soldiers as messengers. They were tough, wiry, professional runners, who could take on any distance and any terrain. One of these messengers, according to legend a man called Pheidippides, once ran from the battlefield of Marathon to Athens with news of a victory over the invading Persians.

'Rejoice, we conquer' was the message he was supposed to have gasped, before dropping dead with exhaustion. He had covered around 25 hilly miles of tough terrain. Certainly, records exist confirming that at least some of this story is based on fact. One historian, Herodotus, wrote a detailed account of a battle of Marathon, but made no mention of Pheidippides' run. He did, however, record that a man called Pheidippides was sent to run 150 miles across mountainous country from Athens to Sparta to try and encourage Spartan support against the Persians.

The 25-mile run from Marathon to Athens actually comes from a separate story related by the philosopher Plutarch some 600 years later. Plutarch told of a messenger called Eucles, who ran to Athens to announce victory. Whatever the truth, it is Pheidippides who is immortalised as the hero today on the marble stone that lies just beyond the southern tip of the village of Marathon and carries the words, 'Starting point of the Marathon'.

But in 1896, despite all their enthusiasm for the Olympic Games and for the newly invented 'Marathon Race', the Greek contingent at the Games in Athens had won nothing. Their last hopes rested on the fourteen Greeks selected to represent them in this 25-mile (40km) run from two trial races.

Generous prizes were being dangled to try and guarantee a Greek victory. The main backer of the Games, Georgios Averoff, was said to have offered his daughter in marriage plus a million-drachma dowry for the winner if he were a Greek. The Greeks badly needed a victory to salvage any national pride and in one Greek runner, Spiridon Louis, it seemed they had found the answer to their prayers.

Louis, aged 24, was the son of a working family from Maroussi, a suburb of Athens. His village was renowned as a fine source of spring water and twice a day he would accompany his mule carrying buckets of water into Athens. It was an 8-mile journey each way and Louis built up considerable stamina. Louis also served in the army under Colonel Papadiamantopoulos, the official starter for the race, who had urged his protégé to take part in the trials for the Greek marathon squad.

The fifth day of the Athens Games, Marathon Day dawned in glorious sunshine. Long before the stadium was open at 10am, the Greeks were out in huge numbers abuzz with talk of the race. Every seat in the stadium was taken and thousands more scrambled onto the hills looking down over the finish. The road itself between Marathon and Athens was narrow, unpaved, rutted and thick with dust.

The day before the big event, the contestants were taken to

Marathon, and most of the Greek runners went to a church service on the morning of the race, where the priests offered up prayers for a home win. Out of the eighteen starters, fourteen of them were Greek, including Spiridon Louis.

With the Greeks were four foreigners: Gyula Kellner of Hungary, Edwin (Teddy) Flack of Australia, Arthur Blake of the USA and Albin Lermusiaux from France. The Frenchman insisted on running in white gloves in honour, he said, of the King of Greece. After speeches in Greek and French, the runners set out in bright but cool conditions, with the Frenchman going off at a crazily aggressive pace.

At the official 15km mark, the Frenchman was 3km ahead of the field and timed at an impressive 52 minutes. Well behind at this stage was Spiridon Louis, who was handed a beaker of wine and a hard-boiled egg by his stepfather. Blake, the American, gave up at around 20km, his feet covered in blood, and at 25km Lermusiaux was still ahead, though paying heavily for his early pace with Flack gaining on him every minute. The Greek, Louis, was reported to be more than 6 minutes down on the leaders, but as they approached the 32km mark, Lermusiaux hit the wall of exhaustion so familiar to marathon runners and was overtaken by the Australian. Flack now had a very comfortable lead, and with only 6km left, it seemed certain that he would win.

But a mile or so later, Louis suddenly appeared at Flack's shoulder, looking 'very fresh and running well'. They ran side by side as the road dipped downhill towards the city of Athens, and at around 5km from the finish, Louis was handed some slices of orange by the girl he was later to marry. Shortly after this, Teddy Flack ground to a standstill, defeated and broken by the surprising speed and freshness of the Greek, who had seemingly come from nowhere.

Back in the stadium, the Greek Royal Family arrived early enough to watch some of the track and field events. The crowd of 60,000 were quite subdued, politely applauding the victories of the foreigners and still unaware that Flack had dropped out. But even as he was brought to the finish in a hospital wagon, the Colonel accompanying Louis galloped ahead to the stadium with the news that a Greek was leading the race.

From outside the stadium, cannon boomed to announce that a runner was in sight and Louis appeared, his white vest drenched in sweat and covered in dust. The crowd erupted and the roars from the stadium were echoed by the thousands perched on the hills outside. Hats, flags and handkerchiefs fluttered like doves; women threw their jewellery at Louis like fans at a rock concert and the Crown Prince Constantine and Prince George leaped from their seats to run alongside him to the tape.

His time was 2:58:50. A full 7 minutes behind him came another Greek, Vasilakos, followed by a third Greek, Belakas. In fourth place was the only foreigner to finish – the Hungarian Kellner, who ran in tired and angry, shouting that Belakas had never overtaken him and must have hitched a ride or taken a shortcut to have come home third. The Crown Prince, deputed to sort out the row, rapidly concluded that Belakas had indeed cheated and he was stripped of his third place.

Spiridon Louis, though, was hailed as a hero and presented with a silver medal and a crown of olive branches. He turned down the offer of a bride but accepted free meals for life, haircuts for life and a plot of land. When the King asked him what real reward he would like for his efforts, he chose a horse and cart to replace his donkey. Spiridon Louis reckoned he had already done enough travelling on his own two feet and never raced again.

That same Oxford student, George Stuart Robertson, shared a flat with Teddy Flack during the Athens Olympics and took a great interest in the Marathon race. 'There were runners accompanied by a lot of Greek officers on horseback and my friend Flack was accompanied also by the butler of the British Ambassador on a bicycle,' he said. All his long life, Robertson was convinced that Spiridon Louis – along with other Greeks – had been assisted by soldiers accompanying them. Whatever the truth, it was the legend that won out and the legend of the Marathon certainly saved de Coubertin's infant Olympic Games.

The longest race and the most gruelling event, the Marathon is now one of the highlights of each Olympics and traditionally takes place on the final day. Its instant popularity led to races modelled on it appearing all over the world. Held only once every four years, it is the Olympic Marathon that attracts the most international attention, and from its earliest days it was this contest that generated the best stories. Already, in New York and in Italy, two boys, Johnny Hayes and Dorando Pietri, were shaping up to clash in the biggest Marathon story of all.

– CHAPTER 11 –

TORN APART
BY PASSION

For Dorando, the Marathon and Teresa were his two great passions and now, almost every night, he would take himself off to train just outside of Carpi. Sometimes friends would walk across and watch the lonely figure pounding away in the twilight.

He would run beyond the town walls, past the Porta Mantova and San Nicolò and by the vast icehouse rented by the butcher from Carpi, who stored meat there. When the weather turned cold, his men would drag ice and snow into the stone structure and pack it in layers of straw, for they thought icehouse meat could be kept fresh for the best part of a year.

Almost always, Dorando ran alone. The truth was that no one could keep up with him. Whenever he ran, he would dream of his life with Teresa; he would put in the miles to make himself unbeatable. He dreamed of wining the Olympics, marrying his girl and making his mark in Carpi, just as his father had always hoped. Other boys would go to the gym club to get strong; they would take part in boxing or fencing, or work out on the parallel bars or the rings. They had fun, but they weren't as driven as he was. Dorando was always a loner and when he wanted to make himself strong, he would contrive to find some task that might also earn him money. Sometimes a pastry cook would want a heavy load of charcoal lugged halfway across town. The boy to send for was Dorando, and for him, the few lire pressed into his hand made the exercise even more enjoyable.

In 1905, Dorando had enough ability to warrant a trip overseas and his first international success came at the age of nineteen when he won a 30km race in Paris in pouring rain. He started to look like a real prospect for the 'Intermediate' Olympics, planned for Athens the following year. But the Paris race was followed by a row as the French objected to the Italian teenager who spent his entire time running. They muttered that he was really a professional and tried to strip him of his victory.

In November 1905, Dorando received his call-up papers for military service. Already he was something of a celebrity because of his running, and the head of the Italian Athletic Federation, Mario Luigi Mina, stepped in to make sure that he spent his two years of military service with a regiment in Turin that was renowned for giving athletes enough time and space to train and race. So he found himself assigned to the 25th Reggimento Fanteria, which he joined on 3 December. There, he raced in the colours of the Atalanta Club.

It was a wrench for Dorando and Teresa to spend the best part of two years apart. It was a long time, but Turin was not that far from Carpi and Dorando relished the thought of being able to give more time and energy over to his running and being able to train alongside some of the best runners in Italy.

On 31 December 1905, on a 500-metre circuit marked out on the Parco del Valentino, he made an attempt on the Italian one-hour record. A big crowd turned out to watch the new runner attack the record, but it was a filthy night, very cold and windy, and the conditions made record-breaking close to impossible. Even so, he only just missed breaking the Italian record set two years before in November 1903, when he covered 17,137.22 metres.

Military service and the odd snatched trip from Turin to Carpi to spend precious hours with Teresa meant that he cut back on his racing programme in 1906. But this still gave him plenty of time for training and his strength and stamina were increasing by the month.

At the beginning of April, Dorando applied for permission from the War Ministry to go to Rome for Olympic Games' trials. He secured himself a ticket for the Intermediate Olympics in Athens when he won the trial marathon, said to be over 42km, in 2:42:6 on a beaten earth track at the Piazza di Siena. He could hardly contain his excitement on being congratulated by the Italian King Vittorio Emanuele for his performance in the trial, nor when Queen Elena presented him with a commemorative sash awarded to all the winners of the Italian Championships that year.

Better than that, he was given a whole month off military service to prepare for the Games, which meant that he could spend even more time back in Carpi with Teresa. But this decision prompted some criticism back in the town. Already he was public property, someone chosen to uphold the honour of

Italy. They didn't like the idea that distractions might spoil his Marathon prospects. 'Why aren't you out there running?' they would taunt, if they saw him walking with Teresa. Or they might say, 'You should be in bed – but go there on your own!'

The club members of La Patria were now fully caught up in his growing success. Magazines they put out in the area played up the triumphs of the working-class boy, a boy with no advantages, who by his own efforts was a champion of the people and looked certain to bring glory and esteem back to Carpi.

Dorando proudly showed the Rome newspapers to his mother, father, Teresa and, it seemed, half the population of Carpi: his name had been added to the list of 59 athletes leaving for Athens.

He left on 20 April 1906, just two days before the start of the Games, on the steamship the *Sicilia*. His hopes were high. Dorando took with him a small bag and in it he had carefully packed cheese, salami, bread and balsamic vinegar, everything he might need for the voyage and for the race. At last, he was off to the cauldron of Athens.

As the boat pitched in the swell of the Mediterranean he was violently seasick. He couldn't wait to get his feet back on dry land and start running again.

– CHAPTER 12 –

THE BARON'S LOST VISION

After the excitement of the Marathon in the first Olympics in Athens, the next two Games almost saw the vision die on its feet, and this time even the Marathon couldn't save it.

The Paris Olympics of 1900 was the most ill planned of all modern Games. They were so disorganised that, bizarrely, many of the more than 1,000 competitors from 22 countries didn't realise they were taking part in an Olympic Games at all! The big problem was that they were run as a sideshow, almost an afterthought to the International Exposition, held in the city that year.

Following the highly successful Games in 1896, plenty wanted to hold the competition permanently in Greece – the athletes of Athens actually circulated a petition asking for just that. But de Coubertin insisted that for the Olympics to be truly international, they had to be hosted in turn by all the leading nations of the world. Added to that, of course, he was French, and had committed himself to holding the Olympic Games as part of the 1900 International Exposition in Paris.

The French government, which was supervising the Exposition, took over responsibility for the Games but treated them very much as a secondary attraction, as insignificant compared with the exhibits at the International Exposition, which included the first line of the Paris Métro underground system, the Gare de Lyon and the Gare d'Orsay, as well as the Grand and Petit Palais.

At first the organisers didn't even bother to have the sports called Olympic Games. The events were termed simply an 'international championship' and nowhere on the official programme did the word Olympic appear. Baron de Coubertin himself was stuck in an obscure committee post and it was only at the last minute that he was called in to salvage his Games when it became all too obvious that none of the facilities were ready. At last, they placed him in charge of the committee overseeing the sports and told him that he could call the games Olympic. The Baron did what he could, but it was too late for him to unscramble all the confusion.

The track and field events were scheduled to be held on the grounds of the Racing Club of France in the Bois de Boulogne. If you planned a picnic, the surroundings and the site were beautiful, but they were not so attractive for the Olympic Games. For one thing, there was no track. The idea of desecrating their grassy meadows with a cinder track was more than the French authorities could stomach.

Despite the lack of preparations, the number of contestants in these Games had increased to 1,319 (including eleven women) compared with the 311 who turned up at Athens four years before, and the number of countries competing had risen from thirteen to 22.

The Americans didn't bother to send a strong team to Paris, but even so, four members of their squad – Ray Ewry, Alvin Kraenzlein, Irving Baxter and J. Walter Tewkesbury – dominated the track and field programme. Out of 23 events, they collected eleven first places, five second places and one third place.

But the uniforms of the Americans made almost as great an impression as their performances. 'The natty costumes of the Americans,' one reporter noted, 'were a decided contrast to the home-made attire of some of the best European athletes who, instead of donning a sweater or bathrobe after the trials, walked about in straw hats and light overcoats'.

The Parisian spectators appeared to be appalled by the enthusiastic cheering of the American supporters. 'What a band of savages!' one onlooker said. And as if all this didn't damage de Coubertin's vision of the Olympics enough, he discovered that a series of athletic events had been organised for 'non-amateurs'.

The shambles of the Paris Games was made even worse by the Marathon, which was run over a distance of 40.260km (25 miles and some 30 yards), over streets encircling the city. Originally, the race was scheduled to be run over 40km from Paris to Versailles, but at the last moment, after the American, British, Swedish and South African runners had carefully studied and even practised over part of the Versailles route, the French switched to a different course.

They planned to send the runners four times around the grass track at the Racing Club and then take a circular route around Paris, returning back to the track.

One of the most obstinate myths about the 1900 Games is the claim that Michel Théato, who won the race for France, was a baker and that he used his knowledge of Paris to take shortcuts. This seems an unlikely story. The idea that this runner should gain an extensive knowledge of Parisian streets in a city where, even now, you are never more than a leisurely stroll from a shop selling fresh bread and croissants is unconvincing, and the 'rumour' seems to have its genesis in an account by J. Walter Tewkesbury, a hurdler from the USA.

Tewkesbury may have had a fine touch in giving the press the odd colourful story. Finding there were no hurdles for practice at the Croix Catalan stadium, he claimed to have shocked passing Parisians by training at the local cemetery, using the gravestones as hurdles. His 'evidence' that Théato had cheated was that there was no sign of sweat on his clothing whereas all the other runners were sweaty and dirty.

In fact, photographs of the event, with Théato in them, show the runner looking suitably exhausted in a dark, sleeveless vest. And any study of the route shows that it would have been almost impossible for anyone to take a shortcut as the course ran round the periphery of the town. Théato would have had to run straight through the centre of Paris to the other side to gain any advantage. There were also six control points, where the runners' numbers were noted, and the runners were followed throughout the route by journalists.

Théato, who finished ahead of Emile Champion (who was actually paced in this race by a professional called Ducros), was born in Luxembourg in 1877. He was said to have worked as a cabinetmaker and a gardener, and probably did not have French citizenship at the time of the race. But he was a member of the

Saint-Mandé Athletic Club and the Racing Club of France, and certainly looked French and spoke French.

The race went into history as the *Marathon des Fortifs* because the route followed the 'fortifications', the defensive walls from the Franco-Prussian War of 1870 that are today the site of the inner ring road (*périphérique*) around Paris. But in 1900, Parisians used the fortifications for tipping their rubbish! No one bothered to cordon off the route and runners had to make their way past herds of sheep and cows being driven to the slaughterhouse. Perhaps even worse were the jeers and insults directed at them.

On a fearsomely hot day, confusion set in early when the Swede Ernest Fast was leading but he was given a wrong direction from a policeman from Marseilles, who didn't know Paris. It was said that the policeman, on learning that the runner he had misdirected had lost, killed himself some days later.

Théato started cautiously and finished nearly 5 minutes ahead of his French team-mate Champion and more than half an hour in front of the hapless Fast. But one American reporter wrote: 'It may be that the chief reason for the Frenchmen's success in this event is that they were familiar with the course.'

Other American observers were less charitable, claiming that Arthur Newton of the New York Athletic Club, who finished fifth in the official results, actually overtook the French runners including the winner early in the race, took the lead around the halfway point and was never passed the rest of the way. They say that when Newton reached the finish, the three Frenchmen and the Swede were waiting for him.

The rumour that Newton should have won the race grew stronger each time it was told and seems subsequently to have entered Olympic lore. But if you go back to the original accounts of the race, published in the papers by eyewitnesses, you get a very different view of the claim that the race should have been awarded to an American. One such account appeared in the *San Francisco Chronicle*, dated Paris, 19 July 1900. The newspaper reports:

> The victory caused much elation among Frenchmen who celebrated their first and only win in the sports with characteristic enthusiasm. French spectators invaded the track and carried Théato around on their shoulders while the cheers resounded across the ground. The three American competitors, to whom the course was quite new and proved a severe handicap, fared badly.
>
> Newton made the best showing, keeping pace with the leading batch of Frenchmen until about 20 miles had been covered. By this time all the weak runners had been weeded out. Newton, who had not been feeling well for several days, was overcome by the heat and exertion and was obliged to drop behind. He struggled on pluckily to the end but reached the goal nearly an hour and a quarter after the winner.
>
> By this time the spectators imagined that all save those who had arrived had abandoned the race and many went home. Newton's arrival therefore passed almost unnoticed, except by the Americans, who gave him an encouraging cheer as he entered the track for the three laps which formed the conclusion of the race. This he did walking.

Michel Théato was given a finishing time of 2:59:45, but even he had no idea that the event in which he was running was part of the new-fangled Olympic Games – in fact, he was not to learn until twelve years later that he had become an official Olympic champion. It was Théato's first marathon. He retired from racing in 1902 with knee problems and took a job as gardener in the Bois de Boulogne. During the Great War, he worked as a carpenter and subsequently, suffering from alcoholism, was reported to have died in an asylum in 1919.

Things grew even worse for the reputation of this marathon long after the finish when one American, Dick Grant, who finished sixth and according to the contemporary account was very close to collapse, brought an unsuccessful lawsuit sixty years later against the International Olympic Committee, claiming that a cyclist had knocked him down as he was about to overtake the Frenchman who won the race.

But if the Paris Marathon of 1900 provided drama, farce, myths and dirty tricks, the Marathon in the next Olympic Games showed that far worse was yet to come.

– CHAPTER 13 –

THE SHAMBLES OF
ST LOUIS

Baron Pierre de Coubertin had visited St Louis, in Missouri, and he didn't think much of it. He feared that the Games there – their next destination – would be an even greater disaster than Paris.

You didn't have to run far to share his low opinion of St Louis. It was notorious for its torpid, sweltering climate during the summer months. The water was unhealthy, fevers persisted, and consequently, energies were sapped. Perhaps most disturbing of all to him was the fact that St Louis did not have any real sporting tradition, for it was outside of the American east and mid-western sporting establishment.

De Coubertin wanted his beloved Games to go to Chicago, and on 13 November 1900, the *New York Sun* told its readers that the Games would be held in Chicago. But de Coubertin found himself caught up in the turmoil of American politics and he was no match for the opponents who overruled him. James Sullivan, the Secretary General of the American Athletic Union, was rumoured to be secretly furious that he had not been chosen as a member of de Coubertin's International Olympic Committee and so he set up his own United States Olympic Committee and the newly elected US President, Theodore Roosevelt – who had a passion for sport – agreed to become honorary president.

St Louis, with a population of over half a million by 1904, was the cotton capital of the US. Founded by French traders, it was due to celebrate the 100th anniversary of the acquisition of Louisiana by President Thomas Jefferson from Napoleon I for $15 million. It was considered madness to conduct two major international events at the same time in two different American cities, and the rows and the horse trading over where the Olympics should end up guaranteed plenty of press coverage.

When the story that St Louis could snatch the Games broke in early November 1902, the press loved it. Soon every newspaper reader knew about de Coubertin's new movement and eagerly devoured each detail of stories about the Olympics. Sullivan strongly backed the Games going to St Louis and Roosevelt, when asked to arbitrate, opted for St Louis too. On 10 February 1903, de Coubertin reluctantly cabled the US Olympic Committee: 'transfer accepted'. These words ended some two and a half years of wrangling and shattered Chicago's lingering hopes for winning civic prestige and worldwide attention.

But de Coubertin never attended the 1904 Games and it was said he never forgave Sullivan for laying on another sideshow to the St Louis World Fair. The official appointment of Sullivan by St Louis Fair officials, in mid-July 1903, as president of the Organising Committee was salt to his wounds.

For his part, Sullivan was delighted to find his picture published from one end of America to the other. But on the other hand, de Coubertin – who was Sullivan's theoretical boss on Olympic matters – was by now ambivalent about the widespread attention on the other side of the Atlantic being paid to his creation. The good news for de Coubertin, however, was that nothing like this had happened before. At last, his movement had 'arrived' in America and thousands of American boys, Johnny Hayes among them, thrilled at the stories of past Olympic heroism and the prospect of more to come that appeared in the newspapers every day.

Because of the time and expense involved in sending a team to the United States, European representation in St Louis was minimal. An overwhelming majority of the 617 competitors representing twelve countries were Americans. The Americans sent 525, which meant that there were only 92 competitors from outside the United States – and 41 of these were from Canada. Britain, then the second-strongest track and field nation in the world, did not bother to send a squad. They were represented by just one athlete; he was in fact Irish and competed for the Irish-American Athletic Club based in New York. France didn't send a team either, while Germany and Hungary sent only a few athletes, mostly swimmers.

The American domination was more than impressive; it was in fact ridiculous. Never before or since has any one nation demonstrated such overwhelming superiority in the Olympic Games. In recognised Olympic events, the United States collected a total of 77 gold medals, precisely 70 more than the next country, Cuba.

Cuba also provided one of the most colourful entrants in the

91

Marathon. Felix Carvajal was a postal delivery boy in Havana, on his feet all day and proud of his endurance. When news filtered through to Cuba that the Olympics were to be held in St Louis, Carvajal announced that he was going to run the Marathon. But first he had to get to St Louis, and with no official Cuban team, Felix had no money. So the ambitious post boy turned up in the public square in Havana and began running round in circles as Pagliani had done back in Italy.

Soon Carvajal had a crowd watching him, so he clambered onto a wooden box and told anyone who would listen that he was off to St Louis to win the Olympic Marathon. It worked. Soon enough he was on a boat for St Louis via New Orleans, where he discovered that New Orleans is famous not just for fine food, but also for gambling. He ate well enough, but lost all his money on the gambling tables. Despite this setback, he didn't give up: he worked a little and he begged a lot.

At the Olympic camp, Carvajal became something of a mascot for the weight- throwers in the US team. They shared their food and lodgings with the little Cuban, who was just 5 feet tall, and tried to teach him a bit about running. On 30 August, the second day of the 1904 Olympic Games, and with the temperature and humidity in the nineties, Carvajal showed up for the start of the Marathon wearing a faded, long-sleeved shirt, a pair of long trousers and a pair of low-cut street shoes with heavy heels.

The start of the race was delayed as Martin Sheridan, a New York policeman and a discus thrower, took a pair of scissors to cut Carvajal's trousers off at the knees to allow him to run in makeshift shorts.

The sound of the starter's gun let loose complete chaos. There were 31 in the field, all of them Americans except for one Greek,

Demeter Velouis, and the Cuban, Carvajal. Men on horseback charged off in front of the runners to clear the course; trainers on bicycles wobbled beside the runners to give refreshments and encouragement; while doctors in cars drove off behind the runners to pick up the dropouts.

'The roads were so lined with vehicles,' one witness recalled, 'that the runners had to constantly dodge the horses and wagons. So dense were the dust clouds on the road that frequently the runners could not be seen by the automobiles following them.'

The Cuban went off in the lead and was reported to have clung onto it until the 25th kilometre, when he fell back and was said to have snatched peaches from spectators to quench his thirst. Later in the race, he was reported to have climbed into an orchard and raided it for apples, which gave him stomach cramps. Eventually he finished fifth, one place ahead of the Greek.

Another runner found the heat and the pace of the leading group too hot to handle. Fred Lorz from New York, a happy-go-lucky bricklayer, well-known among fellow runners for larking around, started fast but pulled up somewhere around 9 miles with cramp. He hitched a ride in a car for 11 miles but when the car in which he was travelling broke down 5 miles from the finish, Lorz started to run again.

In blistering heat he trotted in, looking strangely cool. He was cheered as the winner, did a victory lap, was carried in triumph and photographed with Alice Roosevelt, daughter of the American President. Lorz later claimed he had run in as a joke and was ultimately believed. The ban they had put on him was lifted and he went on to win the Boston Marathon the following year in 2:38:25.

A quarter of an hour later, Thomas Hicks, an English-born

Bostonian, staggered into the stadium close to complete collapse. His trainers had fed him the white of an egg, sulphate of strychnine and brandy. Barely aware of anything around him, Hicks eventually made the finish of that marathon in 3:28.53 for the 40km course. He had to be carried to a dressing room and four doctors worked to revive him. When he was finally strong enough to leave the stadium, he was driven to a bed at the Missouri Athletic Club and slept all the way there in a state of semi-consciousness that appeared to be typical of athletes who had been dosed with strychnine.

If the Americans won almost everything, including the chaotic Marathon, their dominance disappeared on 12 and 13 August, when the organisers staged two so-called 'anthropological days'. The anthropological days featured competition among pygmies and Zulu tribesmen from Africa, Ainus from Japan, Patagonians and Moros and Igorots from the Philippines.

'In no place but America would one have dared to place such events on a programme,' de Coubertin observed. 'But to Americans everything is permissible.'

Back in Europe, he was given an eyewitness account of these events by the Hungarian fencer Ferenc Kemeny. 'I was not only present at a sporting contest,' he said, 'but also at a fair where there were sports, where there was cheating, where monsters were exhibited for a joke.'

'Ah well,' sighed the Baron, 'that outrageous charade will, of course, lose its appeal when black men, red men and yellow men learn to run, jump and throw and leave the white men behind them.'

By the time the St Louis Festival ended, the Olympic ideal must have been close to rock bottom. The 1900 Olympic Games in Paris had attracted an international field, but had been dreadfully organised and badly attended. In contrast, the 1904 Olympic Games in St Louis had been properly organised and reasonably attended, but completely failed to draw an international field. By now, even de Coubertin must have been losing faith in his Olympic dream.

– CHAPTER 14 –

THE GREAT AMERICAN WINNING MACHINE

In half-desperation, de Coubertin reconsidered the offer by the Greeks to be permanent hosts for the Games. After the disastrous side show of St Louis in 1904, the Baron was prepared to settle for a compromise.

Starting in 1906, a plan was put forward that every four years there should be an 'Intermediate' Olympic competition that would always be held in Athens. Although these wouldn't be the official Olympic Games, they would serve to keep the Olympic flame burning bright, and not spluttering as in Paris and St Louis.

De Coubertin, though, kept his distance. He didn't attend the 1906 Games and was also absent from an International Olympic Committee session in Athens, where some delegates questioned his leadership. In the event, he managed to cling to power, but some historians suggest that he considered the Games of 1906 to be a mutinous affair and used his influence to make sure they didn't get full official Olympic recognition.

Originally, the Baron had chosen Rome for the Games of the Fourth Olympiad in 1908. As he explained, in his usual inflated language: 'I wanted Olympism, after its return from the excursion to utilitarian America, to don once again the sumptuous toga, woven of art and philosophy, in which I had always wanted to clothe her.'

The idea of holding these 'Intermediate' Olympic competitions every four years died after this first one in Athens, but by then the success of London in 1908 had secured the future of the Games. Yet the 1906 competition in Athens served a significant purpose. Once again, the Greeks laid on an efficient organisation, fine crowds and handsome pageantry. The great European powers, including Britain and France, returned to support the Games and, considering the shambles of 1900 and the lack of interest in the Games of 1904, it seems reasonable to conclude that once again the Greeks saved the Olympics.

For Wyndham Halswelle and Dorando Pietri, this would be their first taste of the Olympics and the opening ceremony provided quite a feast. King George and Queen Olga of Greece, together with Crown Prince Constantine and his brothers, presided over the pageant. Alongside them were the British King Edward VII and Queen Alexandra with the Princess of Wales. The refurbished Panathinaikos Stadium was packed and thousands more watched from the surrounding hills.

Halswelle nodded his approval at the ranks of Greek soldiers in gleaming armour and Dorando drank in every detail to relay to Teresa, back home in Carpi. Matt Halpin, manager of the United States Olympic Team in 1906, proudly stated, 'When I dipped the Stars and Stripes passing the Royal Box the King staked me to a smile that made me feel that I belonged.'

After the parade of 900 athletes from 21 different teams, the gathering watched a demonstration of gymnastics by Danish girls. 'Short-skirted and neat-legged,' according to one English reporter.

They were then treated to a demonstration in physical fitness by John E. Fowler-Dixon, a 56-year-old Englishman. John (known as Jimmy) Fowler-Dixon walked 1,500 metres in 8:45 seconds, then rested for 20 minutes and ran 1,500 metres in 5:46. Fowler-Dixon was a member of the Thames Hare and Hounds in London, the oldest cross-country running club in the world, founded in 1868. The most hard-line citadel of true blue amateurism, this was truly the club of the gentleman amateur.

There wasn't much room for the gentleman amateur in the American team at these Games, though the Americans were well represented in Athens. In the track and field events, for example, they had 31 athletes taking part, a larger representation than any of the other nineteen countries with the exception of the home nation, Greece. And, in all, America had 38 athletes competing in five sports.

But above all, for the first time, the American athletes regarded themselves as members of a team. They wore team uniforms, they had a team manager and looked and travelled together like a team. Their travelling expenses had been raised partly through voluntary contributions to an Olympic fund established by the American Committee for the Olympic Games.

The Americans descended on Athens to win. They had little time for de Coubertin's romantic vision that taking part was more important than winning. They came to claim victory, not just as individuals but as part of a squad.

When de Coubertin resurrected the Olympics in 1896, he had hoped the movement might foster a brand of internationalism in which nations discovered tolerance and peace through the games they played. He opposed sinister strains of nationalism and favoured instead patriotism – a love of country, which celebrated national pride without the chauvinism that belittles other national cultures.

But very quickly, de Coubertin's ideas ran headlong into the aggressive athletic nationalism pushed by American champions of their culture. Approaching Olympic competition from a different angle, Americans turned the Games into spectacles celebrating American values. De Coubertin's subtle distinctions between nationalism and patriotism passed them by, with American journalists and commentators soon totting up results from international playing fields and trotting them out as proof of national superiority.

In the first of de Coubertin's Games, in 1896, America was represented by a handful of athletes, but that didn't stop the American press from spinning their performances as a triumph of the American spirit. There began the long American tradition, still in the main practised today, of designating track and field events as the 'real Olympic Games'.

In 1900, in Paris, with the Olympics attached to the great turn-of-the-century International Exposition, the Americans asserted dominance in the track and field events, and once again claimed total Olympic victory. The *Chicago Tribune* complained that: 'The facility with which the American athletes carried off prizes finally grew monotonous.' The fact that at the Paris Games France actually won 26 first places to the United States' 20 did not in the least trouble commentators.

For American Olympians, there were no misgivings about foreign mismanagement of the 1904 Games. Once again, the United States had won its cherished track and field Games – what the *St Louis Post Despatch* called the 'Olympic Games proper' – by embarrassing margins, and for the first time the US reigned victorious by a huge, lopsided margin in every category of Olympic sport. After those games, James Sullivan, leader of the American Olympic movement, proclaimed, 'When one looks over the list of Olympic winners and then over the list of eligible men in the world, there are perhaps two men living today who are not in the stadium, who could have won Olympic honours.'

In 1906, as American organisers sent their first unified national team to the Intermediate Games, they vowed to 'spread-eagle their old world rivals'. The American team returned to a telegram from President Theodore Roosevelt: 'Hearty congratulations to you and the American contestants. Uncle Sam is alright.'

The truth was that once again 'Uncle Sam' actually missed out on the overall championship of the Games. The US gained a total of twelve victories in Athens, second to France's fourteen. But the self-image the Americans had fostered as Olympic winners was unstoppable. Their greatest potential rivals were from Britain, the traditional cradle of modern sport, but many Americans believed the British sheltered behind arcane rules crafted to protect a class system, the gentleman amateur and imperial status.

In Athens, Britain managed to place second in the traditional track and field events, but two of the three British victories were actually recorded by Irishmen. Con Leahy won the high jump and Peter O'Connor took the hop, step and jump. After his victory, O'Connor produced an Irish flag and asked that it should be raised to salute his triumph. The Greeks, though, stuck to protocol and raised the British flag. But this battle to be seen as the world leaders in Olympic sport, to use medal winners to assert national superiority, was a taste of deep trouble to come.

– CHAPTER 15 –

HUMBLED BY DISTANCE

For the Greeks who poured in their thousands into the Athens Olympic Stadium in 1906, the Marathon race was again the great attraction. Memories of Spiridon Louis' magnificent home victory twelve years before were still fresh in everyone's mind.

Athens virtually shut down on Marathon Day – 1 May. Most of the stores were closed, and once again the papers were full of hopes for a Greek victory. If the champion were Greek, he was promised prizes that included a huge statue of Hermes, a loaf of bread every day for a year, free lunch for six each Sunday for a year and free shaves for life. Not surprisingly, of the 53 starters, around half of them were Greek.

Dorando Pietri was welcomed to Athens as the guest of the Italian Consul. He was provided with a hamper of food from the Consulate on the eve of the race to ensure that the local food wouldn't upset his stomach. The day before the race, the runners were taken to the town of Marathon, where they spent the night in the residence of the Greek foreign minister, Georgios Skouzes. Two carriages were sent to escort Dorando to the race, and Italian sailors from the *Varese* went out on the route to act as stewards so that he didn't get lost on the way to the race and to ensure he was not misdirected once it was underway.

But as he warmed up for the start, Dorando feared he might well be in trouble: he had stomach pains and they mystified him. He had had them on and off ever since he had stepped off the boat from Italy and he wondered if they might be the after-effects of seasickness.

He confided in his friend Francesco Verri from Mantua (who won three gold medals for cycling in these Games and who was to pedal alongside him in the Marathon) about the pains as they made their way to the start. But as soon as he began running, the pain seemed to vanish and Dorando set out confidently at 3.05pm, with temperatures recorded at 27°C and still rising. Relief that the pain had vanished kicked in and excited him; he felt he could still win, after all.

No one was able to keep up with Dorando in those first few miles and with every step he seemed to build up a bigger lead. The unpaved road was hot and dusty; cinders and coal dust had been used to patch the many ruts and with every passing car, horse or even bicycle, the clouds of dust gripped at his throat. Just after 10 miles, when he had built up a lead of close to 5 minutes, Dorando realised something was very wrong.

He sucked at his handkerchief, which he had soaked before the start in balsamic vinegar. Then he wiped it across his lips and eyes but the dryness in his throat made it difficult, sometimes even impossible to breathe, and now the pains were back in his stomach. By turns he trembled as if with fever, broke into dripping sweats and shuddered with cold. Sometimes the pain throbbed in his stomach as if pincers were tearing away at his gut.

He slowed down, trying to nurse himself through the pain. His cyclist friend shouted to him that there were others behind, closing on him and trying to cut him down. In desperation, Dorando accelerated again, defying the pain that was gripping him.

At 24km, he slumped, his eyes hopelessly scanning the verge of the road for any hint of shade, but his legs buckled and he rolled to the side. For a moment, the joy of stopping with the dazzling sun blocking everything else out seemed even sweeter than winning, but he was a beaten man. His Olympics were over.

Dorando had gambled everything on victory, but the man who had just passed him there on the verge was a gambler too. Before the Games, the problem that had haunted William Sherring, the Canadian who robbed Dorando of his victory, was money. How could he possibly afford to go to Athens?

The Canadians wanted to send two marathon runners to Athens: Sherring and Jack Caffery. A proposal to raise money by a civic fund in Hamilton was vetoed and a benefit concert raised only $75 – not nearly enough to send both men – and so Sherring was given the money.

According to family lore, Sherring took a tip from a barman and bet the $75 on a racehorse at odds of 6:1. The horse, named Cicely, won – giving him a payout of nearly $500. He quit his job and, by February 1906, he was travelling third class on a cattle boat for Athens.

Another version told by Jim Sherring, a nephew, is that his

uncle – who would gamble on anything that moved – may well have bet the money on a horse, but there is no way it would have won. He believed his uncle got himself to Greece by signing on a steamship as a boiler room loader to pay his passage across the Atlantic. When he wasn't shovelling coal, he trained by running around the deck.

William Sherring, who was 5 feet 7 inches tall and weighed only 115lb, worked as a brakeman on the Grand Trunk Railway in Canada and had been running competitively for eleven years before he won the Olympic Marathon. He finished second in the 1900 Boston Marathon to Jack Caffery, who was also from Hamilton, and held the Canadian record for 10 miles.

Sherring's decision to get out to Athens early was an inspired one. He arrived at the end of February 1906, a month before his team-mates, while the American team didn't get there until 19 April – three days before the start of the Games. The Marathon was run on 1 May, giving Sherring two months to train in Athens. He was able to get acclimatised to the food, the weather and the course between Marathon and Athens, which he trained over many times. Always slightly built, Sherring's training and lifestyle caused him to lose over 20lb during his two months in Athens.

The night before the race, he slept in a barn in the town of Marathon, and in the morning, he ate a few eggs before his run. When he entered in the lead at the stadium, far in front of his rivals, Prince George trotted the final lap with him. As a non-Greek, Sherring was ineligible for the statue of Hermes, the free bread or the free meals, but apparently he did receive a free goat from the Greeks and was rewarded with a free house when he arrived back home in Canada.

The Greeks quickly celebrated his victory and greeted him enthusiastically everywhere he went. He received a gold medal, a sprig cut from an olive tree from the sacred grove at Olympia, a marble statue of the Goddess Athena, four silver cups and honorary Greek citizenship.

Sherring received a hero's welcome, too, during his return trip to Canada, which included stops in London, New York, Montreal and Toronto. The City of Hamilton gave him a purse of $5,000 and the City of Toronto added $400. Shortly after he had received these gifts, Baron Pierre de Coubertin wrote a letter to the Governor General of Canada deploring both the Canadian celebrations and the gifts for Sherring.

Back in Athens, the large contingent of Italians – businessmen, traders and their families living there together with many Italians who had travelled across to the city to see Dorando win – were bitterly disappointed. They simply couldn't believe that he had dropped out.

'He must be ill,' they muttered. 'Perhaps he's been doped.' But then their sympathy turned to anger and even contempt. The Consulate felt that Dorando had let them down. 'We expected you to win,' they said coldly. 'We never expected you to drop out, to give up.'

For Dorando, the pain was worse than anything he had met out there on that hot, dusty road to Athens. He couldn't wait to get back to Teresa. His bid to win his Olympic race was over, and for him, the problem was that he didn't know why. Would it happen again, he asked himself over and over.

He boarded the boat home, heavy with doubt and with no winner's medal to take home to Teresa. As the boat pitched, he hung onto the rail and was once again horribly seasick.

– CHAPTER 16 –

ERUPTIONS IN ATHENS

For Wyndham Halswelle, victory in Athens 1906 seemed certain. 'Keep yourself out of trouble,' Jimmy Curran had warned him, 'and the watch tells me you can't lose.'

Halswelle took the document out of his pocket once again. He read it with a mixture of excitement and mounting confidence; he'd never had a passport before. This one, which was issued specially to allow him to travel to Athens for the Olympics, was signed by Sir Edward Grey, Principal Secretary of State for Foreign Affairs. The document requested that Halswelle be allowed to 'pass freely without let or hindrance' and that 'the athlete be given every assistance and protection'.

These were the first Games for which the British Olympic Association was responsible for sending a Great Britain team to the Olympics. Prior to this, individuals always travelled privately, paying their own way. Even so, the competitors received no government assistance, but like other competing nations in these Games, they were offered a contribution by the Greek organisers. The forty-strong team was led by the British Olympic Association Chairman, William Henry Grenfell, Lord Desborough. He arrived on the SS *Branwen*, a yacht owned by fellow fencing competitor Lord Howard de Walden.

Halswelle, in contrast, had travelled out aboard the SS *Baron Castle* and regularly worked out on the deck with two cyclists. They would do plenty of skipping, stretching, walking and even managed a little running while aboard.

On arrival in Athens, Halswelle stayed at the British Consulate. The British were well aware that this was no ordinary athlete, for he had been selected for the 100, 400 and 800 Metres, a range of events no other British athlete has since matched. Halswelle had a tough programme that involved six races in seven days. He competed first in the 100 Metres and made it through to the semi-finals; he then had tough heats in both the 400 and 800 Metres.

In the 400 Metres, he came up against the American Paul Pilgrim, a protégé of Matt Halpin, the New York Athletic Club official serving as manager of the American Olympic team. Pilgrim, aged just twenty and a member of Halpin's club, was added to the already-strong American squad despite the fact that he had no great reputation, had achieved nothing nationally and was regarded very much as an outsider in the 400 Metres final.

Because Harry Hillman, the defending champion from Amercia, had bruised his knee during the boat trip to Athens and failed to regain his best form, Wyndham Halswelle was the pre-race favourite. His most dangerous rival seemed to be Nigel

Barker, an Australian who returned the fastest time in the preliminary heats.

Hillman, who had won the 400 Metres in the St Louis Olympics of 1904, got off to a good start but his leg weakened halfway through the race. Halswelle found it difficult to get past the injured man, who onlookers say was blocking him, but then he and Barker pulled away and swept towards the finish. Victory for Halswelle appeared certain but suddenly, and quite unexpectedly, Pilgrim put on a furious sprint, barged his way past the leaders and won by more than a metre. Halswelle was second and Barker came third. Pilgrim had run 53.2 seconds to Halswelle's 53.8.

In this race, there were no starting blocks, no lanes and the race was run on a 300-metre cinder track with impossibly tight bends. This was the only 400-metre race (off scratch with no handicap) that Halswelle ever lost, and he was angry about what he considered to be blocking tactics. When Jimmy Curran read about the race in the *Glasgow Herald* he was angry, too, but his anger was directed at Halswelle for not staying out of trouble.

The next day, Pilgrim won the 800 Metres with his team-mate James Lightbody coming second. Halswelle could manage only third place, and once again, he lost out to two Americans in the rough and tumble of a race where he found himself the only Briton in the field. The British, who had stood at the track side and watched as Halswelle was jostled in the home straight of the 400, shook their heads in anger too.

'Damned unfair, not a way to run a race!' observed the one spectator, who probably knew more about the conduct of British sport than anyone then alive. He was the leader of the British team, the fencer Lord Desborough, who was there not only as a team leader but as a winner of the team silver medal in the épée at the age of fifty.

Desborough, born in 1855, was the epitome of the nineteenth-century gentleman amateur. Exceptionally talented, he would have a sporting go at anything and the breathtaking range of his achievements makes even the greatest all-rounders of the era look like blinkered specialists. As William Grenfell, the future Lord Desborough was President of Athletics and Rowing at Oxford, he raced the 3 miles against Cambridge and rowed No. 4 for Oxford in the famous 1877 boat race, the only one to end in a dead heat. The next year, he was in the winning boat.

Desborough also won the punting championship of Great Britain three years in a row, sculled from Oxford to Putney (105 miles) in one day, stroked an eight across the English Channel and fenced for Britain in the Olympics. He climbed extensively in the Alps, romping up the Matterhorn three times by three different routes, went big game hunting in India and shooting in the Rocky Mountains. In one season's stalking in Scotland he bagged 100 stags, and he caught 100 tarpon during three weeks' fishing in Florida. As a schoolboy, he shone in Harrow's cricket and football teams, threw the hammer out of sight and set a school mile record that stood for 61 years.

Desborough also swam across the Niagara Falls – twice. He did it twice only because an American lawyer travelling with him across the Atlantic could not believe that he had done it the first time, four years before. Never one to shirk a challenge, Desborough volunteered to do it all over again. They met at the Falls but the weather was foul with heavy hail and snow. The next day was worse, but against all advice he went ahead anyway. Eventually, to the relief of his challenger, the English Lord clambered out on the Canadian side, exhausted and frozen but, as ever, fit enough to be crowned one of the greatest all-round sporting champions Britain has ever produced.

When his competitive days were over, Desborough played with sports administration. He was at various times President of the Amateur Athletic Association, the Lawn Tennis and Croquet Association, the All England Club, the Amateur Fencing Association and the MCC. In his spare time, he founded the Royal Life Saving Society and was the man behind the Channel Swimming Association. As a war correspondent for the *Daily Telegraph* in Sudan in 1888, he once confronted the advancing enemy alone, armed only with an umbrella!

He was not a man to stand by and see a runner such as Wyndham Halswelle being knocked about on the track, and although the British team didn't protest over the conduct of the 400 Metres, Lord Desborough was to be presented with a unique opportunity to put his vision of fair play before the world.

For the Italians, and for Dorando Pietri, part of the attraction of the Intermediate Games in Athens in 1906 was the knowledge that the next Games were to be held in Rome. It was at the 1904 session of the International Olympic Committee held in London that the Games of the fourth Olympiad were formally awarded to Rome, but on 4 April 1906, on the very eve of the Athens Olympics, Mount Vesuvius near Naples erupted, devastating the surrounding area.

This disaster is the reason usually given for Rome's withdrawal as host for the 1908 Games, but while it didn't help, it was only half the story. Baron de Coubertin was a strong champion of the Games going to Rome and had plenty of support from Pope Pius X, King Vittorio Emanuele and, not surprisingly, the Mayor of

Rome. But the Prime Minister, Giovanni Gioletti, who held the purse strings for many new government projects, was dead against it. It was clear to him that the Italian government simply could not afford to subsidise the venture and when Vesuvius erupted it gave Gioletti all the excuses he needed to dump the costly Games.

Faced with the problem of finding an alternative host city with both the facilities and the will to step in and stage the Olympics in only two years' time, the International Olympic Committee sounded out the British. The man they turned to was Lord Desborough. He had been elected to the International Olympic Committee in 1905 and was ideally placed to consider the suggestion.

Desborough was able to float the idea immediately with King Edward VII, a great sports enthusiast and a close friend. He had the added advantage of being able to discuss the matter in even greater detail with his fellow members of the fencing team, who were all staying aboard the *Branwen*. They included Charles Newton-Robinson and Theodore Cook, both members of the Council of the British Olympic Association, and Lord Howard de Walden, a future President of the Amateur Fencing Association, together with two future Vice Presidents of the Association, Sir Cosmo du'Gordon and Edgar Seligman. The consensus of opinion from this very influential group was that the International Olympic Committee invitation for London to host the Games could be accepted, provided they got support from the governing bodies of British sport.

As soon as he was back in London, Desborough put the matter of hosting the 1908 Games before the British Olympic Association, formed only the previous May. With remarkable speed, a British Olympic Council was formed with the sole responsibility of organising of the Games, and on 19 November 1906, a letter was sent to the International Olympic Committee advising them that London was prepared to take over the Olympics. De Coubertin was delighted: he had long admired the British way of conducting sport and he believed Desborough was capable of laying on the best Games yet.

For Dorando Pietri, with his eyes set on winning a marathon in front of his home crowd, shifting the Games from Rome to London was yet another blow. The expense of travelling to London and racing on foreign soil did nothing to ease the pain of defeat. As for Wyndham Halswelle, licking his wounds in Athens, it was a chance to redeem himself at a properly conducted meeting on a level playing field when back in London.

For the British and Desborough in particular, this was a great opportunity. Britain had much more collective experience in organising large sports events than any other country. They could boast the Henley Royal Regatta, the All England Tennis Tournament at Wimbledon and the thirty-year-old Amateur Athletic Association's National Athletic Championships, all of which had fine and long traditions. Desborough was confident that the image of the Olympic Games could be restored and enhanced, and could hardly wait to get hold of de Coubertin's infant Olympics and shape it the British way.

There would be no more cheating, no more professionalism and no more dirty tricks. With all the confidence of a man who had spent his life in sport, politics and public life, Lord Desborough was certain that Britain would show the world how to run the Games.

– Chapter 17 –

Meet Mr Fair Play

More exclusive even than a seat at the Olympic stadium in 1906 was an invitation to visit the SS *Branwen,* moored up in the Bay of Athens and within easy reach of the Games. Great parties were thrown on the magnificent yacht, owned by Lord Howard de Walden, who allowed Lord Desborough, the newly appointed head of the British Olympic delegation, to play the aristocratic host. Even His Majesty, King Edward, would sometimes join him on board to share a bottle of champagne, which they would sip in the cool of the evening over the finest cigars while they chewed over the day's events in the stadium. Desborough had gone out of his way to sympathise with Wyndham Halswelle over the conduct of his opponents in the 400 Metres. He thought the young soldier was a fine man, the sort of athlete the Empire could be proud of.

Another fine upholder of imperial standards was one of the

fencing squad staying on the *Branwen*, Theodore Cook. Desborough was sure that Cook was the man to ensure that if the Games were to come to London, they would be run very much in the British way, with the concept of fair play running through every detail of the Olympic programme.

Ever since the beginning of the modern Olympics in 1896, the organisation and control of the competition for each event had been the responsibility of the host country. All the officials, all the judges and all the score-keepers were drawn from the citizens of the host nation. Desborough wanted to ensure that the situation in 1908 would be no exception. The control of the competitions should, he believed, be exclusively in the hands of British officials.

He had a good knowledge of the shambles that had existed at both the 1900 Games in Paris and the St Louis Games of 1904, and he was determined there would be no repeat performance in Britain. Desborough wanted to see the management of events safely in the hands of the British and had a fear of it falling into the hands of foreigners. He had learned what had happened in St Louis, where everything had been run entirely by the Americans under the leadership of James Sullivan, but Desborough was confident that the Games in London would attract a truly international field of athletes. He knew that not only would the facilities have to stand up to the strains and pressures that the Games would impose upon them but so, too, would the rules and regulations governing the way the competitions were conducted.

Of all the world's nations, it seemed, the Americans were the most concerned with reinforcing their national pride by winning at sport. International co-operation was all very well, it seemed to Desborough, as long as America could claim the bulk of the medals. Headlines betray the strident nationalism being peddled in the press immediately before the Games.

AMERICAN ATHELETES SURE OF SUCCESS, TRAINER MURPHY AND MANAGER HALPIN CONFIDENT THAT PREMIER HOURS WILL BE WON BY US

BRITISHERS FEAR YANKEE ATHLETES

'WE WILL KNOCK SPOTS OFF THE BRITISHERS'

Certainly, there was no lack of competitive spirit and not too many doubts about the outcome of the Games among the American press or delegation. But the English were a little more reticent when it came to commenting on the philosophy of Baron de Coubertin's Olympic creed. *The Times*, in London, reported:

It is commonly said, and indeed is put forward as a conclusive argument in favour of the modern Olympic movement, that international athletics encourage international amity. This is only the case if they are organised in so orderly and impartial a manner that every competitor, whether he has won or lost, goes away satisfied and feeling that every opportunity has been given and every courtesy shown to him.

This record gathering of the world's finest athletes is not only likely to be conducted from beginning to end in a spirit of perfect harmony but will, it is expected, result in the formation of a universal code governing the conditions of all kind of amateur athletics. Some day it may be possible to look back on these Olympic Games of 1908 as having given a powerful impetus to the brotherhood of the world.

The Herculean task of championing this brotherhood of the world and sorting out the rules for the Games of 1908 was given to the journalist, academic and sportsman Theodore Cook, born in 1867 in Exmouth, Devon. His mother had been an artist who had exhibited at the Royal Academy, his father a headmaster. Cook had a high profile in the sporting world: as a classical scholar at Wadham College, Oxford, he had founded the University Fencing Club in 1891 and later became a leading figure in the administration of the sport. In 1903, he went to Paris as the non-playing captain of the first British Fencing Team to compete abroad, and in 1906, he played the same role at the Intermediate Olympic Games in Athens.

After success as a rowing Blue and a fencer at Oxford, he moved into journalism and was given a staff appointment on the *St James's Gazette*, where he was later made editor. He then joined the staff at the *Daily Telegraph*, writing columns on fencing and rowing under the pseudonym of 'Old Blue'. Following the London Games, Cook was appointed editor of *The Field*, a paper that used to boast that it was written by gentlemen and read by gentlemen.

As a member of the British Olympic Association, chaired by Desborough, he took over the detail of drafting the rules for the Games and plunged into the venture with enormous energy and enthusiasm. He wrote the preface to the *Code of Rules*, which he proudly claimed to be the first attempt to govern international competition. Cook was particularly involved in the attempts to codify the regulations regarding amateurism, too, and subsequently, as the editor of the official report on the 1908 Olympic Games, he was given the task of refuting American claims of cheating by British officials.

Cook took his proposals for the rules of the Games and the conduct and definition of amateurism to the International Olympic Committee (IOC), in session at The Hague in 1907. There, they gave approval to the arrangements being made by the British organisers. The design of the medals, for instance, was to be left to the discretion of the British Committee. More significantly, it was agreed that British colonies should have separate representation, both at the Games and on the IOC. This angered German representatives, who saw no reason why states such as Saxony and Bavaria should not have the same status as Australia, and their cause was backed by the Americans, who appeared ready to take every opportunity to put one over on the British.

Perhaps most significantly of all, it was agreed at The Hague that the judges of the Games should be entirely British. There was a Greek motion that a fully international jury of appeal should be appointed, but the British lobby had it thrown out. A provisional programme based on the 1906 Games was approved during the session at The Hague, even though some of the events originally talked about never materialised. Among these were motor racing, a competition for flying machines and golf. There was also talk of including cricket and bandy, a precursor of ice hockey, in the programme.

Even as Cook and Desborough sat with the International Olympic Committee forging the 'rules of sport', world leaders were also meeting at The Hague to hammer out the 'rules of war'.

In 1899, an international conference had been called at the

request of Russia to discuss rules to limit warfare, and in 1907, a second Hague conference was called, this time at the request of the American President Theodore Roosevelt. It was attended by some 44 countries and once again arms limitation was the goal. These peace conferences were bold attempts to look at what exactly a war crime constituted and who decides what is legal during a conflict.

The Hague conference made a number of declarations and conventions about the laws of war, which were adopted by many states. There were prohibitions of aerial bombardment and the use of submarines, mines and poison gas. Both the 'rules of sport' and the 'rules of war' – beaten out at The Hague during the high watermark of Edwardian England – are still applicable, at least in principle, today. The Edwardians were great rule-makers and none greater than Theodore Cook, Mr Fair Play. The Edwardians considered it their duty to impose what they believed to be civilised rules upon the nations of the world. Of course, such optimism was swept away a few years later with a world war, in which mustard gas, aerial warfare, tanks and, above all, the machine gun were introduced to blow the heart out of fair play. Old rules were clearly no longer enough.

But Theodore Cook had done what he could to ensure that the 'rules of sport' were there for everyone to read, even if some chose to ignore them. Cook was one of those Victorians who took the scruffy, often sordid world of sport and shook it into respectability. By the time he and his allies had finished, sport left the Victorian age codified, controlled, genteel even. Taking their blueprint from the public schools and universities, rules, regulations, laws and dress codes were all tightly controlled by men like Cook, who believed they should hand out commandments that would control not only the playing of games, but by implication, govern the game of life itself. These rules were more than technical; they had a moral dimension and they dictated your state of mind.

You were required to try hard, but not too hard. You had to exert yourself without seeming to make too much effort. Winning was all very well, but not making a fuss about winning or losing was better still. There was no doubt that Cook considered the finest embodiment of this ethos to be found in the English gentleman amateur. He would have agreed with the author George Orwell that sport is inevitably bound up with the rise of nationalism.

'Serious sport has nothing to do with fair play,' Orwell concluded in *The Sporting Spirit*, an essay written in 1945. 'It is bound up with hatred, jealousy, boastfulness, disregard of all rules and sadistic pleasure in witnessing violence. In other words, it is war minus the shooting.'

'Anyone winning in London,' said Theodore Cook, 'will win by the rules. They will be strictly, though fairly, enforced and properly judged. There will be no problems. We want to see the best man win.'

But for Cook, the best man was unlikely to be a foreigner. For him, few beyond Britain understood the ethos of fair play.

– CHAPTER 18 –

I WILL WIN OR I WILL DIE

Dorando Pietri was no longer certain he was the best man or that he could win. It was no good, he could not go on as before: the undeniable fact was that he had no stomach for the training.

It had all been very well looking at the schedule he had laboriously pencilled out in the warmth of a café with his friends, the men who made his shoes and shared his dreams. There, they would outline his hard work – so many kilometres to run, so many hills to climb, and so many hours spent with the Indian clubs. But Dorando couldn't get out of his head all the hours and effort he had seemingly wasted, and now his spirit revolted. In the two months that followed his failure in Athens, his friends, the Miselli cousins Tullio and Ondino, talked him into a couple of easy races that were much shorter than marathons and against indifferent opposition.

He began to feel some of his confidence coming back and so, on 26 August 1906, he decided to test his doubts over the marathon distance. It was a disaster. When a man drops out of a marathon, as Dorando had done four months before in Athens, it leaves a scar that can sometimes take a lifetime to heal. The race in Arona started well enough, but after the first half dozen miles, he found he was re-running the fears that had haunted him in Athens.

Every time he felt the pressure of the runners around him, he would wonder, is it all going to happen to me again? The fact that he didn't know what had gone wrong gnawed at his stomach and filled every mile with uncertainty. Just before he reached halfway in this marathon, which had been measured at just over 41km, Dorando shook his head. His shoulders dropped and he stepped off the course, a broken man.

'Look, Dorando, you're a bit unfit, that's all,' said his friends. But this was no consolation. Failure, he knew, should be a teacher and not an undertaker – but he found it difficult to learn the lessons.

On his return from Athens in May of that year, Dorando had given a long interview to the Carpi weekly newspaper *Luce*. He didn't want to make any excuses: he rejected all the rumours that he had been suffering from food poisoning and said that he had gone well at the start, setting a furious pace out in front of the field. But while in Athens, he had been hit by sudden stomach pains just after 10 miles, and forced to sit it out as the Canadian, Sherring, won.

'Was it the chilled water that you drank? Was it sea sickness?' the reporters asked him. 'Did Sherring take drugs? Was the day too hot?'

The fact was that Dorando didn't know the answers, and the doubts and bafflement were killing him.

He tried again at the end of September, this time over 25km. For this event he had forced out the miles in training and the press and other athletes had him down as favourite to win, but he was beaten into second place by his old rival Pericle Pagliani. There were some in Carpi who thought he was finished. Pagliani won again over the same distance on 21 October, but this time Dorando waited on the sidelines, praying his doubts would evaporate.

La Patria, and particularly the man who controlled the purse strings at that club, were highly critical of Dorando's performance in Athens. He'd let them down, they said and they considered him a waste of money. La Patria let it be known that they wouldn't support him for London, even if he made the team. The president of the club was a man called Marri Mario, a socialist, a figurehead and a politician, who considered sporting failure bad for his image. But London was a long way to go and without some financial support, Dorando wasn't going to make the start, let alone run and finish well.

It appeared that only Teresa and Tullio seemed to understand what he was going through. Tullio Miselli was one of the family who hand-made Dorando's running shoes. Later, when Pietri was famous, they would make a dozen pairs or more at a time, since he wore them out rapidly with all his mileage, and so many were stolen as souvenirs. But in those dark days after Athens, Tullio was always there with a free pair of shoes and, more importantly, the advice and encouragement that kept Dorando going. Tullio was always at his side and he always had confidence in his friend. 'We must send Dorando to London,' he told others at the club. 'We've got to find a way.'

It was a year after he dropped out of the race in Athens before Dorando started to get back to his real form. But from the end of May 1907, he once again seemed unbeatable. In the next twelve months, he ran close to twenty races over many distances and appeared invincible. Though still haunted by the targets he had set himself, now he sometimes ran with anger in his heart. He was angry with himself for the painful memory of Athens, constantly reminding himself of what he hadn't done, of what he hadn't become.

When dreams go unfulfilled they can leave an enormous hole in the soul, and even Dorando's love for Teresa couldn't fill his. But he had realised that fearlessness is not just the absence of fear, it is the mastery of fear, about forcing yourself to get up one more time. He always knew he could face physical pain and that out there on the road he could show bravery that would make lesser men surrender. But as he shared his fears with Teresa, he knew that he had to face not physical danger but emotional pain, disapproval, poverty and doubts, rather than surrender his dream. So Teresa backed him when he did what for him was the unthinkable and went out onto the streets of Carpi to ask for the funds to get to London.

Dorando vividly remembered Pagliani and those begging bowls in the piazza at Carpi, but fired up with pride and anger he started training harder than ever to compensate. On 11 September 1907, he was discharged from the army with the rank of corporal and resumed running and competing with La Patria. He was racing on the Piazza di Siena track in Rome by mid-November. There, he won a 5,000-metre race in 16:27:5, on 17 November, and the day after, he won a 20-km race in 1:6:27, beating his old rival Pagliani by almost 3 minutes.

But problems with the longer distance still haunted him. The Italians planned their first marathon championship over 40km, which would also double as a trial for the London Olympics, on

3 June 1908 – seven weeks before the Games. There were only three starters: Dorando, Umberto Blasi and Augusto Cocca.

The race started well enough with Dorando and Blasi matching strides and pulling well away from Cocca. Once he reached halfway, though, Dorando knew he was in trouble. The dryness that gripped his throat matched the fear that his dream of making it to the Olympics was vanishing with every stride. At 19 miles it was all over; Dorando was forced to withdraw and could only watch as Blasi pulled away to win the race easily in just over three hours.

Furious with himself, he shook his head as he told Teresa his dream was over.

'You can't give up now,' Tullio pleaded. 'You've got to get out there and race again!'

Dorando allowed himself less than a week to recover and come to terms with his failure. Then he pushed himself once more, training harder than ever. On 28 June, he won a 5-mile race (7,960 metres) by over a minute. He was convinced he was going well.

In a last desperate bid to win his place for the Olympics, his club arranged for him to run a solo trial over 40km on his home ground in Carpi. 'I'll go for the Italian record,' Dorando proclaimed. It was the only certain way to impress the selectors.

With the Olympic race just over two weeks away, 7 July dawned fearsomely hot. But Dorando had no choice: if he were to make it to London, it was now or never, and he ran at a reckless speed, covering the first half in 1:14. He kicked out the miles relentlessly, his terror of failure chasing him every inch of the way.

As he ran into the finish, he was joined by Tullio, himself a sprinter and a champion over 100 metres, who ran alongside his friend as he raced in. Dorando, with 40km already in his legs, outkicked his friend to cover the 40km in 2:38.

'You'll win the marathon in London,' said Tullio, confidently, 'because if all the best runners in the world get to the finish together, you can beat them. You've got the speed to do it.'

For Dorando, there was yet more welcome news. La Patria, on noting his return to form, had at last relented and said they would back him and would help with the fare to the Games. At last he was on his way.

His older brother Ulpiano was already in London, where he had been working in the heart of the great city as a waiter at the Cecil Hotel. Ulpiano could speak English, he knew his way around and he had all the sophistication of living in the capital of the British Empire. Dorando was sure no one was better equipped to look after him.

As he set out for the railway station, heading for the most important race of his life, he said goodbye to his mother and father.

'If you don't feel good in the race, drop out! Be sensible, take care,' said his mother.

Dorando's father heard her warning and turned to his son with a knowing wink.

'We two knew better,' said Dorando after the London games. 'My father knew that I would win or I would die in the attempt.'

Then Dorando made his farewells to Teresa. 'You know what I said,' he told her, 'I will win or I will die trying.'

For a moment she was silent. She bit her lip and then she smiled at him. 'Send me lots of postcards from London,' she said, 'and stamp them with love. I will be waiting. And I will pray for you.'

– CHAPTER 19 –

A TICKET TO LONDON

It wasn't dying that bothered Wyndham Halswelle, it was getting to the start line. When he came home from Athens in the late spring of 1906, he found that Jimmy Curran was still angry about the way he had allowed himself to be pushed around by the Americans on the track. Together they vowed to train harder than ever.

'You need plenty of races,' Curran said. 'Run everything, learn to look after yourself – they don't give any medals for saying "After you!"'

At the Scottish Championships that year, Curran encouraged him to enter the 100, 220, 440 and 880 Yards. These events were held on the same afternoon and Halswelle won them all. He also took the 1906 Amateur Athletic Association (AAA) 440 Yards title, and in the following season, 1907, he added the 100 and 220 Yards in the Scottish Championships.

Then, on a cold Scottish evening, Halswelle ran a race too far. Perhaps he hadn't warmed up enough, perhaps it was the delay over the starting time of the race, or perhaps he was going stale on the heavy sprint work Curran prescribed for him, but one moment he was moving like a champion and the next it felt as if a bullet had hit his leg.

His momentum carried him hopping and lurching forward but he knew it was serious. He pulled up and watched the others fly past him on the track. Curran ran towards him and threw an overcoat around his shoulders. For Halswelle, the 1907 season was over. The leg injury was painful, crippling for a runner, and even though he kept off it for the best part of two weeks, it still left him limping badly.

'Maybe we should try a touch of gentle running,' suggested Curran.

But Halswelle didn't agree. 'I've done quite enough running,' he snapped. 'If this is the only way to beat the world, forget it! Ever since you've got hold of me, you've tried to turn me into somebody else. If you're so keen on the Yankee methods, then go and join them! They'd love your methods over there. Go and teach them how to win your way.'

Curran said nothing. He knew there would be plenty of criticism from those in the sport who considered he had pushed Halswelle too hard and that the injury might be the result of over-training and too much racing.

It was an approach that would never have done for Lord Desborough. Throughout his life he often remarked that training was one step away from cheating. What he liked about a man was a sense of effortless superiority, the belief that he was good at games because of an innate God-given ability. It was something a gentleman should be born with, he believed. You didn't really need to practise.

'That's the trouble with chaps like your man Curran,' Desborough would say. 'He'll push you until you run yourself into a tizzy, then you'll go stale and your legs will be finished. And there's no point in whining if you take advice from a man like that and get knocked back. You need a rest.'

Half convinced, Halswelle listened to such warnings and took the remainder of the season off to let his leg heal. He took massage from the rubbers sent his way by Curran and he took long, easy walks in the Pentland Hills beyond Edinburgh.

'We'll get the leg right for the summer,' promised Curran, but as Halswelle looked forward to the Olympic Games in London, his easy confidence in his ability and his training had taken a powerful kicking.

Confidence is vital for any champion. Dorando had lost his on the road between Marathon and Athens, and was still fighting to get it back. Halswelle saw his own confidence ebb away on a chilly track in Scotland. But even as he nursed his injured leg at the end of November 1907, Johnny Hayes, in America, was gaining confidence every time he raced and he had just won his first marathon.

It was not the first marathon he had run. Enthused by the press coverage of the Olympic Games in St Louis, Hayes couldn't wait to get involved in some of the foot races held locally in Manhattan. He enjoyed them tremendously, but soon he and others he ran with realised that the further Johnny Hayes went, the better he got. He lacked the blazing speed of a sprinter or even the flow of a miler, but as the distances got further, his stamina shone through. 'Johnny,' they would say, 'can run for ever.'

In truth, he was not much use at anything less than 10 miles, but once runners had been at it for an hour or so and most were grimacing at the effort, Hayes would come through with a grin and often a wisecrack as he passed them. Not only that, he usually finished fresh and in good shape.

He had joined St Bartholomew's Athletic Club as soon as he started running. Always dedicated to his Catholicism, Hayes had been grateful for what the Church had done for his brothers and sisters, and had a lifetime involvement with the Knights of Columbus, a Catholic fraternal organisation. He came across plenty of hardened veterans who could see that what he needed was a race that would really test his long-distance stamina, and they talked him into entering the Boston Marathon.

When he turned up there, on Thursday, 19 April 1906, it became immediately obvious that he had found a distance that suited him. He finished fifth in 2:55:38, in a race won by Timmy Ford, an eighteen-year-old from Cambridge, Massachusetts, who ran chewing a straw.

Hayes earned himself a handsome silver cup and a lot of prestige within St Bartholomew's Athletic Club. But the race didn't make the headlines in the Boston newspapers, for the day before the run, San Francisco had been hit by an earthquake and the disaster dominated press reports for weeks to come.

The next year, Hayes was back again, and this time he improved to third in the Boston race, which was won in an exceptionally fast time by an Onondaga Indian from Canada, Tom Longboat, considered by many to be the best marathon runner in the world. Longboat ran 2:24:24 for the 25 miles. Hayes came home in 2:30:38 and went home with an even larger silver cup.

Longboat never returned to defend his Boston title. The following year, the New England Athletic Union banned him for taking money, but he was reinstated in time to run in London in 1908.

Hayes notched up his first marathon victory in the Yonkers Marathon, held over 25 miles in New York on 28 November 1907. He won it comfortably in 2:44:45. At one point, as they passed the New York Orphan Asylum, Johnny veered away from the other competitors to run over a horseshoe lying in the middle of the road.

'Never underestimate the luck of the Irish,' he grinned after the finish. In second place in 2:57 was Fred Lorz. He was the joker who had famously hitched a lift and been first into the stadium in the 1904 Olympic Marathon.

After his victory at Yonkers, there was a lot of pressure on Hayes to join the Irish-American Athletic Club, where he could get better facilities, more sophisticated coaching and top-class competition. He also started to take training advice from the former Swedish-American champion, Ernie Hjertberg, hired by the New York Athletic Club as their trainer in February 1907. Hjertberg had him out three nights a week, running between 5 and 15 miles at a stretch, with long walks on other days. Hayes started to use the Irish-American Athletic Club's track at Celtic Park in Queens, and by the time of the 1908 Boston, on 21 April, he was being talked about as the favourite.

He employed his trademark tactic, which was to start slowly at a pace he knew he could maintain and then work his way relentlessly through the field. In the early miles, he was cruising along in 32nd place, but he worked his way past the runners who blew up, exhausted, and was described by the *Boston Herald* as finishing 'as fresh as a daisy in a meadow'. In the event, Hayes ran a fine time and considered he could have gone even faster, had he not been impeded by the cars choking up the path through to the finish. He finished second in 2:26:4, just 21 seconds behind Boston's nineteen-year-old Tom Morrisey.

This time, Hayes won not just an even larger silver cup, but selection for the Olympic Games in London in July of that year. For Johnny, it was the experience of a lifetime. To his friends at St Bartholomew's and Bloomingdales, he seemed full of confidence.

Always modest, Hayes was never one to boast about his own achievements. He was reported to have said to his friends at Bloomingdales, the store that nominally employed him before he left for London: 'I know to a breath how far I can run and how fast. I intend to go right out with the pacemakers, to keep at their heels until I am ready to finish and then go on and win.'

He was tremendously excited by the prospect of travelling to London to race. When the list of athletes selected to represent the United States in London was published, he rushed off to buy an autograph book. He kept pulling it from his pocket with a grin. To Johnny's delight, the team seemed to be packed with the names of the sportsmen who had been his boyhood heroes. He couldn't believe his luck that he was going to cross the Atlantic with men like these, and he wasn't going to miss the chance to get their autographs.

Hayes left his room at 246 East 55th Street and turned up wide-eyed, clutching his red leather-bound autograph book, at the foot of Vesey Street to board the *Philadelphia*, bound at ten o'clock that morning for London. At the quayside, he said goodbye to his brother Willie and his two sisters, Harriet and Alice, and pushed his way through the pressmen to get at the gangplank. The flashes from their giant cameras were like fireworks and he was so dazzled he couldn't pick out Willie or his sisters in the crowd below. The *New York Times* reported:

> The piers and docks of the American Line were crowded with athletes and friends of the tourists. Those who came to get a last glimpse of the men who had donned the regulation dark blue cap with shield in front stayed on the decks of the ship until the final bell rang for all ashore when they rushed down the gangplank.
>
> When the Philadelphia backed out into the river she was joined by two tugs decorated with the American colours and crowded to the rails with enthusiasts cheering the men on the way to the International Games. They followed the ship well down the lower bay, tooting their whistles all the way and giving one long last farewell shriek as the big *Philadelphia* turned to take the dip into the open ocean.
>
> Some trepidation was manifested that Martin Sheridan, the all round champion of the Amateur Athletic Union, had not shown up. It was close on the time when the gangplank was to be lifted when the famous athlete was observed pushing his way through the crowd on the dock and as he boarded the ship a great cheer arose.
>
> Ralph Rose, the giant Californian, held quite a levee on board ship. With his 6 feet 5 inches of stature and 260 lbs of weight, the phenomenal weight thrower told his many inquirers that he was looking forward to the trip with pleasure and was confident that he would eclipse all his previous records. Matt McGrath, John Flanagan, Harry Hillman Jr, Johnny C. Garrels, the big Western heavyweight,

and J. B. Taylor, the coloured runner, had hosts of friends to see them off while Mr and Mrs Ray C. Ewry were cordially greeted. Manager Halpin and trainer Mike Murphy had little time to accept the felicitations of their friends, the apportioning of state rooms and other matters pertaining to the trip occupying the greater part of their attention.

The wide-eyed Johnny Hayes reckoned that if his luck held, he could probably get the autographs of them all. That way, whatever happened when he ran in London, he would have something to show his brothers and sisters when he got home.

– CHAPTER 20 –

SECRETS OF THE GREAT WHITE CITY

On Saturday, 9 May 1908, nearly 150 men, women and children, natives of India and Ceylon, arrived at the Franco-British Exhibition. They brought with them a vast menagerie of elephants, dromedaries, antelopes, bears and monkeys. One of the stars of the party was a dwarf from Colombo, named Maricar, who stood only 3 feet 6 inches tall and was said to have wonderful powers as a doctor. With the Edwardian macabre fascination for physical freaks, Maricar had men, women and children, too, queuing for hours to stare at him.

Five days later, on 14 May 1908, the Prince of Wales, the future King George V, declared the Franco-British Exhibition open and the leading soprano Madame Albani sang the National Anthem in the pouring rain. On 26 May, the Marsellaise and the National Anthem were played for the visit of President Fallières of France and Edward VII.

As the exhibition buildings were all painted white, the exhibition was soon nicknamed 'The Great White City'. The French Chamber of Commerce in London had come up with the idea of a Franco–British Exhibition to celebrate four years of the *Entente Cordiale*. A venue was acquired in north-east London's Shepherd's Bush and work began on the former Wood Lane farmland in 1907.

Within a year, twenty pavilions, over 100 other buildings, rides, waterways, pagodas and the most advanced sporting stadium in the world were built at alarming speed. A work force of 120,000 men worked around the clock, many by floodlight at night. In March, a factory inspector said that there had been hundreds of unreported accidents. The exhibition was eight times the size of the 1851 Great Exhibition. It showcased the industrial and cultural achievements of Britain and France, and drew more than 8 million visitors. Already in place was an integrated transport system with trains, tramways and omnibuses that could deliver 80,000 people an hour to the Exhibition.

'The White City was,' said Ulpiano Pietri, 'one of the great wonders of London,' and he couldn't wait to show his brother around. The two young Italians went through the main gates of Wood Lane and into the 'Court of Honour', where the sight was breathtaking. The court surrounded an artificial lake measuring 400 by 100 feet, which could be crossed in the middle by an ornamental bridge. Small pavilions seemed to float out over the water, each topped with a dome. Artists had moulded the delicate lattice work and decorated every nook with sculpture.

It was all strangely oriental. 'Not at all English really,' said Ulpiano. On one side of the lake, stretching to the entrance gates at Wood Lane, there was a spectacular cascade. It was

Top: Heroes all: Dorando Pietri collapses just yards from the finish of the 1908 Olympic Marathon. He is cradled in the arms of Dr Michael Bulger while Jack Andrew wields his megaphone.

Above: Johnny Hayes, from the USA, won the gold medal in the Olympic Marathon, and became the toast of America.

© *Bob Wilcock, Society of Olympic Collectors*

Left: Wyndham Halswelle, the man who believed in fair play in war and peace.

© *Bob Wilcock, Society of Olympic Collectors*

Top left: The 'hoax Dorando': Imposter Pietro Palleschi, pictured in 1948 at his Temperance Bar in Birmingham.

Top right: The picture postcard sent by Dorando from Turin to the girl he was to marry, Teresa Dondi.

Below: The hand-written card with its message of love concealed beneath the postage stamp.

Top left: Sir Arthur Conan Doyle, a fierce defender of the British during the Boer War in South Africa and the creator of Sherlock Holmes.

© *PA Photos*

Above: Robert Baden-Powell, the hero of Mafeking and the founder of the Boy Scouts, went to the same school as Wyndham Halswelle.

© *PA Photos*

Left: King Edward VII, who on Monday 13 July 1908 declared the London Olympic Games open.

© *PA Photos*

Top: The start of the 800 metres in Athens 1906. Halswelle is third from the right, sporting the British flag on his vest.

Above: Baron Pierre de Coubertin, the founding father of the modern Olympic movement.

Right: 'Jimmy' Fowler-Dixon, going through his paces at the age of 56 at the Opening Ceremony of the Athens Games in 1906.

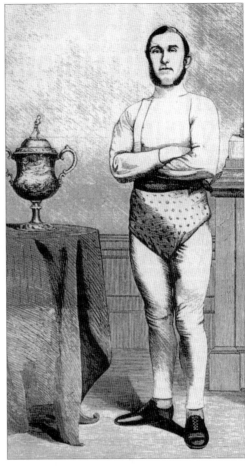

Top left: William Grenfell, Baron Desborough, the guiding light of the 1908 London Games, showing off the skills that made him punting champion of Great Britain for three years in a row.

Top right: Jack White, the 'Gateshead Clipper', who trained a team from the London Athletic Club to compete against the New York Athletic Club in 1895.

Left: The cup presented by Queen Alexandra to Dorando the day after the 1908 Marathon and the commemorative medal presented to all Olympic contestants in the 1908 Games. © *Topfoto*

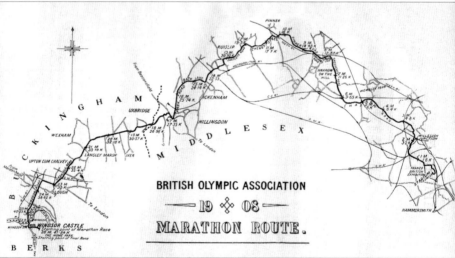

Top: Windsor Castle ready for the start of the 1908 Marathon: Runners amble their way to the line, while the Princess of Wales and the royal children look on. On the table is the signalling apparatus that will send the race on its way.

Below: The official map of the 1908 Marathon course, with the distances marked in miles and kilometres.

The Great Marathon Race!

Fifty-five of the World's Finest Long distance Runners Started from the East Terrace of Windsor Castle, on July 24th, 1908. Dorando, the first to arrive at the Stadium, marked with a cross,

Top: The fifty-five runners set off in the heat of a July afternoon, with Dorando, marked by a cross on this postcard, starting well to the back of the field.

26 miles 385 yards later, both Dorando (*above*) and Johnny Hayes (*left*) are shepherded across the finish by Jack Andrew, Chief Clerk of the Marathon course.

© *Bob Wilcock, Society of Olympic Collectors/ PA Photos*

Sixpence buys you a programme: On Marathon day, 24 July 1908, the demand from the crowd was so great that the Games organisers had to send for extra copies.

impressive in daylight – 'But,' said Ulpiano, 'you should see it at night.'

Imre Kiralfy, the exhibition's co-ordinating genius, was the driving force behind the design of the White City. He had already found fame by producing spectacular events and saw the fair as an opportunity to gain cultural respectability and yet more celebrity. Born in Budapest in 1845, Kiralfy, a Hungarian Jew, was presented as an infant prodigy to Frederick William IV of Prussia. By the time he was eight, he thought he would like to become a conjurer then later a musician, learning the piano and violin. At the age of only fourteen, he heard his own composition performed by an orchestra in Milan. Then, at 22, he went to Paris to visit the International Exhibition in the Champs de Mars, where he finally stumbled on his passion: staging extravaganzas.

He moved on to New York, where he had great success, but soon his stage shows grew too big for theatres and he was taking over Staten Island for his spectaculars. These included 'The Fall of Babylon' and 'The Burning of Rome', which he produced with a cast of thousands.

Back in London, at Earls Court, he masterminded extravaganzas that included 'Empire of India', 'The Victorian Era', 'Woman's International' and 'Paris in London'. But all these extravaganzas were really only a prelude to the great Franco-British Exhibition at Shepherd's Bush.

'One night,' said Kiralfy, 'I lay awake in bed and as if by magic I saw stretched out in my mind's eye an imposing city of palaces, domes and towers set in cool, green spaces and intersected by many bridged canals. But this city was spotlessly white. I saw it all in an instant and the next day I jotted down the scheme of what London was to know as the White City.'

Dorando Pietri had seen magnificent buildings for he had been in Rome and Athens, but when he looked at this dazzling palace with its steel-framed buildings and plaster-cast façades, he merely shrugged. 'It looks,' he said to Ulpiano, 'just like a wedding cake.'

One of the great attractions of the exhibition was the Flip-Flap, a sort of roundabout, on which wagons holding up to fifty people were driven round on the end of long steel arms. The wagons went through the air from left to right so that the passengers got both a shock and a great view of the area from 200 feet up. By the end of the exhibition, over a million people had paid a total of £27,000 to go on the ride. The attraction also inspired a White City hit song entitled 'Take me on the Flip-Flap', performed in music halls by Ella Retford and Millee le Grant.

Dorando and Ulpiano joined the hundreds queuing for the Canadian Palace, with its scenic railway, and the Indian Arena, a 3,000-capacity open-air theatre, where Bollywood-type spectaculars were performed featuring elephants, acrobats and snake charmers from 'our Indian Empire'. Behind India, at the far north end of the Exhibition, was the Irish village called Ballimaclinton, which contained a replica of US President McKinley's grandfather's cottage and raised money to tackle tuberculosis in Ireland.

To the east of the Flip-Flap, near the Canadian toboggan ride, was the most politically incorrect exhibit – the Senegalese village placed in a section devoted to the French Colonies. 'Here in a cluster of mud huts,' said the official White City booklet, 'the 150 African negroes worked as they would back home. A village school showed how France and Great Britain cared for the children of Africa. Visitors could hear and see the weird chants and rhythmic dancing of the young members of the troupe.'

Like everyone else, the two Italians put on their best outfits for this great day out. For men, the fashion in 1908 was lounge suits of worsted or tweed in brown, grey or navy, with a single- or double-breasted jacket and a waistcoat. Shoes were starting to become fashionable but most men wore boots, and bowler hats or straw boaters.

Women would turn up in a fashionably grey or green costume, with braid and button trimmings, white collar and cuffs, a lace blouse, and a fawn felt hat with brown ostrich feathers. A brown handbag, fawn gloves and a parasol completed the outfit.

Young girls would dress entirely in white, usually with black lace-up shoes, and boys would wear knee britches and blouses, with lace collars and cuffs, or a jersey and sailor suits. The working classes would settle for their Sunday best – a white shirt and short jacket for women; a black suit and flannel shirt and cap for men.

To Desborough and his British Olympic Committee, the Franco-British Exhibition was a godsend. Without it, a successful Games would have seemed impossible. The Olympic organising committee pulled off a master stroke when they persuaded the Exhibition authorities to build the Great Stadium, complete with running and cycling tracks, a swimming pool, dressing rooms and spectator accommodation. The exhibition consented to pay for all this at a cost of 'not less than £44,000', but they also agreed to make a grant of £2,000 towards the cost of the British Olympic Association. In return, the Exhibition would get 75% of gate receipts.

This remarkably favourable contract was signed on 14 January

1907. As with all Olympics, the figures on the contracts escalated. Even in 1908, higher, faster, costlier seemed to be the motto once Olympic building started, and some sources estimated the actual cost of construction of Shepherd's Bush subsequently rose to £220,000 and that the grant made to the British Olympic Association was increased to £20,000.

Another headache for Lord Desborough was raising funds for the day-to-day running expenses of the Games. The abortive Rome Games of 1908 had run into trouble over questions of funding, and Desborough was determined his Games would survive without government subsidy. A public appeal was launched, but by the end of June, only £2,840 had been raised from 200 subscribers, most of them personal friends of Desborough's. With just two weeks to go before the opening ceremony, a further £10,000 was still urgently needed.

Conan Doyle used his reputation to lobby the wealthy and influential for funds. Lord Northcliffe, proprietor of the *Daily Mail*, was approached and at a meeting with Lord Desborough, he reluctantly agreed that his newspapers would sponsor a final Olympic appeal. The response was phenomenal and donations poured in from all around Britain and abroad.

The Prince of Wales, the Maharajah of Cooch Behar and the American millionaire Cornelius Vanderbilt all sent money. The professional body builder and strongman Eugen Sandow personally gave £1,500, the largest single individual contribution. The French government sent £680, and the exotic dancer Maud Allen gave all the proceeds from a special matinée performance. Thousands of donations, ranging from a few pounds to a few pence, came from the readers of the *Daily Mail*.

In just over a week, more than £12,000 had been subscribed

and the newspapers were forced to appeal to their readers not to send any more money as the donations reached around £16,000.

When they did their sums, the British Olympic Association walked away with a profit of more than £6,000. The Franco-British Exhibition organisers were the losers in this deal. Their only return on the outlay was just £18,000, as their share of the gate receipts, but despite the cost of the deal, the Exhibition authorities duly subsidised the construction of what was then the finest stadium in the world.

They built a cinder running track of three laps to the mile (586.67 yards, 536.44 metres), a banked concrete cycling track of 660 yards (603.5 metres) and a swimming pool 100 metres in length, which was twice the size of the modern Olympic pool. Above the swimming tank a tower, 55 feet in height, which could be lowered when not in use, was built for the high diving events. Inside the running track was enough space for a full-size pitch, on which football, hockey, rugby football and lacrosse matches could all be played.

There were stages for wrestling and gymnastics, and the archery competitions were held on the grass infield enclosed by the track. The stadium was years ahead of its time and spectators could watch athletics, cycling, gymnastics, swimming and wrestling simultaneously. This gave plenty to look at, though in the days of megaphones, many spectators found the whole spectacle at times confusing.

There were 10 miles of seating for 63,000 spectators in the grandstands, with standing room for another 30,000. The foundation stone was laid by Lord and Lady Desborough on 2 August 1907; work began under the supervision of Charles Perry, the London Athletic Club groundsman at Stamford Bridge. He was considered the best in the business and was the man whom the Greeks had sent for before the first modern Olympic Games in 1896.

In addition to the Royal Box, five other boxes were placed with the best views of the track. The Franco-British Exhibition, the International Olympic Committee and the British Olympic Committee all had their own boxes. Alongside these were the press box and a separate area for the judges.

Beneath the seating were fourteen dressing rooms for the more than 3,000 competitors. There were also separate rooms for the police and ambulance services and five temperance restaurants, but no bars.

The construction of the site in Shepherd's Bush, from the day the foundations were laid until the unveiling of the new Olympic stadium, took just 10 months. On 14 May 1908, the Prince and Princess of Wales dedicated the stadium to international sport.

Before the Games began, ten meetings were held in the stadium, including the British Championships for athletics, cycling and swimming. These served as rehearsals for the Games.

Not for the last time in the history of the Olympics, the Great Stadium of the White City became something of a great white elephant. Following the Games, it fell into disuse. The surrounding exhibition buildings were demolished and the seating capacity of the stands reduced, but no major meetings were held there for many years.

In 1927, the Greyhound Racing Association took over the old White City, and in 1932, the Amateur Athletic Association replaced the old one-third-of-a-mile circuit with a 440-yard cinder track and White City became once more the centre of British athletics. With an eye on the history of the track, the

Greyhound Racing Association staged a 'Dorando Marathon' for dogs each year, and after the stadium was closed the event was moved to the Wimbledon dog track.

In 1971, the Amateur Athletic Association moved their championships to a new athletics centre at Crystal Palace and this finally marked the end of the Great Stadium. The last event at the White City stadium was a greyhound race held on 22 September 1984, which was won by a bitch called Hastings Girl. The site is now the headquarters of BBC Television, from where they transmit live coverage of the annual London Marathon, and from where the latest news of the London Olympics in 2012 will be broadcast.

But what was to outlast even the Great Stadium was the legend of these Games. Here the Marathon was to be run for the first time over a distance that is now recognised worldwide, and here, too, were to be spoken the words that were to define the spirit of the Olympic Games for a century to come.

On Sunday, 19 July 1908, during a lull in the battle for medals and victory at those Games, the Bishop of Pennsylvania – Ethelbert Talbot – preached at St Paul's Cathedral. He quoted a text from St Paul that a week later Baron de Coubertin was to seize upon and re-spin as part of Olympic history. 'The most important thing in these Olympic Games,' ran the sentiment, 'is not the winning but the taking part.'

They were fine words and have echoed through a century of Olympic competition – but they were to be tested to destruction before these stormy Games were over.

– CHAPTER 21 –

NO EARTHLY KING

Monday, 13 July 1908, was a hostile day in Shepherd's Bush. The sky was dark, the wind easterly and the rain lashed angrily against the newly built walls of the stadium. In this weather, the flags, though heavy with rain, slapped their lines against the poles. Men muttered of the madness of marching their finely tuned bodies before a crowd half hidden beneath their umbrellas. Even the King, who wrapped his heavy coat around him and peered out at the thousands who were filing into the Great Stadium, may have wondered if he was wise to be there.

With little more than one week to go before the opening of the Games, Edward VII had been uneasy about attending the ceremony, having picked up on the rumour and the gossip about the animosity between the British and the Americans. He really wanted nothing to do with such squabbles. It was, he felt, beneath him. He was dismissive rather than angry at such behaviour.

Two years before, he had been at the Athens Games and witnessed what he considered to be the bumptious and over-enthusiastic behaviour of the Americans. Did they have to make such a fuss every time they won, he wondered. Did they need to demonstrate their superiority by trying so hard? Must they be quite so pushy? It wasn't the behaviour of a gentleman.

King Edward VII – Bertie to his family – short, rather stout and balding, with a beard so distinctive that it was recognised all over the Empire, was normally relaxed and genial, but he sometimes had a quick and fiery temper.

'Needs a bit of handling,' Desborough would say, and few could manage the King with Desborough's touch. Eventually he got his way with the King, and four weeks before the ceremony, His Majesty agreed to open the Games.

The King and his Queen, Alexandra, from Denmark, travelled by horse-drawn carriage from Buckingham Palace and entered the stadium at 3.49pm. The Royal children were there, too, and many members of the royal households of Europe joined the party, together with packs of noblemen, statesmen and high-ranking officers from the armed forces, ambassadors and representatives of all the competing countries.

The International Olympic Committee members were presented to His Majesty by Baron de Coubertin, and at a fanfare from the trumpets of the lifeguards, who were stationed on the wrestling stage, Lord Desborough bowed to the King and invited him to speak.

'I declare the Olympic Games of London open,' the King said, in a voice that many visitors found surprisingly guttural.

The organisers had rehearsed every detail of the opening ceremony. But the athletes had grown tired of having to march around just to show what was expected of them, and couldn't wait to get on with the real thing. Despite all the planning, there were still problems and there was plenty to moan about.

For weeks, there had been a rumbling row about the Irish athletes, who, under the rules drawn up by Theodore Cook, were told they would have to compete for Britain. Half of them refused to do so. The American team was full of Irish-Americans – Johnny Hayes among them – and the Americans were not going to lose any opportunity to attack the British over the touchy, political hot potato of Home Rule for Ireland.

Then there were the flags and banners. There seemed to be endless disputes and some muddle about what was going on. The press, always eager to whip up a story, pounced on the problems and the gossip. Due to an embarrassing error by the organisers, the flags of Sweden and the United States were not flown during the opening ceremony, and although the problem was quickly rectified and the British Olympic Council apologised, this got things off to a bad start, particularly as far as the Americans were concerned.

Matters were not helped by the fact that the flags of China and Japan, who were not even taking part in the Games, were flying proudly. In charge of the arrangements for the display of national flags in the stadium was Imre Kiralfy, the Director General of the Franco-British Exhibition and the man who had designed the great White City.

Kiralfy knew America well and he had spent many years in New York. He and his wife, Marie Graham, had nine children, but three died in childhood. Three of his sons were born in New York. All three became United States citizens, and one son, Edgar, was actually a sprinter on the American team in 1908. Desborough scoffed at the idea that a man with such strong

American connections could deliberately arrange for the Stars and Stripes not to be flown at the stadium. It was, he believed, nonsense to assume that this was a snub to the United States.

The night before the opening ceremony, a group of American athletes, weary from the rehearsals for next day's march past, gathered to relax over a drink. Among them were Martin Sheridan, a New York policeman and a great discus thrower, and Ralph Rose, the massive shot-putter – 6 feet 5 inches tall, 260lb and a giant of an athlete – both of them leading lights in the Irish-American Athletic Club. They were talking about who should carry the flag in the opening ceremony. Sheridan's name had been put forward, as had Johnny Garrels' and Ralph Rose's. Sheridan urged that Rose should carry the flag.

'You're the biggest and the strongest,' he said. 'There's no fear of you dropping it.' Sheridan added with a grin, 'But don't think you have to bow and scrape to that bunch in the Royal Box. You carry the Stars and Stripes proudly!'

To many, even in the American delegation, Rose seemed an unlikely standard bearer. He had the physique, no one could deny that, but he also had the reputation of being something of a hell-raiser. He had once threatened, after a particularly good evening following the 1904 Olympics, to have an impromptu fight with James J. Jeffries, the undisputed heavyweight boxing champion of the world.

As the wind still whipped across the stadium that afternoon and the band of the Grenadier Guards played 'God Save the King', the standard bearers of the teams grouped in the infield to lower their national ensigns in salute. The eighteen nations then marched in a parade around the stadium and again saluted the King as they passed the Royal Box.

The continental teams marched in alphabetical order with Austria leading the way. They were followed by the British Empire nations – Australasia, Canada and South Africa – with Great Britain as the host country bringing up the rear.

All the teams except for Finland were headed by a standard bearer carrying their national flag. The Finns, who had been conquered by Alexander I of Russia in 1809, were still considered a part of Russia and were refused permission by the Russian officials to march under the Finnish flag. They preferred to join the parade carrying only a placard that announced the name of their team and no flag. It had not been a good week for the Finnish team: they were lucky to make the opening ceremony at all after the boat bringing them to England was stranded off the port of Hull with a damaged boiler.

The huge figure of Ralph Rose marched proudly past the King in the procession, but there was no noticeable sign of the Stars and Stripes being dipped. Most in the Royal Box affected not to notice; those who had a close eye on the banner thought they might have detected the flag was lowered. Others thought that maybe, despite all the time spent rehearsing, Rose had simply forgotten. In the pageantry of the great opening ceremony it was, in the opinion of the British press, a mere detail not even worthy of a mention. Their reporters were more concerned with recording that other great English preoccupation, the weather.

But the Irish-American lobby in the US team weren't going to let the gesture of Ralph Rose slip by like that. If the British press took no notice then there were still plenty of Americans there to note what had happened. Martin Sheridan was one of those who made sure the American press did not miss what he believed was a very significant detail.

So Ralph Rose, whose gesture had not warranted a mention in the British press, woke up the next morning to find that his action featured in several US papers. Certainly, it did not appear in all of them. Some American papers reported that he had carried the flag and implied he dipped it like everyone else. The *New York Herald*, in its Paris edition of 14 July 1908, reported: 'Then came the Americans, Garrels carrying the sign and big Ralph Rose the flag and the manager Matt Halpin in top hat and frock coat heading about seventy of the team.'

The *New York Sun* stated: 'Ralph Rose, the giant shot-putter of the Olympic Athletic Club of San Francisco, was at the head of the little body of Americans carrying the Stars and Stripes.'

The Sportsman said: 'Several of the nations dipped their flag as they arrived opposite the royal party, while others contented themselves with a military salute. Next came the United States whose flag was borne by Ralph Rose, the giant shot-putter, and it was a thousand pities that a large squad of competitors should not have been in their athletic costumes.'

But others, especially the Chicago papers, one of which was carrying eyewitness reports from Martin Sheridan, were quick to play up the so-called incident. Writing in the *Chicago Tribune*, Amos Alonzo Stagg said: 'Ralph Rose, carrying the American flag and leading the American contingent, failed to dip the flag in passing the Royal Box.'

And Martin Sheridan himself, writing in the *Chicago Record-Herald*, said: 'Ralph Rose carrying an American flag in the stadium failed to lower it when passing the King's stand as those of all other nations did. Rose did not give any reason for not lowering his flag.'

The myth-makers were already at work. What happened next

is a supreme example of the growth of a legend and what happens when politics, sporting pressure and a good story get mixed up. Ralph Rose, it seemed, claimed no one had told him what to do during the ceremony, but of course there were two rehearsals of the ceremony – one on Saturday, 11 July, and another shortly before the actual ceremony on Monday, 13 July. A detailed description of the opening ceremony was published in every British paper, so it's hard to see how Rose could not have known that he was supposed to dip the American flag.

But if Rose didn't dip the American Flag, why was there so little British reaction to this apparent affront to their King? No British newspaper reported anything about the American flag not being lowered at the ceremony and so there was no row among the British about Rose's supposed breach of etiquette. The *New York Herald* even noted that: 'As the procession came into the stadium, each country received applause, that for America and the colonies being particularly enthusiastic.'

But the *Chicago Tribune* reporter, Amos Alonzo Stagg, writing from England on 14 July, commented: 'There is one incident of the Games which has received little comment in this country but which may explain in part the markedly noticeable unpopularity of the Yankees with the spectators aside from the fact that they were winning a majority of the events. That incident took place in the parade of the athletes of all nations on opening day. Ralph Rose, carrying the American flag and leading the American contingent, failed to dip the flag in passing the Royal Box.'

So in North America, Rose's apparently defiant act was well reported and even applauded, while the British appeared not to have been aware of or concerned by it. Like so many Olympic legends, it grew with time and just about any Olympic history a century on will quote Martin Sheridan's famous remark: 'This flag dips to no earthly king.'

If Sheridan ever said these words, there is no evidence of it in any 1908 source. In fact, there is no real reference to this American 'tradition' and Sheridan's splendid words until after World War II. Sadly, both Rose and Sheridan died from pneumonia while quite young – Rose in 1913 at the age of 28, and Sheridan in 1918 aged 37. Both men never married and they both died without children.

Martin Sheridan was one of the most famous athletes of his generation and one of the best loved. When he died, in New York on 27 March 1918, he was the subject of very detailed obituaries and yet not once was the legendary remark, 'This flag dips to no earthly king' attributed to him.

It took the best part of fifty years for the press to begin quoting the famous remark. The first description of the American 'tradition' of not dipping the flag appears in 1952, describing the opening ceremony of the Helsinki Olympics. In July 1952, the *New York Times* reported: 'As always the United States colours were not dipped as they passed the Presidential box.'

References to Sheridan making the famous quote started appearing in the newspapers as late as the 1960s. In the *New York Times* of 13 October 1968, Arthur Daley wrote: 'The backbone of the United States team in 1908 was supplied by the brawny weight-men from the Irish-American Athletic Club of New York, all with deep roots in the Auld Sod. They took a firm stand and issued explicit orders to the flag bearer. "Ye won't bow the American flag to a British King," bellowed Martin Sheridan, the discus champion. It didn't bow then and it has not bowed since.'

Sometimes a myth can be so strong that it can come through

and overtake the truth, and it's the myth that carries off the prize. Did Martin Sheridan ever say those ringing words, or were they the creation of an imaginative reporter some half a century later, wishing to add an anachronistic footnote to Olympic history? The chances are this quote was embellished, rehashed and grew with the years, that it was tidied up and used as propaganda. As a piece of propaganda, the story and the Martin Sheridan remark were too good not to be true, and these days the legend has evolved into truth.

There was, of course, plenty going on in July 1908 that could be hijacked by athletes and journalists on both sides, wanting to put across their take on who was winning the great battle of Shepherd's Bush. If the opening ceremony had been soured by squabbles about kings and flags, there was little prospect of peace breaking out the next day, for this was when the brawny weight-men of the American squad clashed with the British police in a war of their very own.

– CHAPTER 22 –

THE TUG-OF-WAR NATIONS

O ne of the great joys for Dorando was the sight of London policemen, so tall and so solid in their heavy boots. In his letters to Teresa back in Carpi, he would write of their reassuring and colourful presence on the streets of London.

Inspector Harry Duke of the City of London Police was no ordinary policeman, however. He was a cross-channel swimmer and a wrestling champion, but his pride and joy was his police tug-of-war team: he was their mentor and their coach.

But what got the British policemen into the headlines on both sides of the Atlantic in 1908 were their boots. They were standard issue police boots, the sort used by Bobbies up and down the land in 1908 to pound the beat, but they caused a furore.

In 1908, the tug-of-war was a fiercely competed Olympic event. It proved a great spectator sport at athletic meetings in Britain and was a favourite whenever a ship pulled into a port in some far outpost of the Empire or when a regiment was sent to some faraway colonial outpost. This was an exciting team event and one that always had supporters cheering and urging on the battling squads. And as with all competition for the 1908 Games, Theodore Cook had carefully drawn up the rules of engagement.

The rule regarding footwear in the tug-of-war event read: 'No competitor shall wear prepared boots or shoes or boots with any projecting nails, tips, point, hollows or projections of any kind. No competitor shall make any hole in the ground with his feet or in any other way before the start.'

In the first pull of the Olympic competition, the Americans faced a British team composed of Liverpool policemen. The *New York Times* reported that the Americans complained that the British wore heavy boots with steel rims, violating the regulations regarding footwear. After being pulled over with ease by the team of Liverpool policemen, the Americans appeared to give up. Angry and muttering among themselves, they walked off the field. The heated protest made headlines in the American papers. The *New York Times* read:

ENGLISH UNFAIR IN OLYMPIC GAMES. US protests against method of holding the Tug of War. Liverpool team wears monstrous shoes that arouse ire of Americans who kick in vain.

The report continued: 'A serious controversy has arisen between the American athletes and the BOC [British Olympic Committee]. America's chief cause of complaint is the arbitrary manner in which their protest against the flagrantly unfair method of conducting the tug of war is dismissed.

The British Olympic Committee ruled that the British team, all bona fide Liverpool policemen, wore footwear that was standard issue and used regularly on the beat. The American protest was dismissed as trivial by the British, with *The Times* of London covering it in just one paragraph:

> In the tug of war, a team of eight stalwart policemen easily pulled the great hammer and discus weight throwers of the US over the line. The Americans protested against the result of the first bout on the grounds that their conquerors were wearing boots, but this objection was, of course, overruled.

American papers made much of what they claimed were examples of British unfairness in the tug-of-war. The Liverpool police were described by the American press as wearing 'great heavy boots, so heavy that it was with great effort that they could lift their feet from the ground'. Another paper said, 'They had on monstrously heavy boots with great pieces of iron. This added so much to their weight and gave them such a grip on the ground that no team could move them.' The Americans saw it as 'a put-up job in which the Americans were not intended to have a chance to win and had none'.

James Sullivan, head of the American team, said: 'Our athletes went to England in the face of every sort of opposition, fair and unfair, that the English officials could devise. If we had taken meekly everything that they tried to do, we would have lost. We had to fight for our rights.'

If the American team had been aware of how meticulously the British squads had been groomed for victory in the tug-of-war, they might have been even angrier still, for it turned out that the training of the British squads had been very un-British, as their preparation was virtually professional in its thoroughness. In the final of the tug-of-war event, two British teams – both from the police – came up against each other, with the City of London force meeting the squad from Liverpool. Both squads did much to underplay their preparation.

It turned out that the City of London team had been training specifically for this event for five months. They got together in the chilly days of February and under their coach, Harry Duke, trained regularly, leaving nothing to chance. Among the scratch American team, more or less assembled on the day, were shot-putter Ralph Rose, who had been chosen to carry the Stars and Stripes, and hammer-thrower John Flanagan, both of them Irish-Americans. For them, the shock was the realisation that with or without their boots, the British teams were not quite so effortlessly amateur as they liked to pretend, and that far from being bumbling amateurs, they went out to win in a very professional fashion.

With the addition of medals and national teams came a high degree of competitive rivalry between countries, and during these Games a fierce feud developed between the Americans and the British. With many of the decisions of the British judges and referees coming under continual scrutiny from the American delegation, the Games represented a clash of values, culture and style.

The American style was certainly something the British found amazing. In the London *Times*, it was noted that: 'The enthusiasm of the Americans is a noteworthy feature of the Games. They keep everything and everyone alive with their shouts of encouragement and applause. And even the phlegmatic natives of these islands are stirred by their example.'

Amid the cheers there were plenty more protests to come.

The Americans became increasingly agitated by the English system of scoring to determine the overall winner of the Olympic Games. American athletes were entered almost entirely in the track and field competitions, so their contingent believed the 'Games Trophy' should go to the winner of those exclusive events. The British, however, wanted to include all events, but a lot of these had no American entries and consequently little American interest.

Once again, the reporting reflected all the national prejudices. While there was much sound and fury in the American press about who was winning the overall total of gold medals in the Games, there was little mention of this news in the British papers.

In retaliation, the Americans devised their own system of scoring. James Sullivan spelled out how the United States planned to calculate who won the Olympics. 'We came here, as we went to Paris and Athens, with a field team and are making a fight in the field events, caring nothing for the other sports,' he declared. 'We asked that the Championship Trophy be put up for the field sports separately but this request was not acceded to, so we will simply take the score in the field events counting first five points, second three points and third one point, and figure out the American score on this basis.'

Officially, of course, countries cannot 'win' the Olympics. Athletes supposedly compete as individuals and no official team scores should have been totted up or national standings announced. In reality, nations send teams to compete one against the other in the Olympics, and while scores may not be officially sanctioned by the International Olympic Committee, inevitably, nations use their victories to promote nationalism.

This gave the American press plenty of opportunity to scoff at what they considered playground and arcane events. At the end of the 1908 Games, one American newspaper ran a picture of John Bull under the heading 'And We Thought Uncle Sam's Boys Won'. Underneath, the report read:

This picture proclaiming John Bull as winner in the Olympic Games appeared in a recent number of *The Standard*, an English paper. And to think that even President Roosevelt was deluded into welcoming home the American team as 'The Victors'. But then we Americans did not include in the athletic events, which decided the championship, such manly sports as Archery, Croquet, Hop Scotch, Jack-Straws, Mumblety-peg, Diablo and Ring Toss. In this kind of event the British athletes really do excel.

Olympic events, of whatever sort, continued in steady downpours and problems with the weather, and low attendance continually preoccupied officials, spectators, athletes and promoters. The British papers were clamouring for ticket prices to be lowered to bring back the crowds, and during the first five days of the competition, the United States lodged four official protests. There was the failure of the British Olympic Committee to display the American flag at the opening ceremony; the Americans disputed the regulations for the pole vault competition; the English monopoly of scoring and judging was also protested against; and, of course, the tug-of-war again caused fury among the American delegation.

There were also plenty of unofficial complaints and insults flew thick and fast, especially from the United States officials.

Because heats were drawn in private, they complained that they were rigged in favour of British competitors. There were also loud suggestions of illegal coaching, rule-breaking and British chauvinism. The Americans even made complaints about the mandatory knee-length running shorts the British had advocated, by wearing, as a protest, mid-thigh outfits. And Forrest Smithson, an American student of theology, protested at the decision to run the final of his event on a Sunday. He ran anyway, and proceeded to break the world record for the high hurdles, supposedly carrying a Bible in his left hand! The only evidence of this legend is a photograph clearly staged after the event.

Eventually, the American officials, whose protests were the loudest, were actually barred from the infield, leaving James Sullivan to state that British 'conduct was cruel, unsportsmanlike and absolutely unfair'. On 25 July, *The Times* of London commented:

> The only unpleasant feature of these Games so far has been the unseemly behaviour of the American contingent. The 1,500 metre race they succeeded in winning by unfair jostling, and when this incident was, in the spirit of sportsmanlike courtesy, passed over and condoned, they proceeded to make themselves ridiculous and offensive by protesting against the boots worn by the team of London policemen who pulled them around the arena in the tug of war.

This war between America and Britain grew increasingly bitter as the Olympic contest continued. Every day, headlines announced more American victories or more 'robberies' because of 'British fair play'. Typical headlines included: 'ANYTHING TO

BEAT THE AMERICANS', 'NEW SCANDAL MARS THE OLYMPIC GAMES', 'UNSPORTSMANLIKE CONDUCT OF BRITISH', 'AMERICAN ATHLETES OUTSPOKEN AGAINST BRITISH VERSION OF FAIR PLAY' and 'BRITONS CALL IT NO RACE WHEN AMERICANS WIN'.

One American humorist, the writer Finlay Peter Dunne, invented a character, Mr Dooley, who describes the Games as: 'Truly a glorious spectacle – waiters rushing with buckets of tea for the English athletes, English officials lodging preliminary claims of "foul" against the American team and so forth.' 'The Americans,' Mr Dooley announces, 'Succeeded in rolling up a score of eight points and eleven disqualifications in more or less obsolete forms of sport known as field and track athletics such as jumping, running, pole vaulting, hurdling etc.'

But the English, chuckles Dooley, claimed the American championship by winning such events as 'Wheeling the Perambulator, the Tea Drinking Contest and the Long Stand Up whilst the Band plays Gawd Save the King.'

The intention of such satirical writing was to reinforce the view that behaviour on the sports field could indicate national character, and that while the national character of the Americans involved the belief that winning was very important, the British could counter this only by cheating or triumphing in obscure events.

Many in Britain believed that the Americans saw international playing fields not as meeting grounds for engendering tolerance between national cultures, but as arenas to convince themselves of their own superiority and the virtues of American civilisation. They felt that America's athletic missionaries competed not as de Coubertin's romanticised patriots, but as evangelists of the gospel of Americanism, a culture in which winning is all.

The British response to all this strident nationalism was one of restrained, if somewhat patronising, superiority. Under the headline 'PRAISE OF BRITISH FAIR PLAY', the *Daily Mail* noted, perhaps a little pompously:

> If the American athletes were pleased, the American spectators were delirious with joy as one event after another fell to their lot. They gave the British a liberal education in the art of manifesting pleasure. The fairness of British sportsmanship has not only been vindicated, it has received a high mood of praise from the most influential and important of our visitors to the Olympic Games. Indeed, many distinguished guests were of the opinion that if anyone had suffered it had been the British competitors who had been, so to speak, sacrificed to ensure the utmost justice for foreign athletes. They could not remember more just and fairer decisions at any previous international meeting.

The English writer G. K. Chesterton, writing in *Colliers Magazine* of 12 September 1908, penned an indictment of American athletic nationalism, asserting that American sportsman embodied 'the vices of statesmen and fanatics, the sins of men inflamed by patriotism or religion'. An American sportsman, said Chesterton, 'cannot shake hands after the fight; he feels towards his conqueror as a man towards the invader who has robbed him of his God.'

This didn't deter President Roosevelt, who welcomed the American team back from the 1908 Games, advising them to stop complaining of British unfairness. 'We don't need to talk,' the President gloated, 'we've won.'

But the Americans were also capable of extending their attacks on the English way beyond Britain to the Empire. The United States regarded the 100 Metres as very much their own territory: they had won the event in all previous Olympic Games. When the South African Reggie Walker, just nineteen years and 128 days old and coached by the legendary Sam Mussabini, won the top sprinting event, he was greeted by headlines in the US that included: 'WALKER IS ON THE PAYROLL OF A WEALTHY MAN' and 'WALKER WINS BY BEATING THE PISTOl'.

As the American newspapers caught the spirit of the 1908 Games, even the jokes took on a biting, competitive edge. The Americans famously despaired of the British weather, particularly in that July of 1908, and jibes began to appear in the papers:

English man: There's been another highway robbery in broad daylight. Why, such a thing couldn't happen in England.
American: No? I understand you never get any broad daylight in England.

And they constantly mocked British claims of fair play. 'Andrew Carnegie is about to establish a "hero fund" in England,' ran the joke in the American papers. 'The first prize ought to go to the Englishman who will cheer when an American athlete wins an international event.'

But the British could give as good as they got, and often they chose to make their point in a very English way. After the City of London police won the gold medals in the tug-of-war, their captain and coach, Inspector Harry Duke, proud of his team and sturdily booted, marched up to some of the American squad.

'If you'd like to, gentlemen,' he said, 'we are happy to have a rematch. We'll remove our boots, of course, and take you on in our stockinged feet.'

– CHAPTER 23 –

TESTING POSITIVE
FOR PROFIT

The man everyone feared most in the Olympic Marathon of
1908 was the Onondaga Indian from Canada, Tom
Longboat. They feared him because he was the best, and they
feared him even more because he ran for money.

The Victorians considered competing for money to be a low-
class pursuit, and as international delegates debated the rules for
the first modern Games held in Athens in 1896, the British
delegation argued that manual labourers should be flatly
disqualified as only the wealthy could afford to exert themselves
without hope of financial gain. The other delegates decided that
the cost of travel would be enough of a deterrent to filter out the
working classes, and for decades, all Olympic competitors were
required to sign an affidavit to swear that they had never been
paid for taking part in sport and that their training had not been
subsidised in any way.

The problem for Tom Longboat was simple: he was universally acknowledged as one of the fastest marathon runners in the world. Coming up to the Olympic Games in 1908, he was at his peak, but no one could agree if he was still an amateur.

Longboat, referred to in contemporary Canadian newspapers in derogatory and dismissive phrases such as 'the Injun' and 'Heap Big Chief', was born on 4 June 1887, in a log cabin on the Six Nations Reserve south of Brantford, Ontario. His father died when he was still a young boy, leaving his mother to raise two sons and two daughters. Tom, it seemed, loved to run everywhere as a boy, and in 1906, at the age of nineteen, he entered a 20-mile race in Hamilton Bay as a complete unknown.

His bizarre appearance did nothing to impress onlookers or the other athletes. One writer described him as cutting 'a pathetic figure in a pair of bathing trunks, with cheap sneakers on his feet and hair that looked as if it had been hacked off by a tomahawk'. It was an outfit that certainly appeared to fool unsuspecting bookmakers. Some of them were offering odds of 60:1 on Longboat, while others, amused by his entry, let backers name the odds themselves. One such bet between an unnamed bookmaker and a man named J. Yaldon was taken at $1,000 to $2. No bookmaker would ever make that mistake with Tom Longboat again.

Even after he had started, Longboat's running style of low arms and splayed feet caused lots of knowing chuckles, but within the first mile, spectators realised that he could run – and fast. He won the 20-mile race with a time of 1:49:25 and came within seconds of setting a new course record.

A few days later, Longboat won the 15-mile 'Ward Marathon' in Toronto. He followed that by taking the 10-mile Christmas

Day race in Hamilton in 54:50, breaking the Canadian record by an impressive two minutes. Within a few months, he had established himself as the odds-on favourite for the Boston Marathon in April 1907. Reporters enthused about him as 'the running machine' and 'the Indian Iron Man' and most bookies were wary of accepting any sort of bet on him.

A crowd estimated at 100,000 turned out to see him win the Boston, and Longboat more than lived up to their expectations. During the race, a bizarre incident occurred when a train pulled out across a level crossing on the road. The first nine runners in the field got past, but the rest, including Johnny Hayes, were held up for several minutes. Longboat crossed the finish line in Boston in 2:24:24⅖, smashing by a full 5 minutes the course record set in 1901. Behind him came two Americans, Bob Fowler and Johnny Hayes, finishing second and third respectively.

On his way back to Toronto, travelling by train via Niagara Falls, Longboat talked to Lou Marsh, a *Toronto Star* writer who had gone to cover the marathon for his paper. 'Do you know what was wrong with those other fellows?' Longboat said to Marsh. 'They didn't have the grit. Some of them are fast enough but they couldn't stand the pace. They couldn't stick. That is what wins races like this, you've got to get out and run and stick through to the end to win.'

Toronto turned out in force to celebrate his victory. Sports historian David Blaikie wrote of his performance:

A sea of celebrating humanity engulfed Longboat as he stepped from the train. The champion was placed in an open car, a Union Jack about his shoulders, and taken to City Hall in a torchlight parade. Young women gazed at

Longboat in rapture as bands played and fireworks exploded around him. A gold medal was pinned to his chest and the mayor read a congratulatory address highlighted by an announcement of a $500 gift from the city for his education.

Longboat's ability soon won him an invitation to join the Irish-Canadian Athletic Club controlled by Tom Flanagan, who took over his training and management. But the big question for Flanagan and Longboat was: would he turn professional? It looked a likely prospect. At this time, races between professionals for big purses were sell-outs in North America and fortunes were to be made. But the 1908 Olympics were looming in London, and Longboat was odds-on favourite to come out a winner.

Already people were asking tough questions about his amateur status. Tom Flanagan, his trainer-manager, installed Longboat at the hotel he owned, where he lived rent-free. Many of the races Flanagan arranged were pure show-business, staged to attract heavy betting, and rumours of his professionalism were widespread. No one could be certain what the deal was between Flanagan and Longboat, and whether amateur rules were being violated, but after Longboat ran a controversial race in Boston, he was disqualified by the New England Amateur Athletic Union.

The ban declaring him a professional prevented him from running the 1908 Boston Marathon, in which Johnny Hayes came second, and caused huge controversy in Canada. Flanagan moved quickly to salvage the situation and established Longboat as the proprietor of a cigar store to demonstrate that he was quite capable of earning a living. The store featured Longboat's name in giant letters in the front window and was located in the Princess Theater building. There, he sold cigars in tins with a photo of himself on the lid. He also sold souvenir pictures of himself dressed as an American Indian and others in running clothes.

But the business soon burned itself out. The joke in running circles was that Longboat smoked most of the stock himself, and eventually the store passed into the hands of a businessman who removed his name from the window.

But Longboat was in good company. The Greek athletes who served as models for de Coubertin's 'amateur ideal' were never as pure as he wished to believe. Theoretically, the only prize awarded to champions in the ancient Olympics was a crown of olive branches, but victorious athletes from that first Olympic era were well compensated with money, food and prestigious jobs once they returned to the city states they represented. Between Olympic Games, they were allowed to compete in other games offering valuable prizes.

In nineteenth-century Britain, amateurism was redefined as a concept to reinforce the class system, to prolong the influence and control of governing elites. In contrast, sport betrayed a legacy of less-civilised origins; it was a rehearsal and a substitute for fighting. When leisure was restricted to the privileged few, sport could still cling to its military roots. The tournament was a wonderful workout for the medieval knight, and Edwardian team games were still considered to be ideal character building for subalterns leading their men over the top when bullets replaced cricket balls.

The rhetoric of leadership was rich in its sporting imagery as amateurs were urged to play the game, show moral fibre, uphold fair play and know if 'it's just not cricket' on the playing field or on the battlefield. Highmindedness was a characteristic of the amateur bodies that sprang up in Britain in the 1880s – the Amateur Athletic Association, the Amateur Boxing Association, the Amateur Rowing Association, the Amateur Swimming Association and the Lawn Tennis Association all set their faces firmly against any payment of athletes, seeing it as a corrupting influence. The consequence was that it kept the tradesmen or the working classes out of their sports long after such rules had baffled much of the world beyond Britain.

The survival of amateurism in athletics was also artificially prolonged by the growing influence of the Olympic Games. Baron de Coubertin was a huge admirer of the ethos of the English public school system. His International Olympic Committee invited a representative of the Head Masters' Conference (the Association of Head Masters of the English Public Schools) to attend their early meetings, and they chose Robert de Courcy Laffan as a representative to the IOC.

Ever since de Coubertin came up with his Olympics, aristocrats of the movement have struggled to define the true significance of the Games, for ways to give them a purpose. There has long been a tug-of-war between Olympic ideals and Olympic reality. One of the harshest and most long-lived of de Coubertin's commandments was the non-negotiable rule that every athlete had to swear that he was an amateur before he could compete. Athletes could not even be paid for time taken off from their other work.

Often the line between the amateur and the professional was blurred. When Dorando Pietri won the so-called 'Amateur Marathon road race' in Paris (actually 30km) in 1:55 on 15 October 1905, he finished 5 minutes ahead of Emile Bonheure of the Sporting Club de Vaugirard. Though he was hailed the winner of that race back in Italy, clearly there was trouble over Dorando's status. The French claimed he was a professional and, according to the *Manchester Guardian* of 18 October, the race was awarded to the Frenchman Bonheure with Charles Wigginton of Birchfield Harriers promoted to second place.

So, as with Longboat, there seemed to be question marks, even as early as 1905, over the 'amateurism' of Dorando. In New York by this time, Johnny Hayes had a token job that gave him all the time he needed to train and rest. And in Edinburgh, Wyndham Halswelle was happy enough to use Curran as his professional coach.

But in 1908, in the days when the Games were awash with blood, sweat and tears rather than urine samples, it still seemed possible to enforce strict rules on amateurism. The concept was all-powerful then and the debate on the ideal raged on for years in the Olympic movement. The most infamous case was that of Jim Thorpe, a Native American who won the Pentathlon and the Decathlon at the 1912 Olympics held in Stockholm. The Swedish monarch himself, King Gustav IV, marvelled at Thorpe's abilities and proclaimed him: 'The greatest athlete in the world'. But two years after the Games, Olympic officials stripped Thorpe of his medals and wiped his name from the record books after they learned that he had played semi-professional baseball while he was in college, for $2 a game. Thorpe's disqualification caused an uproar, but Olympic officials refused to give way.

Even after Thorpe, the Olympics continued to throw out athletes who failed to live up to the amateur vision. Paavo Nurmi, 'the flying Finn', also fell victim to that ideal after winning nine gold medals for distance running in the 1920s. He had hoped to crown his career with an attempt on the Marathon in 1932, but once he was accused of taking cash rewards, he found that despite his fame, he was no longer welcome. The great Swedes Gunder Hägg and Arne Andersson, too, were banned in 1945 when they threatened with every run to smash the 4-minute-mile barrier.

Under-the-table expense payments were common throughout the twentieth century and thousands of competitors were admitted to the Olympics provided they went along with the pretence of amateur purity. The system kept immense power in the hands of the officials of national federations and out of the hands of the athletes. It wasn't until 1986 that the International Olympic Committee took the final step and removed the ban on professionals. Now, the international federations that govern each Olympic sport must decide whether or not to allow professionals in their events.

In 1908, the slightest whiff of professionalism was enough to get you thrown out of the Olympics forever. Testing positive for profit was far more of a threat to your future than taking any illegal drug, and even a century ago, no matter how big a star you might be, men like Longboat, and perhaps even Dorando and Hayes, had to bend the rules to be allowed to take part in de Coubertin's elite Olympic Games.

– CHAPTER 24 –

BY ROYAL COMMAND?

There was a force even more potent than that of Baron de Coubertin at the 1908 Games, and one that attracted far more attention: it was the British Royal Family. And it was the force of the Monarchy that gave rise to so many colourful stories – some fact, some legend – that link this marathon and the debate over its distance to the Royal Family.

Thanks to the dominance of Lord Desborough, the influence of the Monarchy could be witnessed everywhere. It was flagged up in the pageantry and protocol of the opening ceremony, when the Royal Box at the Great Stadium had almost the whole world bowing and scraping.

The King, Edward VII, chose to stay the weekend of the opening ceremony with Lord and Lady Desborough at Taplow, near Reading. It was handy for the race meeting that Saturday at Sandown Park. The King was a regular at Desborough's shooting parties and had installed his favourite mistress, the sensual Lillie Langtry, nicknamed the Jersey Lily, just a bracing walk from Desborough's home, so His Majesty was always up for a visit to Maidenhead.

The sporting friendship with Desborough went back a long way. Two years before, the King and his Queen, Alexandra, had been at Athens as guests of the Greek Royal Family at the 'interim' Olympic Games, where they had been photographed with Olga, the Queen of Greece, on His Majesty's arm. With them, too, were the Prince and Princess of Wales.

King Edward's enthusiasm for the prospect of the Olympics shifting to London was crucial for the British decision and his enchantment with the Olympics, and the marathon in particular, was evident. The Royal party were all there in the Athens stadium when William Sherring, of Canada, carrying his running shoes in his hand, trotted in at the finish of the Marathon. Sherring sported a battered trilby and a wide grin as he came in almost seven minutes ahead of the next man, the Swede, John Svanberg. Prince George, the second son of the Greek King and Queen, 6 feet 5 inches tall and resplendent in his uniform and cap, joined in and ran the last lap in the stadium with the Canadian.

Sherring, to the disappointment of the local crowd, was not a Greek victor, but even so, Prince George repeated what he had done with Spiridon Louis in 1896. By running alongside the winner, the Prince again forged a link between the Greek Royal Family and this showcase event, the Marathon.

No one applauded this Royal gesture to the Marathon more than King Edward. Everyone in the Royal party – His Majesty, Queen Alexandra, the Prince and Princess of Wales – agreed the race was a marvellous spectacle, quite the climax of the Games.

And they admired the way that the Greek Royal Family identified themselves with the event.

The race from the field of Marathon to the capital city of Athens had a ring about it, and even then in 1906, as Desborough and King Edward toyed with the idea of the Games coming to London, it would have been difficult not to think about what might make a memorable starting point 25 miles or so from the capital. Runnymede perhaps, might be the English equivalent of Marathon, dripping with history and tradition. Or nearby Windsor, home of the great castle, could offer the right distance.

As the plans began to form that were to shape the London Games, a marathon race from the site of a Royal Castle to the Royal Capital seemed calculated to delight, even flatter, King Edward, and keep him firmly onside as a supporter of Lord Desborough's Games.

A request had been made from Finland to the British Olympic Council that 'the marathon race should be held on the road' and there had been some debate in the British press about the difficulties of clearing the roads in the London area for the event. But by August 1907, *The Sporting Life* was suggesting that the Polytechnic Harriers, who had their headquarters in London's Regent Street, would be an ideal athletic club to arrange the Marathon. Since 1897, the Polytechnic Harriers had been controlling and authenticating walking races between London and Brighton, with the first run – a trial for the 1900 marathon – over the same route in 1899, and they seemed the ideal candidate. By the late summer of 1907, the British press were speculating about the London route and picking up on the debate that increasingly seemed to favour a start in Windsor.

The details were under the supervision of the four officials who formed the Olympic track committee: Percy Fisher, Charles Val Hunter, George Schofeld and Harry Venn. The Amateur Athletic Association (AAA) decided that a number of 'trial races' would be held to select the British representatives for the great race. The Polytechnic Harriers were allotted one of these and eventually the task of masterminding the 1908 route was given to Jack Andrew, honorary secretary of the Polytechnic Harriers and a representative on the AAA committee.

The anticipation of the Marathon being run in London played to the British view that they had the best distance runners in the world, and the first of these trials took place over a distance of '20 miles' in Manchester on 21 March 1908. Organised by Salford Harriers, it started and finished from the Saracen's Head public house in Warburton, and the route was measured on an Ordnance Survey map. It was won by Fred Lord, a 29-year-old Yorkshire man, in 1:50:23, but when the course was re-measured, however, it proved to be only 19 miles.

The second trial, on 28 March, a week after Manchester, was a 'closed' race, open only to members of Ranelagh Harriers, a south London club. This was won in 2:08:30.2 by Frederick Thompson – an established walker who fancied trying the novel event of the Marathon. Further trial races were held on 4 April in Liverpool over 18 miles, and by Blackheath Harriers in Kent over 24 miles 670 yards. On 11 April, another club, Derby and County, held a 'closed' race over 22 miles 1380 yards.

There still seemed to be no clear criteria for the selection of the British team to contest the marathon, but on 25 April 1908, a trial from Windsor to Wembley was organised by the Polytechnic Harriers, which clearly carried more significance than any previous rehearsal, both for the distance and the route.

This trial was started by Lord Desborough and attended by the Prince of Wales. The *Windsor and Eton Express* reported: 'The race will begin in the Long Walk 290 yards from the Sovereign's Entrance, when the competitors will ascend the slope to reach the Park Street Gate and hence on to Wembley – a distance of 22 miles 1420 yards.'

Evidently, this was a trial not only for the runners but also a dummy run over much of the route, which was clear from the map included in the programme for the race. In April, the stadium at the White City was still under construction, so Jack Andrew took the runners off the proposed route at Sudbury Station to finish on the trotting track at Wembley Stadium.

The Times reported of this trial race that the course was 'about 3 miles under the distance which will have to be covered in the marathon race proper on July 24th' – so it was clear that Andrew intended the Olympic race to be close to 26 miles. There were some problems with the route originally devised for the Olympic race, with too many tramlines in the last few miles and surfaces of tough cobbles. Andrew worked out an alternative route across the heath of Wormwood Scrubs – though easier on the feet, it would, however, add several hundred yards.

On a cold and filthy day amid squalls of snow that left runners ankle-deep in slush at some points, the trial was won by Alexander Duncan of Salford Harriers. The first six finishers were picked to join the twelve-strong team of Britons selected for the Olympic marathon announced on 10 June.

There was one final trial on 23 May, organised by the South London Harriers. It followed most of the Polytechnic Harriers course, this time from Eton to Wembley, and again measured 22 miles 1420 yards. Thus, it was clear that before 1908, there was no set distance for the Marathon; it was simply a long race of around 25 miles (40km) in length. The Olympic Marathon distance in Athens in 1896 was 40,000 metres; in Paris in 1900 it was 40,260 metres, while in St Louis, 1904, it measured 40,232 metres.

On 29 June 1907, when *The Times* of London announced the programme for the Games, it noted that the Marathon would be 25 miles (40km) and this information was sent to all the competing nations. But on 1 November, the *Sporting Life* announced the proposed route of the race with a map and indicated that the distance would be approximately 25½ miles, and on 13 November, *The Times* was giving a distance of 25 miles 600 yards.

There had been indications in the autumn of 1907 that Andrew and the Polytechnic officials hoped that Windsor Castle itself, with special Royal permission, would be the starting point of the Marathon, but it was July before the King gave formal consent to the start being on the East Terrace.

On 22 July, *The Times* confirmed the detailed arrangements for the race, indicating that the start would be at the East Terrace of Windsor Castle, 700 yards from Queen Victoria's statue. It announced that the course would go along Thames Street, across the Thames Bridge into High Street, Eton, and noted that the distance was 26 miles 385 yards, which *The Times* confusingly reported amounted to 42,263 metres, as did the Official Games Report and a number of other newspapers which had miscalculated the conversion from yards to metres.

There have been a number of colourful explanations of how the odd distance of the London Marathon was arrived at. Opinion usually divides between those who claim the Royal

Family wished to have a better view from the East Terrace at Windsor Castle at the start, causing distance to be added at the Windsor end, and those who maintain that the extra distance on top of the 26 miles was added when the finish line at the White City was taken to a position in front of the Royal Box, which was on the opposite side of the stadium from the runners' entrance. But this is to miss the subtlety of how the course evolved, what, if anything, was the 'Royal connection', and the complex factors involved in settling on the final distance.

First of all, the concept of running from Windsor to the Great Stadium in Shepherd's Bush had to win acceptance and almost certainly that idea can be traced back to informal discussions held, among others, between Lord Desborough and King Edward VII, which gives some logical reason for the belief, widely held at the time, that the Royals had a part in shaping the detail of the distance covered. But the man who really controlled the distance was Jack Andrew, the organising keystone of the race. His decisions may have made any arguments about the odd 385 yards pale into insignificance.

In a statement made some years after the event to Arthur Winter, the man who wrote the history of the Polytechnic Marathon in 1969 to celebrate its 50th Jubilee Year, Jack Andrew maintained that having settled on a route for the 1908 Games Marathon of approximately 24½ miles, he learned that the London *Evening News* planned to promote a professional race over the same course. In the strict amateur climate of the time, this would not have been popular. Jack Andrew and his colleagues in the Amateur Athletic Association would have wanted no confusion or comparison with a race run for professionals. As a consequence, Andrew claimed he changed

185

both the route of his finish and altered the distance to the now-famous figure of 26 miles 385 yards.

Whether or not time had clouded his memory, it is clear that Andrew was tinkering with the details of both the length of the route and the site of the start. On 8 November 1907, *The Sporting Life* noted: 'It has not been definitely settled where the race shall start, but the Council of the Olympic Association are endeavouring to obtain permission for it to be in the grounds of Windsor Castle. This would be regarded as a gracious concession by His Majesty, but should the necessary permission not be granted the start will be from either Queen Victoria's or Prince Victor's statue.'

When the trial was held in the sleet and hail of April, it started in the Long Walk of Windsor Park. The end of the first mile was on Barnespool Bridge, where the only surviving marker from the 1908 Olympic race still tells you that there are 25 miles to go. Clearly, the race was intended to measure 26 miles to the stadium entrance. The programme for the race that day states unequivocally: 'It is hoped that the King will graciously consent to the start being made from the terrace of the historic Castle, in which event the distance will be about 26 miles to the edge of the Stadium track.'

That hope became reality and the *Windsor and Eton Express* of 25 July notes that, 'The actual starting point for today's race is just below the East Terrace, Windsor Castle, near the bronze figure of Dako [Queen Victoria's favourite dog, a Scottish terrier], who was buried there.'

There may have been a number of reasons why the race, as originally planned by Jack Andrew, did not start from the Long Walk. It is possible that Inspector Hudson, supervising the local police arrangements, raised some concerns about spectators being too thick in the starting area, though it seems his police team would have had no real difficulty with crowd control. But the most likely explanation of the mystery of the Royal connection with this race is to be found in the impact that the 1906 Marathon in Athens had on the British Royal Family, which included King Edward and Queen Alexandra and the Prince and Princess of Wales.

The prospect of letting the children of the Princess see the start of the Marathon, a race that their father and mother had witnessed themselves in Greece, must have been virtually irresistible, particularly since the press were saying that there might not be another Marathon in Britain for decades. The only person who could make such a scene possible was ultimately the King. His name had already been published on a programme produced for the day of the Olympic race: 'The Start will be given by His Majesty THE KING. The QUEEN has consented to present the prizes.' Furthermore, a line drawing of His Majesty appeared on the front of the programme, and inside it is stated: 'The runners will toe the line on a site on the Eastern Terrace of the Castle some 700 yards from Queen Victoria's statue and it is expected that His Majesty will honour the race by himself giving the starting signal.'

The Royal imprimatur on the race was indelible, and the shift of the start – almost certainly discussed between the King and Desborough – from the Long Walk to the Castle grounds was a logical conclusion to the Royal patronage of the race.

The Marathon was always planned to finish on the straight beneath the site of the Royal Box. Previous Olympic Marathon organisers, somewhat cavalier about precise measurements, had calculated the distance from the start to the entrance of the stadium and left the arrangements about what happened on the track within to the stadium organisers. The truth was that a century ago, few beyond Jack Andrew and his crew of surveyors, obsessed with their maps and their measuring wheels, were likely to be too concerned about the odd 100 yards here or there being tacked onto the distance. It was only the British, with their passion for tidying up the laws of sport, their desire for rules and strict measurement, who were likely to lose much sleep over such details.

In the event, to reach the Royal Box from the point where Andrew planned to bring the runners into the stadium would add 385 yards on the cinder track. It meant running clockwise, to give the crowd a longer opportunity to see the runners on the track – and while present-day tracks are run anticlockwise, in 1908 the direction was not that unusual. Lord Desborough himself, who in his younger days had run the 3 miles for Oxford University against Cambridge, did all his training and racing at the old Iffley Road track where they ran this way round – clockwise – on a cinder track, three laps to the mile, just as in the Great Stadium.

Jack Andrew and his team had done their work. They produced a reasonably tough route of 26 miles, to which 385 yards was added on the cinder track to bring the runners to the finish. It was not an easy course: there were many sharp corners, and even with a starting height of 190 feet (58 metres) at Windsor Castle and a finish height of 33 feet (10 metres) at the White City, the undulating course climbed to 197 feet (60 metres twice) at Pinewood and Uxbridge Commons, to give a total height climbed of 318 feet (97 metres).

Underfoot, the going was tough, too. The high streets in the towns and villages along the route often had cobblestone surfaces, and the country roads between the villages were commonly dirt and dust tracks. Measurement of the 26 miles 385 yards, though, had been thoroughly done, with Andrew and his team of surveyors using wheels and Ordnance Survey maps to check the distance. However, the change in the starting location – the move from the Long Walk to the Eastern Terrace of the Castle – may have introduced yet another mystery into the problem of the distance.

John Disley, co-founder with Chris Brasher of today's London Marathon (first held in 1981), believes that when the start was moved to the Castle terrace, the accuracy of the earlier measurement of the course, from the start at Long Walk, may have been jeopardised. He thinks that the organisers made a stab at reproducing the first mile of the course but may have got their calculations wrong.

By using maps, contemporary photographs of the start and detailed descriptions, Disley used twenty-first-century methods to measure that first mile to Barnespool Bridge. His conclusion is that from the start on the East Terrace, the first mile – and hence the marathon course – is 174 yards (159 metres) short.

The mystery of the missing 174 yards and the question of who first suggested shifting the start to the East Terrace may consume sports historians and statisticians for the next 100 years. Whatever the outcome, there is no doubt that the future standard distance for the Marathon was established on that hot summer day in 1908, and announced to the world as being 26 miles 385 yards (42.195km).

For the next two Olympics, the distance continued to vary. In 1912, in Stockholm, it was 40.2km, and in Antwerp, 1920, 42.75km. Finally, it was standardised on 27 May 1921 at the

IAAF Congress in Geneva. The indelible memory of the 1908 race in London, and the many matches over 26 miles 385 yards to follow, both amateur and professional, ensured all future races would be over this distance.

On 24 July 1908, the *Daily Mail* announced:

The Blue Ribbon of the Games, the Marathon Race, will be decided today over a road course from Windsor to Shepherd's Bush. The start will be made from Windsor Castle, East Terrace, 700 yards from Queen Victoria's statue, at 2.30, and the distance to be covered is 26 miles 385 yards, or 42.263 kilometres [sic].

Providing the weather holds fine, a record crowd will see the finish, for no event in the history of athletics has created so much interest in England as the one to be run today.

– CHAPTER 25 –

THE MARATHON CONTENDERS

Headlines in London's *Daily Mail* of 22 July 1908 captured the mood of anticipation gripping the Games: 'THE MARATHON RACE – TODAY'S GREAT STRUGGLE', they announced. 'LONGBOAT TO RUN. LATEST FROM WINDSOR'.

The extravagant press fanfare meant that all the hot money was on Tom Longboat; the bookmakers didn't give a fig for the view that he should be banned as a professional. He was the man the public wanted to see and he was the man they wanted to bet on, too. That day, the *Mail* reported:

Best of all, from the everyday follower of athletics' point of view, will be the appearance of the Canadian Indian, Tom Longboat. This celebrity, who has done great things in his own land and ran 25 miles in 2 hours 24 minutes at the Boston Marathon, has figured prominently in the papers for many weeks. His amateur status has been questioned in America and he competes today under protest.

The dark-skinned gentleman has been in Ireland some considerable time training. He is accounted a dangerous man and, after all that has been written about him, his running will be awaited with much interest.

The papers queued up to interview Longboat and the *Windsor Express* got something of a scoop when they accompanied him on a visit to Windsor Castle on the Thursday before the Marathon:

Tom Longboat, the famous Canadian Indian, arrived at Windsor on Wednesday and put up at the White Hart Hotel. He is a black-haired, dark-complexioned young fellow and rather reserved. He is a natural humorist and enjoys a joke hugely. A representative of the *Express* accompanied the famous runner over the state apartments at the Castle on Thursday afternoon and he said he had never seen a more wonderful place. He was very pleased, however, that he did not live in bygone days when warriors wore armour.

He said he should not like to run the marathon race with 'tin cans' round him. He said it was too spick and span a place to live in and he was afraid he would lose himself. The beautiful ceilings, pictures, tapestries and furniture were admired by him. He said he would not mind sleeping in the State bed tonight after the marathon race. Going through Eton, Longboat asked, looking at hundreds of Eton boys in top hats, 'Where's the funeral?'

Later, the paper reported:

> Longboat had a spin over part of the course and on his
> return he appeared well satisfied. The great runner looked
> in excellent form but he had a nasty bruise on his right leg
> and his feet were blistered. Mr Marsh, his friend, attended to
> these and remarked to a press man who was present, 'If you
> tickle his ribs he will raise the roof, but if you cut part of his
> toe he would not shout.'
>
> Longboat said: I think a runner is like a racehorse, you
> can't tell exactly what constitutes a runner – it is a natural
> gift. I don't want to speak about myself, but I don't think it
> is much good taking long steps in the marathon race. I have
> changed my stride recently to shorter steps and that I find
> easier to get over the ground. I don't care what sort of day
> it is, but I think if it rains it will suit me best tomorrow.
>
> I eat most anything, except pork and veal and potatoes. I
> like good wholesome food and I have a little sherry and egg
> sometimes. I don't like fire water [very strong alcoholic
> drinks], that's bad for runners, I have a little stout. I never
> felt better in my life than I do today and I'm going to do
> my utmost to win tomorrow.

But beyond Longboat, there were plenty of others the crowd had
come to cheer for. At least his presence kept the pressure away
from Dorando. The Italian prepared by taking a few gentle runs,
sightseeing and relaxing in the small Soho Hotel, where Ulpiano
ensured he had a good supply of Chianti, diluted with water to
quench his thirst and soothe his nerves.

Johnny Hayes was confident after his win at Yonkers, and

though he still believed he could have run faster and won the Boston Marathon, he was picking up the bug for winning that seemed to infect all the Irish-American boys at their headquarters down in Brighton.

Hayes had already told his friends in New York: 'I just know I'm going to win and I wish it were 50 miles instead of 26. The next time you fellows see me I'll be wearing the laurel wreath (or whatever they give the winner) around my ears. I've been training my head and my legs for years for a chance at the Marathon.'

And he had allegedly told the *New York Sun*, 'I know to a breath how far I can run and how fast. I intend to go right out with the pacemakers, keep at their heels until I am ready to finish and then go on and win. I am not afraid of any of them but I expect our own boys to make it hot for me. Longboat? I'll bet you the Indian crumples up before he goes 20 miles. Tom Longboat is like a prize fighter who's seen his best days and I don't believe he will have enough in him to go the distance.'

In a letter to one of his friends, Hayes said, 'There won't be any excuse if we don't win. As for myself I can still eat, sleep and run just as good as I did on the other side.' He had every reason to feel confident. 'Our trainer, Mike Murphy, taught us to run natural. "There's nothing easier than running," he used to say. "You walk, then you walk fast, and first thing you know you're running." He used to make us run three hours a day.'

The likely United States' contenders for the Marathon in London came from two races held in the spring of 1908. At Boston, on 20 April, Johnny Hayes was beaten into second place by Tom Morrisey, and as a result of that race the two men were picked for the Olympic team, along with Michael J. Ryan and

Elton Welton. Also joining them were two men from a race on 2 May in St Louis: Sydney Hatch and Joseph Forshaw.

But some of the bookmakers were not so sure of the result, despite the confidence of Longboat and the squad of Americans. Many fancied the veteran long-distance specialist Charles Hefferon.

Hefferon, born in 1878, was running for South Africa. Originally from Newbury in Berkshire, he first emigrated to Canada, where he continued his successful running career and was practically never beaten. He eventually settled in Bloemfontein after fighting in the Boer War. He worked in the Prisons Department, married and settled down. Although he dropped out of the final Marathon trial in Cape Town, held on a fearsome day of torrid heat in April 1908, because of his great experience at the distance he was selected to represent South Africa in London.

But the greatest interest for the British public was the dozen-strong squad of their own Marathon runners selected as a result of the trial races held in the spring. 'The real struggle is expected to be,' said the *Daily Mail*, 'between the United Kingdom, Canada, the United States, South Africa and Sweden. And to narrow it down to two, the probability is that either the United Kingdom or Canada will provide the champion. Long distance running is more popular, both in this country and Canada, than it is in America and South Africa, where the hot climate is unfavourable to such long sustained exertion.'

Despite the draconian rulings on amateurism and training expenses, it seems the British were keen enough to make sure their men were properly prepared, and were ready to pay for it. Official funds were made available for any British Marathon runner who wanted to undertake special preparation. Alec

Duncan, the 24-year-old from Kendal, who had won the Polytechnic Harriers trial and shown great form on the track, went to Brighton to spend three weeks with his trainer, Bob Ramsden. Fred Lord left his job as a stoker in a chemical works near Bradford to train in London, where he put on 5lb in weight. And Alf Wyatt from Bolton opted for Blackpool to train in the sea air. The *Windsor Express* noted with approval that:

> The Britishers are sportsmen, and they are anxious that the best man should win, but they cannot bring themselves to believe that the Indian Longboat is going to have it all his own way. Indeed, the opinion is freely expressed that the best man in the race will be found in the British team.
>
> A competent judge, thoroughly in touch with the men who are going to try to uphold England's reputation in a punishing race, expressed the belief that one of our team could easily beat the record by five minutes. He doubted whether Longboat could manage to wipe five minutes off the track record for 26 miles and he was certain the Indian would have to do it to win. The best half dozen of the British team seemed to be Duncan, Lord, Beale, Barratt and Price, but there is talk of a dark horse. The rules for the race have been framed in accordance with the best traditions of British Amateur Athletics.

The Italians had staged their first national marathon championship in Rome on 3 June 1908 – a race intended to serve as their Olympic trial. Because of Dorando's failure there, it was only just over two weeks before the Olympic race that he had eventually forced his way into the team following his solo run over 40km in Carpi as late as 7 July. His record-breaking run was followed by the long journey over land and sea to London. A century on, most pundits would suspect the Italian was still feeling the effects of the race in Carpi when he set out from Windsor.

Most British papers carried a weather forecast for Marathon Day, a significant factor in this toughest of all events. The *Daily Express* reported on 24 July:

Everything in the way of the weather promises to assist competitors in the great race of today. The most important point of all is the wind. This promises to be light from the west south west, and therefore in favour of the competitors for three parts of the distance. Nothing in the shape of a head wind will be met with all the way. Nothing in the way of rain or thunder was reported over the whole of Western Europe last night, and with the barometer inclined to rise over our islands, a fair to very fine day with a rather high temperature may be expected in the district between Windsor and London today. The warmth in fact should prove somewhat oppressive during the time the race is due to be run, and this should suit the competitors from southern climes.

Spectators were informed that runners 'will keep to the left hand side of the road, will wear loose running knickers and jerseys. They may all easily be identified by the number pinned on their jerseys in front and behind'.

The *Windsor Express* concluded its preview of the race with a stern warning to all runners: 'No competitor, either at the start or during the progress of the race, may take or receive any drug. A breach of this rule, the competitors are warned, will operate as an absolute disqualification.

'Medical men will control the course and if, in their opinion, a man is not in a fit condition to continue the race, he must at once retire when ordered to do so.'

– CHAPTER 26 –

THE GREAT
HALSWELLE AFFAIR

Even as excitement over the Marathon was hotting up, animosity between the British and the Americans exploded like a starter's pistol in the finals of the 400 Metres to produce one of the most bitter rows in Olympic history.

Wyndham Halswelle was back on course by July 1908, but warnings from Jimmy Curran still rang in his ears. 'This is your chance for gold. Stop being such a gentleman, get in there and win it! If you don't, the Yankees will kill you.'

Lord Desborough, too, heaped yet more pressure on him. There had been talk of the Americans ganging up on the Scot. Someone claimed to have overheard a conversation and they passed on the gossip to the officials.

'Don't worry,' they said, 'we'll look after you. We'll see fair play at any price – it's not going to be Athens all over again.' But Halswelle didn't want other people to fight his battles.

He had looked remarkably good in the preliminary rounds. The *Daily Mail* of 22 July enthusiastically described his running in the heats of the 400 Metres. 'Halswelle gave the home country a chance of rejoicing,' it reported. 'A beautifully built man with a broad chest and a fine action, he started easily in his 400m heat. So easily that people who knew nothing of his methods felt some alarm as they saw an American in front of him. Halswelle bided his time, and when it came he went to the front, won by 10 yards and, although he was pulling up at the finish, he was only a fifth of a second outside the record.'

But all the rancour that haunted the battle of Shepherd's Bush came to a head on Thursday, 23 July, at 5.30 in the afternoon, when four men stepped out for the 400 Metres final. The field was made up of three Americans and the one British runner, Halswelle. The line-up was John Carpenter of Cornell University, William Robbins of Harvard College, John Taylor of the University of Pennsylvania and, of course, Britain's Lieutenant Wyndham Halswelle.

All the runners had come through two tough earlier rounds. Taylor, the black American athlete, had won heat one in 50.8, Robbins heat two in 50.4, Carpenter heat fourteen with 49.6, and Halswelle heat fifteen with 49.4. In the second round, Carpenter won heat one in 49.8. Halswelle set a new Olympic record in heat two with 48.4. Taylor won heat three in 49.8 and Robbins won the last heat with 49.0.

Significantly, the races were not run in lanes or in strings (used to divide one lane from another), and the athletes lined up shoulder to shoulder. In the final of the 400 Metres, Carpenter drew the inside position with Halswelle next to him, Robbins in third position and Taylor on the outside.

The British officials had been tipped off to expect 'tactics' from the American runners and there was a history of trouble in this event from the previous Games in Athens in 1906. A series of judges had been ranged around the track, though officials were told that the American coach, Mike Murphy, had urged his men not to run as a team against Halswelle.

The starter, Harry Goble, called the runners together and warned them about jostling and told them that judges were posted to see fair play. The Amateur Athletic Association rule, printed in the programme that day for all to read, stated: 'Any competitor wilfully jostling or running across or obstructing another competitor so as to impede his progress shall forfeit his right to be in the competition and shall not be awarded any positional prize that he would otherwise have been entitled to.'

Despite the rulebook, the starter's gun that day let loose a clash that enraged reporters and eyewitnesses throughout the stadium. Halswelle was practically elbowed off the track by Carpenter, and the horrified British officials rushed to rip apart the tape before the American could finish. They declared the whole event 'No race' and decreed that the final should be re-run. The British press thundered:

It is a painful thing to have to record that the Olympic Games of London have been marred by one of the most disgraceful exhibitions of foul play that has ever been witnessed. Such a race was witnessed for the final of the 400m yesterday afternoon, and it is to be hoped for the good repute of amateur sportsmen all the world over it will never again be seen in any country.

In commenting yesterday upon the prospects of the race in question it was remarked that the running would be closely watched lest there should be a repetition of those 'tactics' on the part of the three Americans opposed to the British champion Halswelle, which two years ago at Athens precluded the latter from having a fair chance. After those lines were in type the writer half regretted that they had been set on paper. They seemed to cast a reflection upon American sportsmanship which he would have liked to think unworthy. Unhappily, it has to be stated that there was only too much justification for the suggestion implied.

Not only were the fears which prompted the paragraph realised, but they were realised in such a way, by so flagrant and open a breach of the first principles of fair play, that a slur is cast upon American sportsmanship in the eyes of all Europe which can never be eradicated.

The report continued:

Carpenter sprang off with the lead followed by Robbins with Halswelle, who was ever a slow starter, third. Taylor was last. Rounding the bend, Halswelle's pace in the familiar manner began to increase. He closed up on Robbins and all looked to see him enter the straight on even terms with Carpenter, if not actually ahead.

Halswelle's customary strong finish would then have settled the race forthwith. As the runners, passing across the vision of those on the stand confronting the straight, sped round the curve a din arose from the tiers of seats at the northern end. For the moment the cause was not apparent, but as Halswelle and Carpenter came into the straight it was seen that the former was running very wide.

An exclamation burst from the crowd which changed sharp and instant into a howl of execration as Carpenter was seen to be running obliquely, driving Halswelle onto the extreme outside edge of the track. At one point Halswelle nearly stumbled onto the narrow strip of grass which divides the cinder path from the cycle track.

The race down the straight was preposterous. No opportunity would Carpenter give for Halswelle to pass him and the latter, plainly showing in his face the disgust which must have filled him, though saying never a word, eased up. It comes to this: that before the chosen champions of more than twenty nations of the civilised world, before an assembly of 25,000 persons, an American athlete deliberately preferred to defeat by foul means a better man than himself.

There is no excuse; there can be no excuse. The thing was open, unabashed, and shameless. It must either be repudiated or defended and of the point of view which can hold such tactics, manoeuvres, call it what you will, worthy of the name of sport, the less said the better. Fortunately Carpenter was not allowed to profit by his 'skill'. Prompt action was taken by the judges, the tape was broken and the American passed the post first to find that his dirty trick was of no avail. Credit is due to the crowd for the manner in which it behaved. Imprecations flew pretty freely it is true, and there was at first a certain amount of booing. But the spectators soon calmed down and recognising that the affair must be for the moment *sub judice* patiently awaited the results of the official deliberations.

Rumours of all sorts were rife of course, one being to the effect that both Robbins and Taylor had given evidence against Carpenter stating that they saw the foul and eased their pace in consequence. Announcement was presently made that the judges' deliberations were likely to be protracted, as the evidence would have to be taken down before being carefully considered. Content with this, the majority of the spectators filed out, leaving only a few handfuls to await the result of the standing jump.

It is impossible to overrate the outrage thus committed upon the best traditions of sportsmanship. In any amateur athletic meeting it would have been a monstrous thing. That it should happen in a gathering inspired by so high an ideal as the Olympic Games is deplorable.

The Times of London was also outraged by the incident. 'A more disgraceful exhibition of foul running has never been seen on an English track and it is becoming increasingly obvious that in future, American "amateurs" will have to be debarred from taking part in athletic contests in this country, which are supposed to be reserved for gentlemen,' it reported.

Unsurprisingly, the American press took a very different view of the row and the background to it. The *New York Times* didn't offer a detailed account of the incident, but instead summarised the American point of view in their headlines: 'Carpenter of Cornell easily beat English crack but is disqualified for foul. Officials claim bump race to be re-run. English crowds boo American performers for no reason whatsoever.'

And unsurprisingly, some sections of the American press went much further. Under the headline 'AMERICAN WINS THE

Beneath the beaming gaze of Lord Desborough, Queen Alexandra honours
Dorando Pietri with her 'Golden Cup' the day after the Italian was
disqualified in the 1908 Marathon.

Top: Johnny Hayes, USA, chasing the leaders as crowds line the streets of London with just over two miles to go to the finish-line of the Olympic Marathon.
© *Bob Wilcock, Society of Olympic Collectors*

Above: Dorando, showing the perfect style that took him to the front of the field in the Marathon.
© *Bob Wilcock, Society of Olympic Collectors*

Left: Tom Longboat, the Onondaga Indian from Canada, reckoned by many to be the best marathon runner in the world.
© *Bob Wilcock, Society of Olympic Collectors*

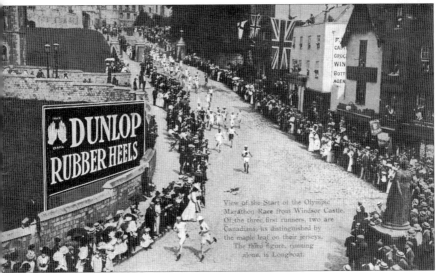

View of the Start of the Olympic
Marathon Race from Windsor Castle.
Of the three first runners, two are
Canadians, as distinguished by
the maple leaf on their jerseys.
The third figure, running
alone, is Longboat.

Top left: Charles Hefferon from South Africa, the silver medallist, enters the
Olympic stadium. © *Bob Wilcock, Society of Olympic Collectors*

Top right: A triumphant Johnny Hayes, winner of the Marathon, carried on a
table by his team-mates. © *Bob Wilcock, Society of Olympic Collectors*

Below: The fast downhill start from the gates of Windsor Castle past Queen
Victoria's statue. Tom Longboat, running alone, is lying third. Dunlop
superimposed their advertising hoarding and sold the shot as a postcard.

© *Bob Wilcock, Society of Olympic Collectors*

Above: The lonely victor: Wyndham Halswelle, GB, walks away from the royal box and his sport after collecting the gold medal for winning the Olympic 400m.

© *PA Photos*

Below: Dazed and confused: Dorando turns the wrong way as he enters the Olympic stadium.

© *Bob Wilcock, Society of Olympic Collectors*

Left: No sweatsuits in 1908: An overcoated John Carpenter, USA, disconsolate after his disqualification in the 400m.   © *Getty Images*

Top right: Spaghetti, wine and dollars put pounds on the frame of the once diminutive Dorando during his post-Olympic career.

© *Bob Wilcock, Society of Olympic Collectors*

Above: Can Dorando beat Hayes? A poster for the rematch that packed Madison Square Garden, New York, on 25 November 1908.

Top left: Teresa and Dorando Pietri in Carpi, in the year of their marriage in 1909.

Top right: Sweet music of fame: The ballad 'Dorando' earned more than $4,000 in royalties.

Bottom left: Side by side: Ulpiano wears a hat and a suit as he trots alongside Dorando for a publicity shot.

Above right: The composer, Irving Berlin, the singing waiter who put the name of Dorando on everyone's lips.

© *Getty Images*

Top left: Princess Victoria Mary, who as Princess of Wales pressed the button that signalled the start of the 1908 Marathon.

Top right: Dorando proudly posing with the cup presented by Queen Alexandra. The cup is now kept in Carpi.

Above: Dorando is rushed from the Great Stadium on a stretcher amid fears for his life.

Top: The runners, many of them in hats, set off for London's Shepherd's Bush against the backdrop of Windsor Castle.
© *Bob Wilcock, Society of Olympic Collectors*

Above: A card advertising the delights of the Grand Hotel Dorando in Carpi.

Left: New York cartoonists captured the hype behind the Great Marathon Derby held on 3 April 1909. The Frenchman, Henri St-Yves, won this race.

400m, Officials call it No Race', one US newspaper included the paragraph:

> When Halswelle found that he could not pass Carpenter, he threw up his hands and in an instant the officials jumped in the air. One broke the tape and immediately there was an announcement of 'no race'. A statement followed that it would be run in an hour. That was alright until it was learned that Halswelle was 'all in' and then came another decision that Carpenter was disqualified and the race would be re-run on Saturday.

The comments from Mike Murphy, the trainer of the American team, were particularly vitriolic. Making the anger of the Americans even worse was the fact that when a meeting of the British Amateur Athletic Association was held to consider the incident, only the judges and Halswelle himself were called to testify. Halswelle's own words on what had happened in the race were:

> Carpenter's elbow undoubtedly touched my chest, for as I moved outwards to pass him he did likewise, keeping his right arm in front of me. In this manner he bored me across quite two-thirds of the track and entirely stopped my running. As I was well up to his shoulder and endeavouring to pass him, it is absurd to say I could have come up on the inside. I was too close after halfway round the bend to have done this. Indeed to have done so would have necessitated chopping my stride and thereby losing anything from 2–4 yards. When about 30 or 40 yards from the tape, I saw officials holding up their hands, so I slowed down.

Murphy used the American press to respond. He told the *Daily Tribune* in New York, 'Highway robbery is pretty strong language, but there are no other words for it. I have been up against the English officials for years and it has always been the same story. They would have robbed us of everything they could.'

He then told the *Evening Post* in New York, 'It shows what the boasted "fairest sportsmen" in the world will do to win. I would rather have seen this happen than win fifty races. It proves what I have always said, that these English officials will do anything to prevent an American or anybody besides their own people from winning a race. If I had my way, every American athlete at that stadium would leave here right away and never return, either to this arena or to England.'

The smouldering antagonism between Britain and America, evident from the day of the opening ceremony, now broke into open hostility and it looked as if the incident might endanger further progress of the Games. Almost from the start, James Sullivan had been complaining about the British. He constantly accused them of cheating and at one point even appeared to blame the London Olympic Committee for the appalling English weather. But after the 400 Metres race, he said, 'Never in my life, and I have attended athletic meetings for 31 years, have I witnessed a scene so unsportsmanlike and unfair.'

It took the judges over an hour of deliberation to decide that Carpenter should be disqualified and the race be re-run without him two days later on Saturday, 25 July. This time, the judges ruled, lanes would be marked and divided by strings to ensure there could be no repetition of such an incident.

The Americans were both baffled and furious. Although the practice of blocking was permitted by the American Athletics

Federation, it was most definitely not allowed in the Olympics. Carpenter and the other Americans could not believe they were not given sufficient opportunity to present their defence to the charges of foul play and Sullivan said he would never allow the other Americans to take part in any re-run.

Even Halswelle had no taste for it, wanting no more to do with the final or, indeed, the Games. It took a lot of persuading from the AAA officials to get him to run and it was only after they appealed to his sense of duty that Halswelle, a soldier and used to acting under orders, reluctantly agreed that he would toe the line.

The last word on the incident should perhaps go to the aptly named *Sportsman*, published in London:

An American tourist once asked the gardener at Magdalene College, Oxford, how the English produced such perfect lawns. The answer was that the thing was quite simple, 'You have only got to mow and roll the grass for three or four hundred years and you will get what you want.' By analogy the same answer may be given to the question, 'Why are present-day Americans such bad sportsmen?'

The fact is that they are a young nation and they will require a good many years' training in sport before they can attain to our level. Regrettable as the fact may be, there can be no doubt about it that the American competitors at this year's Olympic Games and their entourage have not made themselves at all popular. As a distinguished foreign journalist observed the other day, 'They want the whole earth and a bit more.'

There have been continual references in the American

journals to the alleged lack of fair play on the part of our officials, as if men like Lord Desborough and his colleagues were not, as the British know them to be, constitutionally incapable of unfairness... The Americans seem to think that they can bring their own ideas of sport over here and enforce them... We sincerely hope the American competitors will learn a lesson from the incident because otherwise it may become impossible to continue the Olympian Games.

No one objects to the various methods in which American enthusiasm displays itself, such as college cries and songs or statements about 'God's own country', although the more stolid Englishman looked upon all that sort of thing as rather 'bad form'. But fair play is a jewel and we don't intend to forfeit it or even to pawn it.

– CHAPTER 27 –

THE ROAD FROM WINDSOR

On Friday, 24 July, Lord Desborough arrived on the 10.55 from Paddington and stepped from the station in Windsor under a sky already hazy with heat. There was much to do before the start at 2.30.

He had hoped to relax over lunch at Layton's restaurant with the Mayor of Windsor, but that would have to wait. His first stop was the Castle that dominated the town, and the East Terrace to check that all was going to plan. The start of the great Marathon race was to take place just 700 yards from Queen Victoria's statue, and he knew that Lord Esher, Warden of Windsor Castle and supervisor of the arrangements there, would have taken care of any last-minute details.

The streets were already busy. Several of the competitors had been staying in the town, including Tom Longboat, who had been lodging at the White Hart, where he was still nursing a bruised leg and blisters, the result of last-minute training. But most runners came up during the morning, using the railway.

Mayor Bampfylde had appealed to shopkeepers, traders and businesses to close for the day to give everybody a chance to see the race. Eton boys and Windsor schoolchildren were out in force. Police arrangements were under the supervision of Inspector Hudson and guarding the course was down to Superintendent Pearman.

They were expecting heavy crowds right along the route and there was a nervous buzz at the station as the competitors, their attendants and team officials all tumbled out onto the platform. At Windsor, they were met by enthusiastic crowds, a lot of them waving miniature flags of the countries they favoured, with the Stars and Stripes and Union Jacks everywhere. A couple of Eton boys were busy collecting autographs.

Johnny Hayes and a handful of other American Marathon men – Tom Morrisey and Joe Forshaw among them – had travelled up together. Hayes got off the train looking fresh, if a little languid. He had spent most of the previous two days in bed back in Brighton; not because he was ill but to make sure he was well rested. He was planning to take nothing to eat or drink during the journey. 'Before starting,' Hayes said, 'I partook of a light luncheon consisting of two ounces of beef, two slices of toast and a cup of tea.'

Back in Soho, Dorando had a last meal with his brother Ulpiano, complete with his usual doses of Chianti, the night before the race. His breakfast was calculated to build up his strength for the ordeal to come: beefsteak and coffee. In his small bag was a bottle of balsamic vinegar that he used to soak his running corks and handkerchief. He knew it was going to be hot and he needed to keep his lips and throat moist.

In the waiting room at the station, there was a list of the 57 people expected for the start. In the event, two were scratched that morning and 55 walked slowly up the hill that afternoon. The runners changed in the waiting room at Windsor using the cloakrooms and toilets there, courtesy of the station master.

The smell of liniment was everywhere. Some rubbed their feet and even their shoes with grease and powder. Here, too, in the superintendent's office, were the last-minute medical checks on the runners. Each had to send with his entry a medical certificate to say that he was fit to run, but even so the British were taking no chances and wanted a doctor to check everyone.

Dorando took a few deep breaths. This English doctor made him nervous. What if he had come all this way only to be pulled out? He had read the rules about refreshment stops, Oxo feeding stations, where you could get a drink, and the warning not to take drugs or stimulants – and even where you could get a sponge dowsed in eau-de-cologne. He didn't need a doctor – he just wanted to run now.

The last train from Paddington for competitors and officials was the 1.03, which left precious little time for any latecomers to bundle their clothes into a bag for the baggage car by 2pm. Alec Duncan and Fred Lord, England's great hopes, had changed in private rooms away from the railway station and sauntered to the waiting room. Duncan said he would have preferred 'a snowstorm or a thunderstorm' rather than the heat of the day.

Here in the waiting room was the last chance to have a word with the cyclists who would follow the race. There were two of them for each runner and they were being sent 5 miles down the road beyond Windsor before they were allowed to join in. The runners were told that a special omnibus would follow to pick up competitors who had abandoned the race. Johnny Hayes grinned at the prospect of a ride in the rescue wagon. Longboat, confident as ever, was fooling around, while Dorando said nothing.

Inside the Castle grounds, the staff had already been busy. They had carted out half a dozen red upholstered chairs and a heavy gilt table, and parked them on the lawn overlooking the East Terrace. The red chairs and the table were quite close to a small thorn tree and the only indication of a start point apart from Lord Desborough's car, which was brought in close to the pathway on which the runners would line up.

Shortly after 2.15, a royal carriage came across the park from Frogmore, bringing the Princess of Wales, Victoria Mary ('May') of Teck. Her diary entry for that day, 24 July 1908, reads: 'At 2 we went to see the start for the Marathon Race from the East Terrace.' The Princess stepped out wearing a blue-flowered white dress and carrying a pink parasol. With her were Prince Albert, later George VI, nine-year-old Princess Mary and Prince Henry, eight. Prince Albert, with an eye on capturing the significance of the day, had with him a camera and an autograph book.

They were joined by two nurses bringing six-year-old Prince George and Prince John, just three, in a bassinet (a portable cradle). Sir William Carrington and Lady Bertha Dawkins helped them all from the carriage. The Dean of Windsor was there in black to greet them, and the Royal Guards, already stationed on the terrace, dazzled in their scarlet tunics. The King, though, despite reports in the press and on some of the programmes, had not appeared at the start.

An engineer came in and fiddled with the telegraph signalling system placed on the table. Back at Shepherd's Bush, Conan Doyle took his seat in the Great Stadium. For a moment, the

Royal children were more interested in the statue of Queen Victoria's dog, but they clapped when some of the British runners were pointed out to them.

Lord Desborough was everywhere, checking on everything – the timekeepers, the judges, the marshals, all easily identifiable because of the green ribbons around their hats. He appeared more excited and energetic than most of the runners, continually consulting his pocket watch. He went to the car, an open Bentley, as the marshals shepherded the athletes.

They lined up in four lines like a grid. There, in the first row, was No. 72, Tom Longboat of Canada, and No. 29, Tom Morrisey of the United States. Fred Appleby, the Herne Hill Harrier and one of the English favourites, was in the second row, and with him Jack Price. In the third row was Hayes wearing No. 26 for the USA, and No. 71 was Caffery of Canada. In the fourth row, with No. 19 stitched to his vest, was Dorando, and next to him No. 8, Charles Hefferon of South Africa.

Even then, in these tense moments of uncertainty, some jostled to get a better start. They were the ones bursting with nervous energy, the ones who wanted to go off like a champagne cork from a bottle. Johnny Hayes was the voice of calm: 'It's hot, there's a long, long way to go,' he says. 'Don't go crazy,' he mutters to Jack Caffery, standing by him in the line-up.

For a moment Dorando's mind flashes back to that run in Athens. It was hot then, too. He remembers how dry his throat was, how he couldn't breathe, how he'd been in the lead. The memory sends a tremble through his body and despite the sunshine, he shivers here a little at the start. Already it is becoming sappingly hot. That run haunts him still. Dorando's lips move silently as if he is voicing a prayer: 'I will win or I will die.'

Desborough consults his watch. 'To your marks, gentlemen, please,' he booms. 'Five minutes to go.'

Longboat tightens the laces on his shoes. Dorando tugs at the knotted white handkerchief on his head. He grips his running corks; his lips are still moving. Desborough taps his watch. It's already just past 2.30. He looks across at the table, dazzled for a moment as it catches the sun, and then down at the electric machine in his car.

The Princess of Wales presses the button at the table and Desborough jolts into action. He raises his gun and everything falls very quiet; even the chattering children are hushed. At 2.33, a shot ripped into the silence and the crowd, who had been given Royal permission to stand just outside the gates, erupted into a volcano of cheering as the 55 men set out on their gruelling journey to the feet of the Queen.

As soon as Dorando started running, he felt fine again. To move was like a miracle cure – all the apprehension fell away and he could feel the power within him. It was a familiar sensation; it came from thousands of miles of training and running. He embraced it like an old friend. He looked down the field. They had gone off fast, too fast, he thought, even though this first mile was downhill. He glimpsed the loping figure of Longboat, his arms held low, running aggressively. The English runners were up there, too, overexcited by the cheers of their countrymen. There were thick crowds of them here in this first mile, packed tightly, straining for a view, spilling out into the road as Dorando picked a path through this forest of noise.

Where the road opened up, motor cars would rattle by, sometimes alongside the runners kicking up clouds. Dorando dabbed his handkerchief soaked in vinegar to keep the dust from his throat. Sometimes, early in the race, the runners would call out to the drivers and people in their cars, but later as things grew grimmer, they fell silent.

The leading British runners set off at an over-optimistic pace urged on by the huge crowds. Some of the British press, with imperial confidence, predicted their twelve entries would fill the first twelve places – though one of the dozen, Sam Stevenson, a Scot who had already been eliminated in the heats of the 5-mile track race, was a non-starter.

By the time they reached the Canal Bridge at Slough, 3 miles from the start, the runners had sorted themselves out. The Scot Tom Jack, wearing a white hat, who had been up with the leaders at the mile in 5:01.4 and through 2 miles in 10:11, was still in the lead. After 5 miles reached in 27:1, Jack suddenly dropped to a walk. In his wake, Lord, Price, Duncan and Hefferon had been sucked into this suicidal pace. Dorando was struggling to stay on the heels of Hefferon as more than 100 cyclists, the official attendants, joined the runners.

Even at this part of the course, said the *Windsor Express*:

The whole establishment of one or two country houses which were passed seemed to be out to see the sport, while where there were crossroads the motor cars and carriages drawn up presented quite a picturesque spectacle. The whole countryside had turned out from the oldest to the youngest and the schoolchildren, many of whom were waving flags, were most vociferous in their applause. After about seven miles Duncan (who was suffering from stitch) was walking and it was disappointing to find one of Great Britain's champions in trouble so early in the race, but there was a long way to go and anything might happen.

Duncan struggled on, but finally dropped out around halfway at Ruislip. He told his local paper, the *Westmorland Gazette*, 'It was the heat that killed me. If it had been a proper wet day the result would have been different. It was about 80 degrees when we set off and only those who took part in the race could have any idea of what we went through.' The *Windsor Express* noted:

It was a memorable day and there seemed to be a feeling that this, after all, was a thing to be seen in one's own country probably once only in a lifetime, for it will be many years before the revived Olympic Games are again held in England. As one went past, one noticed of course all kinds of nationalities and colour: a turbaned Turk near Ruislip was watching with intense interest, Japanese, Indians and Negroes were scattered here and there.

As we followed the race in a motorcar, now near the leader, now alongside the second or third, now further back, it was amazing to see how many of the men seemed comparatively untroubled by the conditions. Early in the race several had a word to say as we passed, but later on one could sympathise with what the men must be feeling.

At 13 miles, just before halfway, Jack Price was through in 1:15:13, just 38 seconds ahead of Hefferon. But suddenly, around 15 miles, while still in the lead, Price staggered to the side and sat down. Fred Hatton wrote in *The Athletic News*: 'A sudden collapse, the terrific heat of the sun, an equally strong pace were all joining forces that betokened the early retirement of the Birmingham man; spent by his own folly and lack of forethought.'

216

'At last Hefferon got in front,' reported the *Windsor Express*. 'At this time he was running beautifully and seemed quite fresh, and before Harrow was reached he had established a long lead with Longboat, Appleby and Dorando, who had been going most gamely, behind him.'

Up towards Wembley the going was tough and hilly, and by 17 miles, Tom Longboat was walking. The crowd said they had seen him down a bottle of champagne passed to him by his handler. Every time Dorando came up behind him, Longboat would break into a run, a shuffle, but he couldn't get away. And as he slumped to a walk again, Dorando eventually got past.

'So we had Hefferon with his long lead and Dorando going well in his wake,' reported the *Windsor Express*. 'There were constant questions shouted as our car passed. What of Longboat? Who's third? Between Sudbury and Harlesden Hefferon kept his lead, but Dorando was creeping up to him and the last time we passed him before reaching Harlesden he looked in a sorry plight. And so it proved. For in the remaining miles he was passed by Dorando, who struggled towards the stadium first, practically in a state of collapse, and by J. J. Hayes (USA).'

Two hours after Queen Alexandra's arrival in the Great Stadium came the order barked through the megaphone: 'Clear the stadium for the Marathon race!' Progress had been conveyed by the official announcers, who were led by the City of London Toastmaster, who, resplendent in scarlet evening dress and with a booming baritone voice, kept the crowd on 'the tiptoe of expectation'. The *Daily Mail* noted:

To show the state of tension, a momentary bustle, and running to and fro of a few attendants, brought the whole concourse to its feet. What was it, came the half-whispered question. And the answer brought with it a welcome relief of laughter. It was merely the new stock of programmes had arrived to supply the eager but unavailing demands which had been made for a couple of hours past.

At 18 miles excitement was getting to fever height when it was found that the South African was leading. Another mile and the changes were almost kaleidoscopic, for the indicator boards gave the three leaders as Hefferon still 1st, the little Italian Dorando 2nd and then Appleby, one of England's hopes, 3rd. Then came another change. Hayes, of the Stars and Bars, dispossessed the Britisher of his place. At 24 miles we learned, as it seemed by some mysterious agency, that the South African and the Italian were running neck and neck well ahead of the rest.

A few more seconds and a drooping figure of swarthy face is helped by two comrades into the arena. It is the Indian Longboat, who has had to give up and has been brought in by motor car. Close on his heels follows Lord Desborough and members of the Council.

According to the Olympic Committee's official report on the race:

The crucial point of this long and desperate struggle arrived when Dorando came in sight of Hefferon in Old Oak Common Lane. For the whole of the previous 24 miles the route had been more or less lined with spectators whose ranks thickened as the race passed through towns and villages until the road had all the aspect of the Thames on Boat Race day. The crowd was enthusiastic but orderly and it was in response to a tremendous outburst of cheering from the huge throngs of spectators that Dorando made the fateful spurt that took him past Hefferon before they reached Wormwood Scrubs. Soon afterwards Hayes passed the South African as well.

Dorando's premature effort had so exhausted him that he could scarcely reach the entrance of the stadium where nearly a hundred thousand spectators were awaiting his arrival, having only heard from the last telegraphic bulletin posted up in the arena that a South African was ahead and an Italian second.

'Another great hush,' the *Windsor Express* reporter scribbled, 'during which one had the feeling it would be almost a relief if someone would scream. After minutes, which seemed ages, there came the double boom of guns. In the stadium 100,000 people knew what that meant. It was the signal that the runners were in sight.'

– CHAPTER 28 –

THE MAN WHO LOST AND WON

Dorando couldn't forget the words of his mother as she had said goodbye to him in Carpi. 'Pull out, drop out if things are going badly. Be careful, please take care of yourself.'

But the face he now saw was not his mother's: it was Teresa. His lips moved as if in prayer, repeating over and over the mantra, '*Vincerò o morirò*', 'I will win or I will die'. Over the last half-mile, as his eyes strained in the glare of the sunshine for a sight of the stadium, he began to wonder if once again as in Athens his body would let him down.

'I will win or I will die.' His lips moved as he silently mouthed the words, groping for any sort of rhythm that now seemed to have vanished from his stride. The drink he had been given by Ulpiano after he passed Charles Hefferon seemed to have left him dazed and disorientated. He felt light-headed, drunk almost, as if he had taken too much Chianti. But he was used to Chianti. Chianti and water − surely that was what Ulpiano had given him?

One more sharp turn and suddenly he was in the cool shadow of the stadium going through an arch. The cyclists who had been pedalling behind him, occasionally ringing their bells shouting encouragement, had peeled off. They were directed to the stadium via a separate entrance.

He was on his own now, just himself and the sunshine and his doubts and his prayer, 'I will win or I will die'. As he turned at a right angle off Ducane Road to the narrow path that led him to the stadium, the shady darkness was like running into a cool haven on a scorching day. The shade was seductive, welcoming, and there in the passage leading to the stadium, Dorando slumped to his knees and rolled over. The marshals and officials shouted for Dr Bulger, who charged across from the trackside.

'He was in a state of absolute collapse,' said the doctor later, 'quite pulse-less. But in a short time he recovered sufficiently to enter the stadium.'

'You're nearly there, you're nearly there,' Dorando heard the strange English words. They got him back on his feet and he staggered blinking into the sunshine and tottered down the 9 yards of the slope of the cycle track onto the running path.

As he found his feet in the cauldron of cinders, the roar of the crowd was enough, it seemed, to knock him over again. He'd been on the track before. Nine days earlier he had failed to finish in the heats of the 3-mile team race, and he turned, as he had done then, to follow the track to the finishing line. But as he turned to the right, he found people blocking his way, trying to stop him. Policemen, tall giants now in their crowning helmets, officials and attendants, all trying to push him the other way.

'Wrong way, wrong way!' they shouted. He was confused. For a moment he thought he'd gone down again. The idea of turning was a movement that pitched him off balance, threatened to make him fall. A few more steps and then he did fall again.

The crowd that had been alive with noise fell dead quiet. As the men around him stepped forward, Dr Bulger – a big, powerful man who'd played rugby for Ireland – cradled him like a child in his arms. The thin man with the megaphone, Jack Andrew, stood up straight and bellowed down it for help, for more attendants, for people to come with a stretcher.

'You're nearly there, you're nearly there! Let's get you up,' said the doctor. Dorando got to his feet and staggered a few more yards. He tried to focus on the track. It should be flat, he knew that, but as he ran, it was like going up a steep slope, a tough hill. He leaned into it. It seemed to come up to meet him and slap him in the face. He keeled over again.

Now everything stopped, everyone broke off to watch. They held their breath as they got him up again. This time, the crowd was still, and as he fell once more, there was a sigh as deep as any wave. It seemed to come from 100,000 throats. Above the silence, somebody yelled, 'For God's sake, stop him! He'll die. He's dying!'

The whisper 'He's dying' rustled round the stadium as everyone strained to glimpse him. Even in the Royal Box, for a moment, the Queen was half on her feet. Protocol stood for nothing here when a man, the Marathon and death seemed to be all on the track at the same time.

But Dorando got up again. He stood, and squinted down the track to see the tape – he seemed to have no idea where he was or what he was doing. Only his lips moved. They were dry now, caked white, flecked with salt and sweat. They moved, but no sound came.

'I will win or I will die.' The handkerchief was still on his head, the corks still in his hands. It was as if a puppet were trying to run and somehow all the strings had become crossed. He shuffled forwards; every step now was bringing him closer to the finish. Each time a foot landed, the crowd wondered whether he would totter and fall like a baby, or if, it seemed, he could somehow make it across the room to his mother's waiting arms.

Again, he half-remembered his mother's last words: 'Be sensible, be reasonable, don't kill yourself.' But the words he mouthed now were the promise he'd made to himself back in Carpi, 'I will win or I will die.'

By now, every voice, 100,000 voices, were urging him on. But behind him, almost unnoticed except by the Americans, whose cheers seemed to be out of time with the rest of the world's, appeared a runner wearing No. 26 and moving rapidly as he strode out of the passage. It was Johnny Hayes, the boy who knew about keeping himself fresh, knew about pacing his effort, and who was now moving relentlessly towards the shadow of Dorando at around 6 minutes a mile.

The contrast was painful: Dorando an empty shell, Hayes looking, as one reporter put it, 'as fresh as a daisy in a meadow'. Over the last few yards, Dorando's lips were still moving, but no sound came. His legs seemed to be out of control; they twitched with a life of their own.

When Dorando focused hard, he could see the tape. He could see it now, that thin string, and he knew that if he could get there everything would stop. That was the harbour. Beyond was peace, the sleep of death. In a parody of movement, he lurched towards it, carrying his arms high and swinging them, trusting his legs would follow.

Behind him now was a phalanx of policemen, attendants and doctors, closing in on him. Dorando was running again now, and the policemen were running in their heavy hobnails, the nails in the boots biting into the cinders of the track. They were running alongside him, their hands outstretched like slip fielders at a cricket match, waiting to catch him at any time, should he fall.

In his right hand, Jack Andrew clutched the megaphone; his left hand was behind Dorando, waiting to take his arm to push him across the line. Dorando managed to finish and then fell again for the last time.

Behind him, Johnny Hayes was moving steadily round the track, but few noticed him. Even the timekeepers and the judges were hardly concentrating as Hayes crossed the line. Their fingers pressed the stopwatch buttons as if in a daze.

Dorando was out cold, like a prize fighter who had hung on in there for round after round when his seconds should have long before thrown in the towel.

Dr Bulger called for the stretcher and they lifted the tiny, damp figure onto it and threw a blanket across him. As the stretcher bearers ran to get him out, they seemed to be running faster than Dorando had moved since he took his first staggering steps into the stadium.

Jack Andrew lifted the megaphone to his lips. His words couldn't be heard over the excited roar and frenzy of the crowd. 'Here's the result of the Marathon Race,' he bellowed. 'First, and winner of the Greek Cup, Dorando Pietri of Italy, second J. J. Hayes of the United States!'

In the stadium, they chalked the verdict on the boards and walked them around so the crowd could see the results for themselves. But in the American camp, confusion reigned. Jim

Connolly, the veteran Irish-American who had won the first gold medal in de Coubertin's Games, was crying foul. According to him, he practically had to put a boot into the American team managers to get them to go out and complain.

But complain they did. And the British judges debated the painful scenes in the stadium for over an hour. Then the man with the megaphone came out again. The big boards were wiped clean. It was announced that Dorando had been disqualified for receiving assistance and the winner of the gold medal was John Joseph Hayes of the United States. Hefferon, running for South Africa, was awarded second place, and Joseph Forshaw of the United States, who had finished strongly, was given third.

Where once there had been excitement, now there were boos and scuffles in the stands. Those same London policemen who had trotted beside Dorando, willing him to the finish, stepped in with their truncheons to break up the trouble.

At 2.33 that very afternoon, they had used an electric cable to signal the start of the marathon. Shortly after ten o'clock the same day, the Central News Service in London used the electric telegraph to put out a message to the world. The clattering machines spelt out the chilling news: 'Dorando is dead'.

And in the early hours of the morning, Johnny Hayes sat in a bar, unable to sleep for excitement, with his boyhood hero, Jim Connolly. Together they sipped beer, toasting another great Irish-American victory, and swapped tales that would turn that long day into a legend.

– CHAPTER 29 –

A FAIR FIELD AND NO FAVOUR

In the turmoil that surrounded Dorando's struggle to finish, even eyewitness reports are contradictory and confusing. The official report, compiled carefully by Theodore Cook, comes closest to what really happened:

> As it was impossible to leave him there, for it looked as if he might die in the very presence of the Queen and that enormous crowd, the doctors and attendants rushed to his assistance. When he was slightly resuscitated, the excitement of his compatriots was so intense that the officials did not put him on an ambulance and send him out as they no doubt would have done under less agitating circumstances.

Sir Arthur Conan Doyle was in the stands as a reporter for the *Daily Mail*. Despite accounts that have been around for many years, he was not one of the attendants who helped Dorando to his feet and was not on the track as he covered that last 385 yards. The mistaken story, which has been widely published in books, newspapers and on websites, arose because of photographs that confused the burly man in a peaked cap and armband with Conan Doyle.

The man in the pictures is in fact Dr Michael Bulger, the chief medical attendant and the man who raced to Dorando's aid when he collapsed in the passage leading to the stadium. Dr Bulger was part of a prominent rugby playing and athletic family. He was a founder of the London Irish Rugby Club in 1898 and acted as medical officer to that club for many years.

In Conan Doyle's own account in his autobiography, *Memories and Adventures*, published in 1924, he states: 'On the occasion of the Olympic Games of 1908 I was tempted, chiefly by the offer of an excellent seat, to do the Marathon Race for the *Daily Mail*.' Even in his account for the *Mail* he mentions his seat. He continues:

It is horrible and yet fascinating, the struggle between a set purpose and an utterly exhausted frame. Again for 100 yards he ran in the same furious and yet uncertain gait, and again he collapsed, kind hands saving him from a heavy fall. He was within a few yards of my seat. Amid stooping figures and grasping hands I caught a glimpse of the haggard yellow face, the glazed, expressionless eyes, the lank, black hair streaked across the brow. Surely he is done now, he cannot rise again.

From under the archway has darted a second runner, Hayes, Stars and Stripes on his breast, going gallantly, well within his strength. There is only 20 yards to do if the Italian can do it. He staggered up, no trace of intelligence upon his set face, and again the red legs broke into their strange automatic amble. Will he fall again? No, he sways, he balances and he is through the tape and into a score of friendly arms. He has gone to the extreme of human endurance. No Roman of the prime ever bore himself better than Dorando of the Olympics of 1908. The great breed is not yet extinct.

Even as I write there comes the rumour that he has been disqualified. If true, it is indeed a tragedy. But there are prizes higher even than the oak branch and the medal. The Italian's great performance can never be effaced from our records of sport, be the decision of the judges what it may.

P.S. – The rumour then is true. I confess that I cannot see how the judges could have come to any other decision. It was, as matters stood, a fair and square win for the American, since, without help, Dorando must have lain senseless on the track. And yet the tragedy remains.

Almost anyone who witnessed what happened that hot July day in the Great Stadium would never forget it, and most couldn't wait to tell the world what they had seen. One fourteen-year-old girl, Vera Cox, from Longton Avenue, Sydenham, wrote a twelve-page letter to her family after she had seen the race. She had, she said, a good seat close to the Royal Box and noted that 'the American section was very lively with their extraordinary Ra, Ra, Ra,' adding that if you were very lucky, 'every now and then you could hear what the man with the megaphone said'. She wrote:

Eventually, a tottering figure was seen to appear until the noise was absolutely deafening and the excitement seemed almost suffocating. Then, more wondrous still, an almost dead silence succeeded as the people took in what an awful figure Dorando looked. A smallish man in crimson knickers and a crimson handkerchief tied around his head tottered onto the track with his legs almost giving way under him and apparently blind. Officials sort of guided him around the track and then suddenly he fell. After a few seconds he staggered up again. A burst of cheering once more broke forth, and then a few more yards and he was down again. Three times this happened, and each time he was surrounded by officials and friends so that we could not see what happened. But when he got up he was clearly running by himself.

As he got up the third time another figure appeared – Hayes the American, and the crowd was in agony lest Dorando should not win after getting to the stadium so many minutes before anyone else. Dorando with a final effort gave a pitiful kind of spurt, then, just as one was beginning to breathe again, he fell down once more about twenty yards from the tape. Meanwhile Hayes, who looked about as bad as Dorando except that he kept on his feet, was slowly making his way round, staggering from one side of the track to the other.

It was like a nightmare to see the one man lying like a log a few yards from the tape and the other man gradually staggering along behind, slowly but surely closing the gap. Then the crowd around Dorando suddenly moved. Apparently he was on his feet again (this was the time he was helped though it was not evident to us). Hayes was a few yards behind. Dorando apparently unconscious lurched over the last few dreadful yards and fell over the tape. Hayes was a short distance behind.

The crowd roared itself hoarse whilst both Hayes and Dorando lay unconscious on the grass. The ambulance hurried up and they were carried out. Meanwhile the Italian flag went up with the USA underneath for first and second. It was not until two hours after that anyone knew that Dorando had been disqualified. It seemed very hard lines on Hefferon, the South African, that he should have led for so many miles and yet collapsed just outside the stadium, Hayes and Dorando passing him before he was restored to consciousness. It really was a wonderful sight and, although extremely painful, I am very glad I saw it. Hayes and Dorando were really magnificent, their pluck was simply marvellous.

The night before the Marathon and the evening of the race were busy times for Lord Desborough. He took in two banquets in London and both were abuzz with the news and controversies of the Games. Presiding at the fifth and final banquet for visiting athletes at the King's Hall, Desborough found his audience in a boisterous mood. There were endless toasts and singing, and at one point he himself broke into an impromptu rendition of 'La Marseillaise'.

He was anxious to bring some perspective to the issues of sportsmanship and fair play that haunted and threatened to sour the Games. Proposing the toast of the Olympic Games, Desborough said the Games of London would stand out as the most memorable gathering of athletes ever seen in the world. There must be, he said, owing to variations in the manner of conducting sports in various countries, differences of opinion.

But when those differences did arise, the British Olympic Committee endeavoured to settle them according to the policy of 'a fair field and no favour'. The guests stood and raised their glasses as one to toast 'A Fair Field and No Favour'.

The next night, Desborough was again at a dinner at the Grafton Galleries, this time given by Lewis Harcourt MP on behalf of Asquith's Liberal Government. This time, Baron de Coubertin, speaking entirely in French, launched into what sounded at first like an attack on gambling, but then he, too, raised the subject of 'fair play'.

He said that he had read 'of an incident that occurred yesterday', which was a clear reference to Wyndham Halswelle's treatment in the 400 Metres. The great aim of those who promoted the Olympic Games, said de Coubertin, was to encourage chivalry or 'what was so prettily called in England fair play'. Winning, he said, with the rows over Halswelle, Hayes and Dorando ringing in his ears, 'is not so important as to take part'.

After he had finished speaking in his well-modulated French, amid loud cheers, Desborough rose to his feet to say that he had an announcement to make. 'Her Majesty, Queen Alexandra,' he said, 'expressed a desire that the Italian representative in the Marathon race should accept from her as a personal gift a cup, for being practically, if not *de facto*, the winner.' Desborough said he knew that their Italian friends were 'somewhat sore' that the victory was not theirs, owing to a protest, but that did not prevent him from expressing his appreciation of the splendid running of the Italian representative.

Count de Bosdari, in the absence of the Italian ambassador, expressed his appreciation of the gracious promise of Queen Alexandra. 'Italy,' he added, 'had had a very lucky time recently winning the Derby and some of the best prizes at the horse show and all Italians were pleased that those victories had taken place on English ground and in the country of fair play.' 'The result of the race,' he continued, 'had made his compatriots feel very proud' and he was extremely glad 'that it had been achieved on English ground and that they had been able to show their English friends that they were developing a love for sports'.

As Desborough sat down amid wild cheering, Buckingham Palace staff were already at work. Like everyone else, they had heard about the courage of Dorando, and they wanted a cup that was fit for a Queen.

– CHAPTER 30 –

THE MORNING AFTER

At 11.28pm on the night of the Marathon came yet another announcement to the world: 'The Central News is officially informed by the Olympic Games Committee that the report to the effect that Dorando, the Italian runner, was dead is incorrect. A telegram, having every appearance of authenticity, was received at the City Police Headquarters stating that Dorando succumbed this evening.'

It seems that at 9pm that evening, Dorando was sufficiently recovered from the effects of the Marathon to walk to a taxi cab rank and be driven to his apartments in Church Street, Soho. He was up early the next morning, having slept well, and was recovered sufficiently from the race to eat a good breakfast.

Having spoken to Ulpiano, the other thing Dorando wanted to do was to lodge a protest. The *Pall Mall Gazette* takes up the story:

Signor Dorando, the Italian hero of the marathon race, had an hour's conference this morning with Count Brunetta d'Usseaux, the Italian General Commissioner on the International Olympic Council. At the conclusion of the interview, Count Brunetta informed a representative of the *Pall Mall* Gazette that Signor Dorando had decided to lodge a formal protest against the judges' decision in awarding the victory to Hayes.

The protest, the Count stated, is based on the grounds that Signor Dorando did not ask for the assistance that was rendered at the stadium and that he could have finished first without it. The Count took away with him from the conference the written protest and will present it to the Council this afternoon. Signor Dorando, the Count added, will accept the decision of the Council after they have considered the protest, and he wishes to say that he is profoundly thankful for the sympathy that has been shown to him and particularly for the gracious fact of the Queen presenting a special cup.

He will be at the stadium this afternoon to accept the cup from Her Majesty's hands. During the hour of the conference, at No. 8 Church Street, Soho, where it was held, he was besieged by an eager crowd of Italians, some of whom in their impatience to see the hero shouted to the occupants of the house, 'Bring him out, we want to see him.' Eventually the crowd was moved off by the police, but it gathered again and surged round Count Brunetta and gave him three cheers as he drove off with the document of protest in his motor car.

Back at Church Street, Dorando asked Ulpiano to translate the letter that had been sent from Lord Desborough. It said:

> Lady Desborough and I are sending you some flowers with every wish for your speedy and complete recovery and heartiest congratulations on your splendid achievement yesterday, which has the sincere sympathy of every man and woman in the vast crowd of the stadium.

Dorando and Ulpiano scribbled their reply:

> Please accept my thanks for the beautiful roses and your charming letter of congratulations which I shall always treasure in remembrance of your great kindness.

But already in the stadium, there was one final act in the 400-Metres drama. It was early and there were few events on the programme, but the crowd was bigger than usual that morning. There were last-minute hopes that the Americans would show up for the re-run of the 400 Metres, but when Wyndham Halswelle stepped out to take his mark for the start of the race, no other opponent had appeared.

'The southern curve of the cinder path where the fouling had taken place was lined out with avenues of stakes and strings so as to avoid any repetition of those tactics,' the press reported.

'There were cries of Taylor from the stands as it was hoped that the American Negro, who had nothing to do with the ugly business that had prevented Halswelle winning in the first race, would turn out. But there was no sign of any other competitors coming through the entrance way to the track. So Halswelle ran his race by himself to an accompaniment of encouraging cheers all round the track. Whoever asked him to try and attempt to beat the record was no judge of atmospherical conditions. The waving flags told of the strong breeze that circulated the arena.'

Under a headline that announced 'A FINE IF LONELY RUN', the *Daily Telegraph* reported: 'Halswelle tried his best and ran himself out to the last ounce, but the best quarter-mile runner that amateur athletics has yet known was unable to do better than 50 seconds for the 400 metres. This was disappointing to those who did not take circumstances into consideration. A lot of cheering was raised as the Union Jack was strung up to the flagstaff in token of victory.'

Silently, Halswelle looked up at the token of victory. He rested his hands on his knees, his body bowed forward while he fought to control his breathing. Then he stood tall, head held high, and walked silently and alone to the dressing room.

The stands were filling up fast as crowds streamed in for the afternoon's programme. Having officially opened the Games, it had been hoped and planned that King Edward would also preside over the award ceremony that brought to an end the two weeks of competition in the stadium.

It has been strongly suggested that the King, offended by what he saw of the American behaviour and the way that the integrity of the British officials had been challenged, decided that he wanted nothing further to do with the Games. This was almost certainly why he declined to act as starter to the Marathon. A brief announcement made from Buckingham Palace stated that the King would not give the prizes as had been planned, nor participate in the finish of the Games.

In the King's absence, the duty of presenting the prizes on

Saturday, 25 July, fell to Queen Alexandra, and the ceremony began immediately after the Medley Relay concluded the programme of athletics. A strong detachment of non-commissioned officers of the Grenadier and Irish Guard battalions were ready for the reception of the Queen, their scarlet coats and gold trimmings adding a splash of colour around the arena.

High up in the stands, buglers sent out calls announcing that the ceremony was about to begin. In front of the Royal Box, the drums and fifes of the Irish Guards stood in line, waiting for the order to begin the musical salute. Then the band of the Grenadier Guards gave an international touch by playing all the different national anthems of the competing nations. They began by playing the Austrian 'Kaiserhymne' and it became obvious that the national songs would be played in the alphabetical order of the countries. Every time an anthem rang out, the supporters of that country would cheer loudly. Then swimmers appeared to give an exhibition of diving in the swimming tank.

There was a rolling of drums, the banging of cymbals, shrill notes of fifes, and then a group of athletes standing by the Eastern stand, some in their athletic kit, suddenly formed into a marching group. They were the second and third prize winners, and included competitors who had also gained certificates of merit.

As they stepped out to the lively music, they formed a long queue and were loudly cheered. The first award of the afternoon was made by the Duchess of Sutherland, who made a presentation to two ladies; one of them was the famous tennis player Lottie Dodd, who had won medals in the archery competitions. Both ladies received a huge ovation.

The silver medals were given out by the Duchess of Rutland,

239

the bronze medals by Catherine, Duchess of Westminster, and Lady Desborough presented the Diplomas of Merit and commemorative medals. There were gold, silver and bronze medals for the winners, each of whom was also awarded a diploma noting their victory. The winners also received a smaller diploma that they could present to their club or association when they returned home. Diplomas of Merit were awarded to athletes who achieved a standard of excellence but failed to win a medal, and a number of officials and participants in the demonstration events also received this award.

Johnny Hayes went home not only with the gold medal for winning his event, but also a silver replica which was his commemorative medal from the same event. The proliferation of awards meant that no fewer than 1,320 presentations had to be made.

At 4.00 exactly, the Queen arrived to present the gold medals to the winners. As the band of the Grenadier Guards struck up 'See the Conquering Hero Comes', the newly-crowned Olympic champions walked across the grass to receive their awards and each was also presented with a sprig of oak leaves taken from Windsor Forest, tied with red, white and blue ribbons.

Not all the prize-winners were able to be at the stadium for the ceremony, and the British Olympic Council had to announce that they were able to send prizes by post to those competitors who were unable to collect them in person. There were, in addition, twelve perpetual challenge cups or trophies that had been donated, and these formed a wonderful display on a separate table in front of the Queen. It seemed to the crowd that in contrast to the previous two weeks, all the bitterness and rivalry had disappeared and the prize ceremony was a happy occasion in which people could relax and allow some of the wounds to heal.

There were plenty of cheers and laughter when Lord Desborough was presented with his own commemorative medal by his wife. And as the winner of the 20km cycling race, Charles Kingsbury, had already left the Games to take part in the World Championships in Leipzig, when it came to the presentation of his gold, the Queen handed over the medal to his infant daughter while the stadium went wild with cheering.

While the Queen was presenting the awards, there was suddenly a lot of excitement on the far side of the stadium. *The Times* of London captured the moment:

Suddenly, as the Queen was taking the medals from Lord Desborough and handing them to the winners, there was a great shout of 'Dorando', and the man by whose name the Marathon of 1908 will be remembered came out from the gangway under the competitors' stand and walked round the track by himself until he was joined by an Italian admirer bearing the national flag. A mighty roar went up from the whole assembly as he made his way to the tail end of prize winners, and the shouts and cheers and applause and sympathy were renewed again and again when it came to his turn to climb up the broad red carpeted steps, placed almost exactly where he had fallen for the last time at the end of his gallant struggle, and received from the hands of England's Queen the beautiful cup – her own personal gift.

Wrapped in the Italian flag, Dorando cut a dramatic figure as he strode across the grass to the Queen, waving and bowing to his admirers amid tumultuous cheers. Some Americans seemed slightly annoyed at the attention paid to Dorando, both by the crowd and by the Queen, and in retaliation they heaved the winner of the Marathon, Johnny Hayes – in his athletic kit as if ready to run yet again – onto a table, from where he carried the handsome Marathon trophy presented by the Greek Olympic Committee around the stadium, borne by his team mates.

But nothing could take away from Dorando the triumph of the moment when he stepped up to collect his golden cup from the hands of the Queen. There had been no time to get the cup engraved and it was presented to him with a card written in the Queen's own handwriting and bearing the words:

For Pietri Dorando. In Remembrance of the Marathon Race from Windsor to the Stadium. From Queen Alexandra.

– CHAPTER 31 –

THE LION IN
CHAINS

On their return to New York, the American athletes were given a tremendous ovation. Twenty-five thousand people marched in a procession and a million others lined the streets. The athletes were all awarded gold cups and endless speeches were made denouncing the 'foul tactics' of the British officials.

Quite the most bizarre sight was that of James Sullivan, the leader of the American team, at a reception for the returning Olympic squad at New York City Hall. Sullivan chose the occasion to parade a British lion in chains and on a leash – to symbolise the humbling of the British Empire. It was a huge and unmistakeable insult to Britain and the British Olympic Committee, and prompted a response by the British Olympic Council, who asked Theodore Cook to prepare a pamphlet entitled 'A Reply to Certain Criticisms', which set out to answer the more outrageous of the complaints from Sullivan and the Americans.

The day after the Marathon in London, Johnny Hayes was whisked off to the House of Commons. There, he was a guest of the Irish MP O'Malley, and he filled many pages of his little autograph book with the congratulations of dozens of MPs, supporters of Irish Home Rule and leaders of the new Labour movement in Britain, Keir Hardie among them.

In the days that followed, he crossed the Irish Sea to meet his grandfather in his father's old home in Silver Street, Nenagh, County Tipperary. A wonderful crowd was there to greet him and there were speeches, flags, drinking and singing, while the crowds couldn't get enough of their Irish hero. For Johnny it was bewildering and overwhelming, but in the quiet of the bakery, where his father, Michael, and his grandfather had spent their long hot days, Hayes and his grandfather spoke of the orphanage, of life in New York and the gold medal he had brought home to Nenagh.

For the Irish and for the Americans, the Marathon more than any other event seemed to prove their dominance over the British. Hayes' victory and the success of the other Americans symbolised the emergence of the United States as the world's leading sporting nation. And the overwhelming success of the Irish-American Athletic Club demonstrated their role in this achievement. Americans won thirteen of the 23 track and field events, and of those thirteen victories, members of the Irish-American Athletic Club carried off eight.

But Johnny Hayes was the one who won the greatest cheers. New York newspapers gave him coverage that seemed to be setting him up for sainthood. Pictures of him in his Irish-American Athletic Club uniform with the Club's symbol – the winged fist – were everywhere. The *New York Sun* wrote, 'Jack Hayes is as Irish as you find them with black hair, blue eyes, a good humoured and freckled face and a ton of confidence in himself'. Hayes was saluted everywhere as 'a modest chap who doesn't care to babble about his own achievements'.

The newspapers spun the myth that he had worked at Bloomingdales six days a week since he was seventeen and that he was going to be promoted to the position of head of its sporting department. He'd worked so hard at the store, readers were told, that he had been forced to train at night on the roof of the store without a coach. An article for the *Gaelic American*, covering the parade in New York, said, 'The buildings along the route of the parade were decorated with American flags and American flags were carried by many of the paraders and spectators. The Irish flag was also in evidence and the bands played "The Star Spangled Banner", "Hail Columbia" and "The Wearing of the Green."'

E. P. McKenna published a poem called 'How the Yankees beat the World' in the *Gaelic American* on 25 July 1908, portraying the English as bad losers and cheaters who hated America. And Jim Connolly, the former triple jump gold medallist, brought out a piece entitled 'The English as Poor Losers'.

Connolly concluded that in England, 'If your father wasn't a curate or a barrister, or if he wasn't a brewer or a wholesale dealer in jams, or in some way making his living off the government, or if he did work with his hands for a living, be sure your entry won't be accepted.'

The turmoil caused by the events of the 1908 Games stimulated a great deal of soul-searching concerning both the value and the future of the Olympics. On both sides of the Atlantic, serious doubts were raised concerning whether the Games should continue.

The British acknowledged that not everything had been perfect at the Games but felt that the Olympics could contribute to international harmony and understanding, if all nations kept that purpose in mind and made a sincere effort to move towards it. But the American viewpoint was more direct and more negative. Changes, they believed, had to be made or American participation in the Olympic movement would be ended.

The Times in London had this comment: 'The Games have not been all plain sailing. The perfect harmony which everyone wished for has been marred by certain regrettable disputes and protests and objections to the judges' ruling. Let it be granted then in the immortal language of an old and common friend, Euclid, that there have been mistakes on all sides. What else could be expected and what after all does it matter as long as we part friends?'

The American feeling reported in the *New York Times* took a more aggressive view: 'The Olympiad leaves minor heart burnings and altogether, while an athletic success, as a means of promoting international friendship it has been a deplorable failure.'

James Sullivan was even blunter. 'So far as I am personally concerned, this is the last international meeting I shall recommend the Americans to take part in until assured that every country competing shall have some say in the management, so that we shall not hereafter be placed in the false position that we have here.'

Meanwhile, the British believed they had learned some useful lessons and *The Times* commented: 'We have learned that in speed and strength we are far behind the Americans. Even our last confident hope that the older nation was endowed with greater powers of endurance than its mighty rival received a rude shock when our chosen long distance runners were hopelessly outclassed in the severest test of all (the marathon). When we analyse the results of the strictly athletic contests our national pride receives a severe blow.'

But the huge row generated at the London Olympics did result in some permanent and positive changes in the organisation of future Olympics. Regulations were adopted and implemented which altered the responsibility for day-to-day management of many athletic events. No longer would the host nation provide all the judges, officials and score-keepers, and after the rows that had broken out in London, the management of athletic events was delegated to the international governing body for each particular sport.

These changes, together with the rules and regulations drawn up by Theodore Cook, were robust enough to control international sport for a century to come. But above all, the dramas on the track had whetted the public appetite for more and given them a thirst for the drama of international competition.

Even as Ulpiano Pietri was arranging for Dorando's cup to be put on show for a fee at the Hammersmith Palais, he was talking to the Americans, who knew how to make the Italian brothers very rich.

'This is your moment,' Ulpiano kept urging Dorando. 'Make the most of it! This is your time, I will help you.'

Promoters and impresarios, mostly American, were not slow to realise the potential of the athletes who had made headlines at the 1908 Games, and they were keen to stage rematches. And so they approached Wyndham Halswelle. They wanted to stage a rematch, possibly a whole series of rematches between him and John Carpenter, the American who had been disqualified in the 400 Metres.

'We could make it a head-to-head, just the two of you – a showdown,' they suggested. 'The gate money could make you both rich, why waste the opportunity? It's what the public wants.'

But Halswelle tossed their invitation aside with contempt. It was not the sort of thing that warranted any reply, he thought. He'd had enough and vowed to turn his back on the sport. A week after the Games, he ran his farewell race at Ibrox Park, Glasgow, and then retired, disillusioned by the Olympic experience. His only further appearances on a track came in 1910 and 1911, when he turned out in handicap races at his battalion sports.

But the Marathon was the duel the promoters craved and they would happily pay a fortune for a rematch between Hayes and Dorando, just to see who would hit the tape first. It was a mouth-watering prospect.

The figure of 26 miles 385 yards may have seemed arbitrary, quaint, and even absurd to some, but when it came to staging a rematch, this was the exact distance the promoters seized on. As far as they were concerned, this was the 'London distance' and every inch would have to be covered before you could call it a Marathon.

The result of the July race was still fiercely debated and both Hayes and Dorando had won worldwide recognition. The question of who really deserved to win hung there, tantalising the sporting public and the gambling world. It needed to be settled. How much would people pay to see all that again with their own eyes, to witness a battle of wills, with the shadow of collapse or even death hovering at the trackside?

In Soho, as Ulpiano Pietri relaxed over yet another glass of Chianti, he smiled at his little brother. He had already been in touch with the New York impresario Pat Powers… and he knew exactly what Dorando was to do next.

– CHAPTER 32 –

MARATHON MANIA

I n London, three days after the great Marathon race, Sir Arthur Conan Doyle used the *Daily Mail* to launch an appeal to raise money for the defeated Dorando, and a cheque for £308 and 15 shillings was presented to the Italian by Lady Conan Doyle in a ceremony at the *Mail* offices. The cheque was placed in a gold cigarette case inscribed to 'Dorando Pietri from friends and admirers in England. Souvenir of Marathon race 1908'. As well as this, Dorando received a gold medal from the Italian Hotel and Restaurant Employees' Society and some £30 for appearances he made on the music hall stage.

Half of all this money went to the Italian Hospital in London and half to a hospital or charity chosen by the *Mail,* for at this point, of course, despite the feelers put out to various impresarios by Ulpiano, Dorando was still, in the eyes of the Olympic authorities, an amateur.

However, everybody wanted to get their hands on Dorando. He was showered with gifts and offers. Kaiser Wilhelm, the German Emperor, who was staying in London during the Games, personally sent him a cigar from the Savoy with his scribbled congratulations, and Dorando was showered with proposals of marriage, which he detailed with amusement in his letters back to Teresa in Carpi.

The clamour for Johnny Hayes on his return to America was even greater. 'THOUSANDS CHEER VICTORS OF THE OLYMPIC GAMES' read the headline in The *New York Times* of 30 August 1908. A crowd of 100,000 mobbed the streets in one of the greatest ovations in the history of athletics as the returning athletes made their way from 46th Street and Broadway to the City Hall. The *New York Times* reported:

The majority of the men behaved like bashful schoolboys while they listened to the congratulatory words of acting Mayor McGowan. Ralph Rose, the Californian giant, blushed like a schoolgirl when Mr McGowan handed him his reward and a grin of pleasure spread over his face as he listened to the warm tribute paid him. J. C. Carpenter of Cornell, who ran in the disputed 400 metre race, was cheered to the echo and J. B. Taylor, the Negro runner from the University of Pennsylvania, had no cause to complain of the reception he received.

But by far the loudest cheers were saved for Johnny Hayes. The newspaper said:

He had been almost entirely hid among the group of shot-putters and hammer-throwers. The diminutive winner of the great marathon race elbowed his way to the table on which his medal lay. Mr McGowan stepped forward and grasped him by the hand, lifted him up to the table and a perfect uproar followed.

Amid cries of 'Hayes! Hayes! Hayes!' the lad waved his cap and a mighty roar greeted him. He was the only athlete to be honoured in so signal a manner and when he was recognised by the multitude surrounding the City Hall, the cheers again resounded from 100,000. Below the grandstand a band was located and as Hayes received his reward, the stirring notes of 'The Star Spangled Banner' rang out and thousands of children's voices burst into the national song.

The refrain was taken up by the multitude and continued until Hayes stepped down from the table. There were tears in the eyes of the little runner as he realised that the outburst had all been for him.

For Hayes, as well as his ticker-tape welcome at City Hall, Bloomingdale Brothers had decked out its premises with photographs, balloons and bunting to celebrate the success of their most famous 'employee'. President Roosevelt gave a reception at his home in Oyster Bay, Long Island, New York, for the remaining Olympians, where Hayes was presented with a trophy with horn handles. The near-death drama at the White City made the Marathon the hottest sports story of the year.

There was still a festering row about the motives of the doctor and the attendants who had assisted Dorando in the London stadium. A lot of Americans believed they had virtually carried the Italian across the line in their desperation to stop yet another American Olympic victory.

Dorando himself, in his own words quoted through his brother Ulpiano as interpreter, said, 'It was not until I saw the big stadium that the weakness came over me, and then as I had no attendant I became confused. If I had had my attendant to guide me, and give me such aid as I was entitled to, I could have finished without falling again. But they would not allow my attendant to come into the stadium with me.' He was now vehemently claiming that the assistance given him had actually prevented him from winning and that he could have reached the line alone, if not comfortably.

The story was too good to end and the world was agog for more races, more heroics, more collapsing, more dicing with death... The only stage appropriate for this drama was the 26 miles and 385 yards of the Marathon. The New York sports promoter and impresario Pat Powers approached both the Hayes and the Pietri camps, telegraphing them offers too good to turn down to give up their amateur status and take part in a rematch in New York.

In a city where immigrant communities were so strong, the idea of an Italian competing against an American was irresistible. For Powers, this was the ultimate publicity stunt. The vision of the Olympics being revisited as a man-to-man match like a prize fight, a contest to settle all the arguments about who deserved to win and who could win, was a publicity man's dream come true.

Powers booked the old Madison Square Garden, at the time a splendidly classical building with huge columns like an Italian palace, which was situated at 4th Avenue and 27th Street. It could take 16,000 paying spectators, many of whom would have to stand, with trackside boxes for those people who could afford them. The track was tiny, dusty and 176 yards round – ten laps to the mile – which would mean that the runners would have to run 262 laps to cover the London distance.

The *New York Times* of 26 November 1908 reported that 'long before the doors were open for general admission, street hawkers with American and Italian flags were on hand ready for business and the side streets were clogged.' The paper said:

> When the doors were opened the galleries filled swiftly... and crowds flowed in steadily, at prices that varied from a dollar for standing room in the galleries to $10 for arena box seats.
>
> Then the runners and officials grouped for the preliminaries and flashlight photographs. The track was cleared as the photographers filed off the course and within the next half minute Mr Croker fired the starting shot. The rivals took their places on the mark with Hayes, who had won the toss for the position of the inside; and they started on exactly even terms, jogging away, with Hayes making not even the pretence of trying to save his rail position when Dorando with a short spurt, just after the start, drew ahead.

For weeks, the press in New York had been building up the duel, particularly provoking the Italian and the Irish communities into heavy betting on the outcome. Rival bands lined up at the Garden, with rollicking Italian tunes for Dorando and with the 69th Regiment band beating the drum for Johnny Hayes. The crowd was in a frenzy, and the Italians were chanting 'Dorando, Dorando!' and '*Viva Italia!*' The *New York Times* declared it 'the

most spectacular foot race that New York has ever witnessed…
Flags waved and partisans cheered until the big amphitheatre
trembled with the sound. And through it all the rival runners
plodded around the ten laps to the mile track, inhaled the dust and
tobacco smoke with which the hall reeked, in their reproduction
of their struggle over 26 miles and 385 yards of English road.'

Pietri set out leading the race with Hayes patiently following
behind him. Every so often one or the other would produce the
semblance of a sprint, but the positions didn't change. Dorando
was relentlessly pattering round, clocking off the laps, and Hayes
seemed quite content to sit on his shoulder. Hayes appeared tired
after 20 miles and attempted to grab the psychological initiative
from Dorando. Coming up to 25 miles, he actually took the lead
for the first time. But Dorando was up for the challenge and,
once he had assessed the condition of his rival, he moved clearly
ahead and opened up a gap.

The crowd, who'd been watching the duel with an increasing
sense of suspense, erupted into pandemonium as the race drew to
its climax. The *New York Times* reported:

Finishing the 25th mile Dorando led by about four feet, in
the next lap by ten feet, in the next by fifteen and at that
rate he steadily drew further and further away. When they
finished the 26th mile, Dorando crossed the lap end mark
while Hayes was just turning at the bend from which they'd
started, 33 yards back at the straight.

A riot was all but precipitated by the thoughtless holders
of the arena box seats who in the mistaken idea that the race
had ended, hurried from their boxes and onto the track
when the racers still had two laps more to run. The track

officials tried to warn the trespassers back but it was no time for them to be at all gentle, for fierce partisans of the runners already were swarming on the course eager to clear the way for the finish of the race...

Blows were struck and fights sprang up on every side, but the track officials, backed by the police, cleared a lane through which Dorando and Hayes ran in the next lap of the track, and then the invading spectators were crowded roughly back to the aisles between the arena boxes with broken hats and a few bruises distributed among them, while the mass of spectators still swarmed over the scene of the trouble and filled up the track a second time.

Dorando got to the finish of the race to win by nearly half a lap in 2:44.20⅘. This reduced the time of Hayes' victory in the London Olympic Games race by 10:57⅗. It was impressive running. On the tight bends of the tiny circuit, with a surface of loose, dirty sand, and through a haze of smoke and dust, the two runners churned out each mile in 6:16.

It had been a close and hard-fought race and until the last few yards, the outcome was by no means certain. Thousands of dollars changed hands in bets. The runners had gone nearly 11 minutes faster than they had in London, but this time neither of them had collapsed.

The public had had their money's worth, but, they wondered, how much faster could such men go? What would happen if they pushed themselves the way Dorando had in London?

In America, there were still many thousands more people who would happily pay still more dollars for yet another duel, and for the ghoulish opportunity to witness men dicing with death.

– Chapter 33 –

The Sweet Music
of Fame

A ny event that gets people talking, gets them excited and
involves swapping the drama and the details, has to be
good material for a song. And the great showdown at Madison
Square Garden between Hayes and Dorando was very much the
talk of the town. At the turn of the century, Johnny Hayes was an
orphan in the melting pot of New York and he found his fame
through sport. Another pitched into this great melting pot of the
world was to find his fame and fortune through music.

Moses Baline and his family arrived in New York from Temun,
in Russia, in 1893. His son named Israel, but known as Izzy, was
born on 11 May 1888, and was the youngest of eight children.
The family fled Russia to escape the persecution of Jews, and
settled on the Lower East Side of New York. There, Moses Baline,
was forced to work in a market and filled in at times as a cantor
in local synagogues.

When Moses died in 1896, his son Izzy ran away from home and made friends with a low-life singing beggar. Soon he was singing, too, and he hung around popular cafés and restaurants trying to pick up some money. As a result, he was hired to sing in some of the cafés and played to plug von Tilzer songs at Tony Pastor's Music Hall.

In 1906, Izzy was hired as a singing waiter at Pelham's Café, which was a place more than halfway towards being a brothel. The staple attractions were the beer it dispensed, the big-busted girls who were always on the lookout for ways to earn a few more dimes, and the singing waiters. Izzy had to get to work at eight o'clock every night and his shift didn't finish until six the next morning. With a tray in one hand and a serving cloth slung over his arm, he would burst into song. If the customers happened to like what they heard, they would make his tray rattle with the coins they threw onto it.

Everyone at Pelham's was out to make money. In the apartment above the café was installed a lady of easy virtue known as Chinatown Gertie, well known and something of a local attraction. Parties of tourists out to see the shadier parts of town would be taken by a guide with a megaphone past Chinatown Gertie's door. The guide would always tip her with a dollar or two and most of the sightseers, taking their cue from the guide, would follow suit. Later, the man with the megaphone would be back to split the night's takings with Gertie.

So Izzy learned how to play an audience. He knew what the customers liked and when two waiters at a rival café had something of a hit with an Italian song in Italian dialect, Pelham urged the café's pianist to write a melody and he, Izzy Baline, would write the lyrics. The two wrote 'Marie of Sunny Italy' and

Baline plugged the song himself by singing it while he served the drinks.

The song was popular enough to catch the eye of a publisher. A printer's error on the cover of the sheet music, which was produced as a result, changed Izzy's name from 'I. Baline' to 'I. Berlin', a name that Berlin stuck with for the rest of his life. The newly named Mr Berlin made a total of 37 cents in royalties from the song. By the time his next song was published, he had decided that he would change his first name too. 'Israel', he reckoned, had too biblical a ring for a songwriter, and so he altered it to the more popular sounding 'Irving'.

One of Irving's specialities at Pelham's had been the ability to sing parodies of existing hit songs, and not long after the publication of 'Marie of Sunny Italy', Berlin ended up 'accidentally' writing a melody to go with some lyrics.

The name of Dorando was on everyone's lips in New York, and just three weeks after the big showdown with Hayes, he was at it again, in a head-to-head battle with the Canadian Tom Longboat. This time, though, in scenes that sent New Yorkers delirious, both inside and outside of Madison Square Garden, Dorando did indeed collapse and dramatically lost the race to the Canadian Indian.

This was the race that provided the peg for Irving Berlin's song. The song is the tale of an Italian-American barber who sells his barber's shop to stick all his life savings on the gamble of Dorando winning the race.

The Italian barber cheers wildly for his hero, 'He run-a, run-a, run like anything,' but his efforts are followed by disaster, 'Just then Dorando he's a-drop! Goodbye poor old barber's shop.' The explanation for the failure of the Italian to win the race in the

Irving Berlin lyric was that Dorando had been fed with Irish stew the night before the race instead of stuffing himself with his usual spaghetti.

Irving Berlin was certain that Dorando was a hot subject for a topical song, and when a customer at Pelham's offered him $10 for a song in Italian dialect, he jumped at it. And when the customer changed his mind the next day, Berlin didn't give up. He tried to sell the lyric to a Tin Pan Alley publisher called Ted Snyder. Snyder assumed that Berlin also had a tune to go with the words and offered him $25 for the complete song.

Berlin gulped, but not wanting to pass up the opportunity to make $25, he hummed an improvised melody to the pianist in the publisher's office and managed to secure his sale. So Irving Berlin had his first complete song, entitled 'Dorando', and this time it was a big enough hit to earn him $4,000 in royalties.

After the sell-out success of the Hayes–Dorando race in New York, Pat Powers quickly signed up Tom Longboat to make the next challenge to Dorando. The race was scheduled for 15 December 1908.

The build-up was such that on race day, Madison Square Garden was packed well in advance of the event. Italian fans had been sold thousands of fake tickets. Many of them were for a roller-skating event that had taken place there the previous month, and fierce fighting broke out as the crowd stormed the gates. The crush of rival groups of Italians and Irish was so great that the police were unable to draw or swing their truncheons; the barriers seemed certain to give way and were saved only by the last-minute arrival of reinforcements on horseback.

Longboat wore the orange and green colours of the Irish-Canadian Athletic Club and Dorando went to the start in his trademark red shorts, which he had worn at the Olympic Games in London. Race conditions in the indoor arena were stifling. The air was blue and thick with tobacco smoke, and the track was once again ten dusty laps to the mile. But gate receipts swelled to more than $15,000, which kept Ulpiano happy.

Longboat was accompanied by Tom Flanagan, his trainer-manager. One furniture dealer offered him a complete bedroom suite if he could build up a mile lead over Dorando by the 16th mile, but Lou Marsh, the Canadian journalist, advised Longboat to hang back and wait for Dorando to get tired and start to crack. Marsh believed that the Italian was almost certainly still drained by his race against Hayes only three weeks before.

Crowds cheered wildly as the two men ran as if glued together for virtually the entire race. Dorando was sometimes a few paces in front, while Longboat also surged occasionally into the lead. But the real drama took place in the closing minutes of the race.

Just past 25 miles, Longboat made his big break to win the race. His legs were still fresh enough to sprint and once he overtook Dorando, the outcome seemed clear. For three desperate laps, Dorando tried to hang onto Longboat but he failed, and his body was so drained and tired that he staggered onto the track and fell unconscious. Handlers, who still remembered what had happened at the Games the previous summer in London, rushed to carry him from the track while Longboat eased to victory in 2:45:05.

The *New York Times*' report was full of echoes, reviving the memory of that race in London:

It was a frantic, futile struggle for Dorando. He swerved as his legs weakened and then staggered and finally fell to the track, exhausted. There was a glassy stare in Dorando's eyes as his brother and a trainer rushed to the track to help him to his feet. He was urged to make another effort, but was unable to stand, and fell back helpless in his brother's arms. He was too far gone to speak, and in response to the repeated urging, simply shook his head. As he was carried to his dressing room he fainted and was unconscious for some time.

The *New York Times* had placed bulletin boards in Times Square, which was totally jammed with all the traffic at a standstill as packed crowds followed the climax of the race and the sensational collapse in the last mile.

Among those watching in the arena was a woman named Lauretta Maracle. Two weeks later, on 28 December 1908, she and Longboat were married in Toronto. The *Toronto Globe* noted with approval that she was an 'educated woman' and took heart that: 'She does not like talk of feathers, war paint or other Indian paraphernalia. She is ambitious for Tom and if anybody can make a reliable man and a good citizen out of that elusive human being, it will be his wife.'

The dramatic collapse of Dorando in the race against Longboat provided not just an idea and an inspiration for Irving Berlin and his hit song, but had also excited Ulpiano. Every day he was out speaking to the press, issuing challenges, trying to arrange races.

When the reporters asked if he had ever been a runner too, Ulpiano would boast, 'Give me a month and I can beat Dorando easily!' The press printed his every word and when they asked for a photograph of him training with Dorando, he appeared in a smart New York three-piece suit and fine handmade Italian shoes. The dapper Ulpiano trotted for a few yards for the camera alongside his brother, already stripped for a two-hour run.

'They'll print whatever I tell them,' he said to Dorando. 'What happened to you with Longboat is good. You need to fall over a few times – it makes more of a show. Reminds all of those people what happened back there in London, that's what they pay to come and see.'

While the words of Irving Berlin's 'Dorando' were on the lips of New York, Ulpiano knew there was no time to lose.

'This is our time,' he would say constantly to Dorando. 'This is our moment.'

He knew he had to cash in on the fever that gripped the crowd at the track and in Times Square for the Longboat match. And he couldn't wait to talk again to Tom Flanagan and Pat Powers.

– CHAPTER 34 –

RUNNING TO DEATH

'What gasoline is to the automobile, wine is to Dorando Pietri,' Ulpiano told the American press when they stepped off the boat in New York. Dorando is reputed to have told the waiting reporters, with Ulpiano acting as interpreter:

Wine, wine, plenty of wine. That's what makes me run. It is so good it keeps me from getting tired. It makes me run long and fast. When I have no wine, I feel faint. It is the liquid of life.

After my coffee in the morning I drink some good Chianti. It wakes me up thoroughly, then I drink some more and go to the running ground. There, I drink again. When I feel tired I call for more wine, and just as soon as I drink I feel new again and continue. When I have run one hour or two hours, and it is sufficient for the day, I drink

some more and I am as fresh as when I get out of bed. I
drink more at dinner and during the night until I go to bed.

In this way, according to what Ulpiano was telling the press,
Dorando claimed he consumed at least three quarts of Chianti
a day.

'He eats plenty too,' added Ulpiano. 'Four times a day he has a
good meal and sometimes eats as often as half a dozen times a
day. Chicken and beef he has at every meal, and lots of eggs for
breakfast, all washed down with Chianti.'

Ulpiano certainly knew what the press wanted to hear, and he
was happy to spin them any sort of line as long as they kept
printing the stuff and keeping the interest in Dorando at fever
pitch. There had been no plans for a rematch when Longboat
pushed Dorando to the point of collapse in December, but the
race whipped up such excitement that they agreed to meet again
in Buffalo, New York, on 2 January 1909.

It was a crazy schedule with never enough time for recovery.
This was especially true for Dorando, who was running his third
marathon in the space of five weeks.

The seating capacity of the venue was increased from 8,000 to
nearly 15,000 with the addition of extra seats and the sale of
standing room tickets. Longboat was keen to run the same sort
of race as he had run at Madison Square Garden – a waiting game
followed by a strong finish – but Dorando set out at so fast a pace,
covering the first mile in 5:03, that Longboat was pushed to hang
on. So determined was Dorando to prove that he could burn
Longboat off, that they went through the first 15 miles of the
race in 1:26:34:4 seconds – 19 seconds under Longboat's existing
Canadian 15-mile record.

But Dorando was heading for trouble with this ridiculously fast pace. Canadian reporters noticed that he was taking frequent swigs from what they described as 'the little brown dope bottle'. And the race ended suddenly and dramatically at 19 miles when Dorando veered off the track and collapsed into the arms of Ulpiano. Longboat was also in difficulty at this stage. His feet were covered in angry red blisters and he had a knee that was still bleeding from a fall during the second mile. He might well have had to abandon the race himself if Dorando had been able to continue, but as it was, he managed to struggle on to complete the distance and get the bets paid.

Despite this second collapse, Dorando was back on the track to run another full marathon just over a week later, on 11 January, and then another only eleven days after that. He won both of these. The first was in Philadelphia against Welshman Percy Smallwood, who was clearly in trouble and limping after 2 miles. He struggled on for another 10 miles, then dropped out and Dorando went on to win in 2:44:32.4. Next, Dorando journeyed to Chicago to take on Albert Coray, a Frenchman living in America. Coray fared no better, for Dorando took charge of the race and was never headed after the first 3 miles. He saw the Frenchman drop out in dismay at 19 miles with crippling blisters. Dorando kept going and finished alone in 2:56:0.4.

The newspapers marvelled at the apparent recovery powers of both Dorando and Hayes. 'Dorando's work since he has been in America has been wonderful,' said the *San Jose Sentinel*. 'Not least of his accomplishments has been his ability to run race after race, week after week without the slightest hint of going stale. Truly this man is a remarkable athlete.'

Another headline read, 'JOHNNY HAYES DEFIES THE LAWS OF NATURE IN GRUELLING MARATHON SPORT AND IS STILL A GREAT LITTLE ATHLETE'. The report beneath read:

> The general opinion in sporting circles is that long distance running has a tendency to injure the runner's health, but little Johnny Hayes knocks this theory higher than Gilroy's famous kite. The New York hiker, who startled the world with his sensational victory in the Olympic Games held in London last summer, and who now is in training for another race with Dorando Pietri, the great Italian racer who was disqualified in that sensational race and placed second because of interference on behalf of the English judges in an effort to freeze out Hayes, claims that with the right sort of training and proper dieting, long distance running is beneficial as well as remunerative.

Hayes himself declared to a *New York Post* reporter:

> I can make more money running than I can in any other business and as the Marathon has no harmful effects on me, I am going to stick with it.
>
> So long as you train right, and know how to run after you get on the track, long distance running will never harm you. I do not smoke or drink, and I take things easy in training, gradually getting into shape by a steady and consistent course of training, and when I start in a race I never allow the pace of my competitors to bother me in the least. I know just how fast I can run and know that the best possible time can be made in covering the distance. If I see

that my opponent is establishing a killing pace I permit him to run his own legs off for the first part of the journey, and then close on him at the finish. If a man doesn't know how to train for such an event, and doesn't know how to take care of his health, it naturally will affect his heart. But I never have been bothered in the least by my blood pumping station and am now in the finest physical condition.

All this marathon running was not without critics. The *New York Times* ran an editorial warning about the dangers of the sudden popularity of 'the so-called marathon race' in which it said that 'to take part in a marathon race is to risk serious and permanent injury to health with immediate death a danger not very remote. The truth is that exercise should always be purely subordinate to the business and pleasure of life. To make it, or the bodily changes it produces, ends instead of incidents, is a dangerous as well as an absurd mistake.'

But the races went on, and for Ulpiano Pietri the dollars rolled in.

Next in Longboat's sights was Alf Shrubb, the greatest British distance runner at the start of the first decade of the twentieth century. He had set at least fifteen world records and seemed almost unbeatable as an amateur or a professional at every distance between 1 and 15 miles. The Marathon, though, was another matter. Shrubb was a notoriously fast starter and seemed never to have learned the lesson of pacing himself for distances over 25 miles, and Longboat, who looked like a plodder in the early miles, had the beating of him every time they met.

The marathon boom was now exploding, not just in America

but worldwide. Indoor marathons were held in Montreal, London and Berlin. The craze had spread to Britain, too. On 10 October 1908, a professional race was held over the London Olympic route, promoted by the *Evening News*. It was won in 2:37:23 by J. Henri Siret from France, who carried off a purse of £100. On Wednesday, 24 November 1908, the first Great Hampshire Marathon was run and 107 men sent in their entry forms from all corners of the country. This was strictly an amateur race and controlled by the manager of the Southampton branch of the London City and Midland Bank, a former member of the South London Harriers.

After the London race, the *Sporting Life* announced the donation of a handsome silver trophy to the winner of an annual marathon, and on 8 May 1909, 68 runners lined up in Windsor in a race organised by the Polytechnic Harriers, in what was to become over the next six decades Britain's premier marathon. It was won by Harry Barrett in 2:42:31.2 – the trophy is now presented annually to the men's and women's London Marathon champions and has been renamed the Chris Brasher Sporting Life Trophy. Also, the previous week, a marathon had been run in Manchester and won by John Roberts of Sefton Harriers – and like all such races, 26 miles 385 yards was now the accepted distance.

The marathon craze took some unusual twists. On Christmas Day 1908, a marathon was run around the deck of a warship – *The Wyoming* – docked in San Francisco harbour. It took all of 355 laps of the ship to reel off the distance. And on 29 November 1910, the world was given a glimpse of the speeds future marathon runners might aspire to. In Madison Square Garden, five two-man teams ran against the clock to establish a world best for two men, each running alternate laps. Hans Holmer, a Swedish immigrant to Canada, and William Queale, of the USA, crossed the finish line in 2:02:16.2.

Back in Europe, a few months after his wedding to his childhood sweetheart Teresa Dondi, on 4 September 1909, Dorando took in an indoor marathon at London's Royal Albert Hall, on 18 December. This was against Charles Gardiner, a 26-year-old Londoner who was described as the Professional Champion Marathon Runner of all England after he won the third race to be held over the Olympic Games course in May 1909, defeating a Frenchman, Hector Labry, in 2:53:23.2.

At the Albert Hall, a track of coconut matting was laid on the floor of the arena. The central area was filled by people sitting at tables, sipping champagne and writing notes, many of them in evening dress, and there was a bandstand in the middle.

The prize money consisted of £150, with two thirds to go to the winner and one third to the loser over the full marathon on a track of twenty laps to the mile. The race started at 8.15 in the evening and the first mile was covered in 4:39.4. The *Daily Telegraph* reported:

Dorando practically defeated himself from the start. He allowed himself to be persuaded to wear a new pair of shoes of special design. The almost inevitable happened. After going about 14½ miles he got foot sore and upon removing the new shoes it was seen that the skin on the inside of the right foot was worn off. He changed into a pair of old shoes but the damage was done, and although the plucky little Italian plodded on for several more miles, it was evident that he was in great pain.

Dorando eventually pulled out in the 24th mile and Gardiner, amid loud cheering and much waving of Union Jacks, completed the distance in 2:37:1.4, though some question marks were raised over the distance run at the Albert Hall.

Everyone, it seemed, was leaping on the marathon bandwagon, and a number of books with marathon themes started to appear. One such, published by the Religious Tract Society at the beginning of 1909, was entitled *Our Marathon Race* by Dora Bee. It was a novel featuring a group of girls who decide to organise an ad hoc marathon race.

There seemed to be plenty of fuel to keep the marathon frenzy going. After the success of the first Dorando–Hayes professional meeting, fourteen more such races were held in the United States between that evening and 17 October 1909. Of these races, Dorando won four, Tom Longboat three, Henri St-Yves three and Louis Orphée two. Hayes won none.

Henri St-Yves was a pint-sized Frenchman who took on all-comers, including Dorando, Hayes, Longboat and Shrubb, and defeated them all in the Great Marathon Derby of 3 April 1909. Understandably, St-Yves was somewhat bitter about the amount of attention Dorando was getting in the press. He was jealous of his fame as a celebrity.

A report in the *Bulletin* of 17 February 1910, under the headline of DORANDO HAS CASE OF BIG HEAD said:

Withering chunks of sarcasm fairly rolled off the lips of Henri St-Yves yesterday as he paid his respects to the great Dorando who he has challenged to a marathon gallop, but who has artfully dodged him up to this time. 'So ze great Dorando says I'm unworthy to loose his shoe laces?' said the little Frenchman with a cynical smile creeping over his clear cut features. 'How nice of him, he, ze great Dorando and me, ze little Frenchman.'

But Dorando says he will run you a race if you allow him 40% of the receipts, mentioned the writer – just to draw St-Yves on further.

'Ze great Dorando is ze most generous man,' resumed St-Yves. 'He give me, who has bested him three times, just 20%. But I will be more generous. If he beat me I give him all ze money. I don't want a franc, I mean a dollar. Am I not generous?'

St-Yves may have had a point. At this stage, his best for the marathon was 2:32 – considerably faster than anything Dorando had achieved.

'The trouble with ze great Dorando, he has what you call a big 'ead. His 'ead is bigger than his chest. When I finish with him his 'ead will be so small, you can stick it in that inkwell,' taunted St-Yves.

Dorando and Hayes met in a head-to-head for the third time as professionals in San Francisco on 30 January 1910. As with all the previous races, Dorando took command of the contest in the first 100 yards. However, much to the delight and surprise of the spectators, Hayes stayed right on his heels, matching him stride for stride. During the 10th mile, Hayes took over the lead and stayed in front until both the runners made it to 22 miles. Here, once again, Dorando took over, but in the 23rd mile, Hayes swept past him and opened up a small lead, which he hung onto until the last lap.

Then, with about 100 yards to go, Dorando let loose an

impressive sprint and passed Hayes quite easily. Hayes attempted to fight back, but was unable to stay with the fast-finishing Dorando and ended up a mere 4 seconds behind him. For both runners, it was their closest contest, and for the spectators, their finest race. The time was 2:41:35 and, with only a 4-second difference between the two, it offered proof that both runners were running all out in a bid to win.

But not all the people in the arena found the race that exciting. Franklin B. Morse wrote his own eyewitness account of the contest for a San Franciso newspaper:

The big marathon race which was run yesterday afternoon at the recreation baseball park between Hayes and Dorando was as spectacular and exciting as the sight of two old ladies engaged in a long distance knitting contest. It is a safe bet that Dorando can take Hayes' measure in 40 more races provided he is in the same excellent condition he was in yesterday. When Dorando opened up the throttle for his final burst of speed, Johnny appeared to be standing still.

Hayes has been aware of the fact that his limitations as a sprinter have been the cause of his repeated defeats by the Italian, and for this reason Hayes stated to the writer that he had been practising sprinting. Unfortunately for Johnny, he forgot to bring this commodity down with him from his training quarters at the stadium yesterday, for there was nary a sprint in the little Irish-American. He could have been beaten in the last 100 yards by a 10-year-old schoolboy.

Dorando's finish was, in fact, phenomenally effective. Back in Italy, he had been renowned for it before the Games of 1908, when it had been commented on by Tullio Miselli. Johnny Hayes had great stamina and would say that he could run at marathon pace for 30 to 40 miles or more, but when it came to a fast finish, Dorando seemed to have the beating of him, except, of course, in London, where he spectacularly collapsed.

While Ulpiano was leading the life of a playboy in New York, swaggering around America with a procession of women ever ready to help him count the dollars, Dorando, despite his famous powers of recovery, was on a killer racing schedule.

'There were races everywhere every few days,' said Ondino Miselli. 'Dorando would run with horses, with Negroes; he was up to every trick, sometimes they were genuine races and sometimes not.'

The frequency and schedule of the races undertaken by Dorando and Hayes is terrifying. They competed in New York, Chicago, Indianapolis, Philadelphia, Florida, Buffalo and Syracuse. The catalogue continued with Louisville, Columbus, Newark and San Francisco, but it wasn't just America that Ulpiano and Dorando had their eyes on, it was the world.

Dorando moved on to races in London, Bologna, Vancouver, Winnipeg and Buenos Aires, Gothenburg and Stockholm. He won his last and fastest marathon race in Buenos Aires on 24 May 1910, when he ran 2:38:48.2, defeating the Spanish runner Antonio Creuz and Anibal Carraro of Argentina.

'This,' Ulpiano kept reminding Dorando, 'is our time. We make the money now and you are rich for life.'

But during 1910, the popularity of the professional marathon races seemed to be fading. The gate money dropped off as the crowds became tiring of seeing the same men line up against each other time and time again. The great marathon boom seemed to have run its course, and for Dorando and Johnny Hayes, it was time to go home.

– CHAPTER 35 –

VICTORIA'S SECRETS

C arpi made royal preparations for the great homecoming of
Dorando Pietri. According to Britain's *Daily Mirror*:

A public holiday was observed and the whole city assembled
at the station to greet its hero, who was hoisted shoulder
high and carried forth amid a delirious, tumultuous throng.

Through the city his progress was as some victorious
warrior, a veritable triumphal procession until, while the
enthusiasm of his fellow citizens was yet at its height,
Dorando quietly tore himself away to seek out his mother
in the humble dwelling of his parents. And a few hours later,
while the din of his welcome still rang in his ears, the city's
hero donned his white apron, took up his rolling pin and
resumed his work as a pastry cook, as though Olympic
Games, Marathon races, and vast cheering multitudes never
entered into his life at all.

Dorando was back in the city that was home. He'd come back to the girl he loved and he'd fulfilled every hope of his father to make it in Carpi. When he stepped off the train, he was the most famous man in the city and fêted all over Italy. And within a couple of years, he and his brother Ulpiano were to be two of the richest men in town.

On 4 September of that year, 1909, he was married to Teresa. His world had changed, but still he wanted to return to the girl he'd fallen in love with, the girl who had shared his dreams before he'd stumbled into fame. And this time, Teresa's family gave their stamp of approval. On 1 November that year, Dorando and Ulpiano signed a deed for the purchase of a building in the piazza in Carpi, and it was not too long before another crowd packed the square for the opening of the Grand Hotel Dorando.

It had, of course, all been Ulpiano's idea. They would buy a site at the corner of the fine piazza, only a short sprint away from the confectioners where Dorando had worked as a messenger boy, and turn it into the grandest hotel in the region. Ulpiano negotiated with the Swiss family who owned the building. He hired Modena's top architect – a man called Prati – to design the frontage, and he controlled all the finances. As Dorando's interpreter, masseur, self-styled coach, manager and brother, Ulpiano had negotiated to take 50% of everything Dorando earned as a professional runner.

The two men had come back to Italy with a fortune, many millions by today's standards, and Ulpiano was determined to spend it in grand style. The great hotels in New York had caught his eye and fired his ambition. This hotel, he decided, would be a statement of the success of the Pietri brothers.

'It was fabulous,' said Ondino Miselli, who had known

Dorando in the days when he was virtually begging to raise the fare to go to the Olympics. 'There were velvet sofas, marble tables, an electric piano where you put in a 10 cent coin and it played music from paper rolls. There were newspapers for the customers to read, held on a stick with a chain. They had all the table-services – the plates, the bowls, the cups and so on – specially designed by a ceramics company and they were all decorated with the letters UDP.'

The initials stood for 'Ulpiano and Dorando Pietri', but a local wit used to joke that the UDP motif stood for '*Utile Dei Piedi*' ('Useful With his Feet').

'The gentlemen of Carpi found it a fine place and would go there for coffee, but it was intimidating for everyone else, for ordinary people who couldn't afford to go there,' recalled Miselli. 'Sometimes things would look up during the opera season. The artistes, the orchestra people, the ballerinas and a few foreigners would come along; other times it was often empty, but Ulpiano was determined to have his hotel in the grand American style.'

There were certainly plenty of people there for the great opening. Ulpiano was everywhere with a glamorous Argentinian girl, Virginia Ferro, hanging on his arm, gazing into his eyes. She spoke no Italian but she flashed her eyes and her smile as she was introduced to the journalists and the dignitaries who packed the foyer and enjoyed Ulpiano's lavish hospitality.

Dorando stuck close to Teresa. They said little, bemused by the attention from the packs of photographers. The hotel was plastered with photos of Dorando – at the Olympics, vanquishing Johnny Hayes in New York, collecting his cup from the Queen of England. All his cups and trophies were on display, too, with the precious cup given by Queen Alexandra in the proudest position. The men with the cameras queued up to get a shot of Dorando holding the Queen's cup, but when they pressed him to pose next to the photo of him collapsing in the finishing straight, Teresa shook her head and steered him quietly away.

In the heady days that followed the opening of the Grand Hotel Dorando, Ulpiano would lord it at the bar or over dinner, never tiring of telling of their adventures and success in London and New York. But there were other things, too, on Dorando's mind. When he had collapsed in London, the doctors there had told him that his heart had been 'displaced by half an inch'. Despite this strange, perhaps quaint, diagnosis, he showed no ill effects in the days that followed the London race, and his performances in America suggested he was running as well as ever.

But back in Italy, Dorando was worried about the amount of punishment his body was taking and took advice from his doctors. And they all said the same thing: 'You should stop; your heart won't take it'. Given the state of sports medicine a century ago, it is possible that some of these doctors were confusing Dorando's low pulse rate, a result of his training and racing, for serious damage to his heart. Nevertheless, the warnings scared him, and alarmed Teresa even more.

On one occasion, a famous scientist from Bologna – Augusto Murri – came to Carpi to examine for himself the phenomenon that was Dorando. Murri gave him the most detailed examination; he made every test and measurement available a century ago, seeking the elusive ingredient that made Dorando such a champion. And finally he gave his verdict.

'Your heart,' said Dr Murri, 'is like a clenched fist. It's deformed – you must not run any more. If you do, you will die.'

Dorando heard the words, but while Ulpiano was dreaming of

pouring their fortune into his grand hotel, he wanted his brother still to be out there earning the real money. Long after the doctors read the riot act to Dorando about his heart, Ulpiano was there urging him on.

'Just one more race,' he would say. 'It's a big pay day, earn it while you can.' He was happy to make the deals and take his 50%.

But Teresa was furious with Ulpiano bleeding Dorando to death. 'You must stop,' she would plead. 'You don't need it now. Don't let Ulpiano talk you into it any more.'

Ulpiano stopped speaking to Teresa. 'She's never travelled. Doesn't understand the world,' he would tell his friends in the bar. 'Without me, Dorando would be nothing. I was the best thing that ever happened to him.' But Ulpiano was, in the opinion of Dorando's old training friends, his new doctors and Teresa, also the worst thing that ever happened to his brother.

According to Dorando's old friend Ondino Miselli, his last races in 1910 and 1911 were far from easy. 'His engine,' he admitted, 'was showing signs of giving out.' Ulpiano, he said, was encouraging his brother to prolong his racing career with stimulants, probably strychnine, but Dorando had had enough. His running and his desperation to win fame had given him a failing heart, not to mention a declining hotel, and in the years that followed, his dealings with Ulpiano became increasingly difficult.

When the Great War broke out on 1 August 1914, Dorando was called up, but he was subsequently discharged from the army in 1916 because of his heart problems. The clouds of war cast an even darker shadow over the Grand Hotel Dorando, and in 1917, their fortune wasted and their relationship broken, the Pietri brothers sold up.

But Dorando didn't desert Carpi, and Teresa refused to

abandon her hopes for him. She encouraged her husband to put what money they had left into buying a taxi business with a garage and a petrol station. They both found his status confusing. He had left Carpi as a poor messenger boy, a hero of the local socialists, to run in the Olympics, but had come back a rich man, a hotel owner, a capitalist. Now Dorando was still famous, still a great celebrity, but he'd lost a fortune with the hotel.

By the 1920s, there were other pressures, other political movements in Italy, and the emerging Fascist supporters saw Dorando as an icon who might be tempted to their cause. One late autumn evening in 1923, some members of a Fascist cell asked if Dorando would drive them on a mission in his taxi and he seemed reluctant to turn them down. But their venture went disastrously wrong. The journey involved a fight and a beating, and a victim was left dying.

Dorando was known in Carpi – and so, too, was his taxi. He wanted nothing more to do with the business, and he and Teresa cleared out of town on 27 November, fleeing north to San Remo, on the Italian Riviera. Once there, they picked up the pieces and started again. Dorando bought another taxi, another business, and had thousands of postcards printed that featured his finest hours in London and New York. He became the man all visiting tourists wanted at the wheel of their car to take them sightseeing. Of course, everyone wanted to hear about his most famous race and he became a living legend, having to re-live, often many times a day, those dramatic moments from July 1908.

Dorando tasted wealth again; he was content to enjoy his celebrity and grew increasingly fat on the tips. He was granted a government pension, and in 1936, was honoured with a knighthood – Cavaliere della Corona d'Italia. On 7 February

1942, he died of a heart attack at the age of 56. Teresa, the woman the doctors had always believed to be delicate, lived on until 29 October 1979. The couple had no children.

It took a while, too, for Johnny Hayes to find his feet. He raced occasionally, for diminishing rewards, until 1913. Like Dorando, Hayes was a worldwide attraction wherever he raced. On 4 May 1912, he ran in an indoor marathon in Berlin, where he came second to the Swedish-Canadian runner Hans Holmer, with a German, Jakob Kern, placed third. Straight after the race, Hayes left Germany, with $1,500 in his pocket as prize money from the American promoter Richard C. Klegin, to become coach to the United States team of marathon runners in the Stockholm Olympics of 1912.

For three years after his retirement from running, he wrote sporting articles for the *Hudson Dispatch* and he lived for a while with the one-time editor of the *New York Mirror* – Phil Payne – who disappeared over the Atlantic en route to Rome, trying to break a long-distance flying record in 1927. Johnny Hayes met Annie O'Reilly in 1905, married her in 1914 and they had one child, Doris.

After the war, his brother helped him get a job as an agent for the Californian Peach and Fig Growers' Association, and in time he became an independent food broker, working at a tiny office in Manhattan that was decorated with labelled cans of fruit and a print of Van Gogh's *The Reaper*. He enjoyed the work, and during its best year, the business netted him $10,000. But following the depression in 1929, which Hayes always maintained was the result of President Edgar J. Hoover's ideas on the economy being tainted by the British, his business failed and he was once again forced to become a food-broking agent, working at the offices of Holst-Knudsen, who dealt in dried prunes, apricots, olives and canned figs.

Johnny always kept himself in shape. In the 1930s, just coming up to fifty, he would walk every day to work from his home in the Woodcliff section of North Bergen, New Jersey, to his office at 105 Hudson Street, breaking now and then into a run just to keep himself fit. At the age of 78, he was reported as taking a daily dash into the surf and a vigorous swim. The sturdy legs and barrel chest that had carried him thousands of miles in races all over North America and Europe were still, they said, in evidence. Johnny Hayes died a widower at the age of 79, in New Jersey, on 25 August 1965. In 2002, in Nenagh, County Tipperary, the land where his father and grandfather before him were born and raised, they erected a life-sized bronze statue to the man who had won gold in that far-off London Marathon of 1908.

Meanwhile, Tom Longboat volunteered to serve in the Great War as a despatch carrier with the 107th Pioneer Battalion in France. He ran messages between units. Wounded twice, he was mistakenly declared dead, and when he returned to Canada in 1919, he was to find that his wife, believing him dead, had re-married. Longboat, too, re-married, and became a garbage collector in Toronto. He died in 1949, at the age of 62.

Sir Arthur Conan Doyle continued to pursue his passion for Olympism, amateurism and fair play. He staged the lavish West End production of *The House of Temperley* about prize fighting and was heavily involved in the plans for the 1916 Olympic Games planned for Berlin. Though he was invited to be chairman, the Berlin Games never took place, however. When World War I broke out, again Conan Doyle volunteered. Too old and probably overweight, he was turned down, but formed his own militia, a sort of prototype Home Guard. After the death of his wife, Louisa, in 1906, and the deaths of his son Kingsley and his brother Innes shortly after World War I, Conan Doyle sank into depression. He became a supporter of spiritualism and its alleged scientific proof of existence beyond the grave. Conan Doyle was found clutching his chest in the family garden on 7 July 1930. He died of a heart attack, aged 71, and is buried in Church Yard at Minstead in the New Forest, Hampshire. The epitaph on his gravestone reads:

Steel True

Blade Straight

Arthur Conan Doyle

Knight

Patriot Physician and Man of Letters

Jimmy Curran took his professional training secrets to the United States. There, he became a long-lived and legendary track and field coach to Mercersburg Academy, Pennsylvania, where he groomed Ted Meredith of the USA to win gold medals at the 800 Metres and the 4 x 400 Metres relay at the Stockholm Olympics of 1912 and to subsequently break the world 400 Metres record. He appears to have held a teaching post there until his death in 1961. As well as Meredith, three other track and field Olympians won gold during Curran's time at Mercersburg. They were Allen Woodring, who won the 200 Metres at the Games of 1920; Bill Carr, winner of the 400 Metres in 1932; and Charles H. Moore Jr, who won the 400-metre hurdles in 1952. Lord Desborough, Baron Desborough of Taplow, dedicated his life to fighting for the ethos of amateurism and fair play in sport, and lived long enough to chuckle over reading his own obituary in *The Times*. The next day, he telephoned the obituary editor, who enquired, 'Where are you calling from, my Lord?' And the following day, the newspaper published a grovelling apology. Desborough witnessed the Edwardian world with its long summers of gentlemanly sport vanish into the mud of Flanders. His eldest son, Captain Julian Grenfell, a war poet, died aged 27. His younger son, William Grenfell, was killed in action like Julian in 1915. A third son, Gerald Grenfell, died in 1926 as a result of a motoring accident. Desborough also had two daughters. His wife, Ethel Anne Priscilla Fane, died in 1952.

Dorando Pietri won his farewell races in Parma, Italy, on 3 September 1911, and in Gothenburg, Sweden, in October of the same year. He was 26 at the time. In three years as a professional runner, he had earned 200,000 lire in prize money alone – an enormous sum for the time.

He saw his old friends Ondino and Tullio for the last time in Carpi. It was winter and the war was raging. This was always the town where he felt most at home, where he had first found fame and where he had lost his heart to Teresa. Here, he could talk of old times, of life and death, and sometimes he and his friends would go to a hotel there called Victoria's. It was a place run by women for men, a place to relax, to be unbuttoned, and to dream a little.

While in Victoria's, surrounded by girls, playing cards and sipping wine, Ondino made a sketch of Dorando looking serious and thoughtful. Beneath the drawing, he penned a caption. 'Ah, Dorando,' it read, 'are you dreaming of the joys of victory in the

Marathon or are you dreaming of the joys of Victoria?'

Victoria would smile and say to him, as such girls do, the words Dorando needed to hear. 'We all love you,' she whispered, 'you and your little boy's face. You're the most famous man in all Italy but you're still our little Dorando. At home you have Teresa and here you have us. What more can life offer you? A hundred years from now you will still be spoken of here, right here in Carpi. Isn't that what you've always wanted?'

So we leave him now, sipping wine in a bar, surrounded by his friends and his memories. He is telling yet again the stories of that scorching July day in London, remembering how he fell to the track in the sunshine, how he nearly died that night and how pride picked him up long enough to collect his golden cup from the Queen of England. His memory flickers like silent film with glimpses of Madison Square Garden and trotting laps on the stages of Broadway to show off his style.

'But above all,' he says to anyone who cares to listen, 'I was the first.' And no matter how many men come to run marathons, Dorando truly was the first ever to cover that mysterious 26 miles and 385 yards.

– CHAPTER 36 –

THE BATTLE IS OVER

For Wyndham Halswelle, the 1908 Olympics really came to an end on the fields of France in the spring of 1915.

The self-confident Edwardians who sat around at the conference in the peaceful surroundings of The Hague in 1907, drawing up both *The Rules of Sport* and *The Rules of War*, could never have envisaged how soon their codes would be put to the test and tested to destruction. But if *The Rules of Sport* creaked under the pressures placed upon them in London's White City, they were to explode in the days of August 1914, when Queen Victoria's grandson Kaiser Wilhelm II, in whose arms she had died, let loose the might of Germany to challenge the British Empire.

The problems over the conduct of war had long been foreshadowed. Writers, statesmen and soldiers had all warned that unless men fought, as well as played, by the rules, civilisation would break down. H. G. Wells, for instance, had warned of the dangers of war in the air, the threat of poison gas, and the menace of tank warfare. These were truly weapons of mass destruction and they opened up a new and terrible chapter in the conduct of war.

Lord Kitchener, by now 64 and Britain's most successful soldier, who had been military governor of Egypt since 1911, was in London in August 1914 when hostilities broke out, and was immediately appointed Secretary of State for War. He took up office on 5 August, but as the men of Britain answered the call of that veteran Boer War general, few had any concept of the bloodbath yet to come.

Within two days, Kitchener issued an appeal for 100,000 volunteers. This was the Great War to end wars, and just as the Boer War had shaken Britain's faith in the invincibility of the British Empire, so, too, was this war to signal the end of that British dominance and to clear the way for a new world order.

From all points of the world, men flocked to the call of arms. Much to their chagrin, Sir Arthur Conan Doyle and Robert Baden-Powell were far too old to fight, but their influence would still play a part in the Empire's war effort.

In the United States, Johnny Hayes volunteered his winning ways to the struggle, but was told that he was unfit to serve as a fighter because he was colour-blind. Hayes, the man on whose heart was inscribed the difference in colour and status between silver and gold, found that it was his eyes rather than his heart that let him down, and he took a non-combatant role in the 9th Regiment Medical Corps.

In Italy, Dorando Pietri answered the call to fight for his country as an infantryman, but the heart problem his doctors had scared him with in 1909, which put an end to his running career in the summer of 1911, now forced him out of the ranks. He returned to Carpi, limping out of the conflict.

In Edinburgh, Wyndham Halswelle read the first news of the declaration of war in *The Times*. Jimmy Curran first saw it on a placard, and soon the news spread throughout the towns, cities and villages by word of mouth. It was greeted with enthusiastic expressions of support, though even in these first days there were small demonstrations against the war. There seemed to be no great urgency on the part of the British public to gear up for the conflict to come, but there was one group, already in uniform, who were able to react immediately to the declaration of war.

The Boy Scouts, already wearing tunics and training in camps, were ready for action. Baden-Powell had deeply impressed upon them a respect for chivalry and fair play, along with the ability to improvise tactics to chase victory. These young men, heirs to the games in the copse where Halswelle and Baden-Powell played after school, were mobilised straightaway to safeguard railways, coastlines, telegraphs and reservoirs. They used their fitness as runners to deliver messages, and their map-reading skills as despatch riders. In the first four months of the war, some 10,000 ex-Scouts and Scoutmasters answered the call of Kitchener.

But they weren't the only ones to line up to fight. Halswelle, by this time a veteran of 31, observed that thousands of under-age boys were flocking to the colours. He saw dozens of them, little more than overgrown schoolboys, who were asked their age but were rarely required to produce evidence of it. In those boys, he saw the same youthful ideals that he himself had dreamed of as a schoolboy. Boys as young as fifteen were anxious that the war might take place without them. They feared, as he had done so many years before, that they might miss the boat, and after all, as everyone said, it would be all over by Christmas. One under-age recruit for the Queen's Westminster Rifles said later:

> We were a normal lot of healthy young men afflicted with romantic minds and large reserves of pent-up energy. Our real need was to rescue beautiful maidens from terrible dragons, but the beautiful maidens were so capable and stand-offish and all the dragons had been slain long ago, so that when the *Daily Mail* told us that beautiful Belgium had been violated and France was in distress, we all rushed to the rescue. But I think we did it for our own sakes very largely. The uniforms, the bands, the open-air life, and most of all the feeling that one was a devil of a fellow, attracted us irresistibly.

That old war horse, Sir Arthur Conan Doyle, mobilised himself to deliver a recruiting speech on 6 September in the year the war began. He declared:

> There was a time for all things in the world. There was a time for games. There was a time for business. There was a time for domestic life. There was a time for everything. But there is only time for one thing now, and that thing is war.
>
> If the cricketer had a straight eye, let him look along the barrel of a rifle. If a footballer had strength of limb, let him serve and march in the field of battle.

For Halswelle, now a captain and a hardened veteran of those

Boer War battles a lifetime ago, his duty was clear: he had to lead these idealistic young men in their crusade to fight for King and country and for all the values that had made the British Empire great. The old enemy on the track, America, was long forgotten, perhaps forgiven. Here was a new threat – a threat from Germany. A threat not just to life but to everything Halswelle held dear. His mission was to give those boys leadership. He had to catch them as their stomachs churned at the first sound of distant gunfire, and nerves frayed at the spectacle of a mutilated landscape.

But Halswelle understood their fear. Every time the Very lights burst in the sky over the trenches, or the rattle of a machine gun broke the eerie silence, he was back, lining up on the track and waiting for that starting gun. He knew how the heart raced at the sound and he could help them handle it.

War, like the Games, had changed so much. This was a very dirty war, a nightmare of cloying mud that would churn every battlefield into a quagmire of despair. Even worse than the mud were the waiting and the fear: Halswelle knew all about this. He had known them both at all the great Games, but the memories seemed so far away now, so insignificant. What did it matter to win? Who cared if you lost? Would history forget him? Would it remember Dorando? Here in the trench, the men knew waiting and fear of a kind that he himself had only played with long ago.

It rained and rained. Black water ran along the bottom of the trench. Halswelle would stand on an ammunition box risking a glimpse of the enemy, perching there until the box sank deep into the mud. Then he would put another on top of it and stand on that. As the battle of Neuve Chapelle raged in Northern France in the late spring of 1915 and the waiting was at last over, his men would find themselves wrestling with the weight of the equipment they had to drag with them through the mud even as they charged into battle.

On 29 March 1915, the message came from up the line that the offensive was underway. Halswelle reported that that day his men gained 15 yards, a distance Halswelle the athlete could have run in less than a couple of seconds. Then they dug in for three hours before retreating in the evening back to the position from where they had started.

'I lost three platoon sergeants in the first rush,' Halswelle reported. 'I must have started 140 strong; 79 men died to gain 15 yards which were given up again within hours.'

On the following day, Halswelle was wounded by a sniper.

'Keep your bloody head down, sir!' they used to shout at him. Back in the field station, they patched him up. He pleaded to get straight back to the trenches, knowing all too well that fighting was a dirty business – the reason why they were fighting this war to end all wars.

Halswelle knew, too, that when he blew the whistle and they went over the top, his legs would still get him across those crazy yards of no man's land faster than the young boys running behind him. He knew that he could still be first to the barbed wire. All that track work with Jimmy Curran had left him that, if nothing more.

It was on the morning of the second day back in the trenches on the last day of March 1915 that it happened. He and a Lieutenant Henderson were walking along the trench, giving directions and encouragement. The trench was shallow and it was hard to walk upright.

'Ten yards away from where I lay,' recalled Henderson, 'the Captain was struck. His head had shown and a sniper got him about the temple. He dropped unconscious immediately. I called for stretcher bearers, but half an hour afterwards he was dead.'

Within hours, Captain Halswelle was buried in a shallow grave that was hastily dug on a farm behind the line. A contemporary sketch, still treasured by his family, shows a simple wooden cross, his name written on it in boot polish.

Later, members of the Highland Light Infantry exhumed his body and re-interred it in the Royal Irish Rifles graveyard at Laventie, a village 7 miles south-west of Armentières in the Nord Pas-de-Calais.

The bullet that ended his life came from a Mauser rifle cradled in the arms of an unseen sniper. There was no smoke from the barrel of the gun. And on his gravestone there is no mention of his Olympic victory, or of fair play.

AFTERWORD

'To believe this story you must believe that the human race can be one joyous family, working together, laughing together, achieving the impossible. I believe it because I saw it happen.'
Chris Brasher, after the New York City Marathon, 1979

With all the hindsight of 100 years, as we look back on the events of 1908, what runs on in the memory are the stories of heroes. What those athletes did on the track of the Great Stadium in London's Shepherd's Bush was to play the hero and provide inspiration for thousands who were to follow in their footsteps.

Much has changed in the cauldron of the Olympics, but much has stayed the same. These days, television and the Internet will bring every detail of the 2008 Games – the sporting struggle to go ever higher, faster and stronger – from Beijing into millions of homes around the world. More money than ever before will be

297

spent, and yet these simpler Games of 1908 show that the path to an heroic life has little to do with spending a fortune.

In the days before the flickering screens turned half the world into spectators, these Games of 1908 were enough to bring enormous crowds onto the streets and into the Great Stadium to witness at first hand what it is to be a hero. And 100 years on, the thousands who might once have been happy to watch are now hungry to become heroes themselves.

Wyndham Halswelle, Johnny Hayes and Dorando Pietri were the headline heroes of those first London Games. The 400 Metres produced a unique victor: Halswelle, with his true love of sportsmanship and fair play, showed that he needed no competitor to prove that he was a hero, nor that he was afraid to die on the battlefield. And the marathon of 1908 was unusual, in that it produced not one, but two heroes – and two role models for marathon runners of the future.

But the biggest change since 1908 is that running has exploded to such an extent, that each year it produces not just three, but thousands of heroes. Those pioneers showed that heroes are not as exceptional as the world believed in 1908, and that heroism is a path open to all.

Everyone is now familiar with the marathon, the distance made famous by that duel between Hayes and Dorando. We all know someone who has run one, we have all been buttonholed to sponsor some runner's favourite charity. We have seen some of the world's greatest runners gliding across our TV screens, and we all know that the most unlikely celebrities have completed marathons.

Chris Brasher, co-founder of today's London Marathon, was fond of labelling the race 'the great suburban Everest'. It is a distance that is tantalisingly out of reach for the untrained novice, but one that's accessible to almost anyone prepared to lace up their running shoes and clock up the training miles.

Today, hundreds of thousands take on the challenge of the marathon. Some are young and fast, others are older but still ready to tap wells of defiance and endurance that will get them through the distance. All are running in the footsteps of Hayes and Dorando and, like those great champions, yearn to be heroes of their own.

The beauty of sport is that it makes heroism available to us all. But each of us needs to find our own arena, our own event, our passion and our calling.

The journey towards being a hero can, and often does, take a lifetime. But the lure of the marathon is that it can give you a taste of it within three or four hours – the drama, the suffering, the uncertainty: all can be compressed into the 26 miles 385 yards between the gun and the tape.

In 1975, when Britain's Ron Hill ran in the Boston Marathon, in which he had set a course record five years before, he came upon Canada's Jerome Drayton, slumped on a kerb with just 2 miles left to run.

'Get going,' shouted Hill. 'Get up and walk if you have to. But finish the damned race!'

The secret to being a hero is to take whatever the race, or life, throws at you and to survive it to the finish. In the marathon, as in almost any endeavour, to endure is to win. To cross the line, as Dorando and Johnny Hayes knew well, is to win – and the only way to lose is by failing to endure.

Johnny Hayes prepared himself well for his marathons. He put in the miles, he knew about pace, he weighed up the opposition and he studied the weather conditions. Dorando relied more on inspiration. He knew that crossing the line in a marathon was an unforgettable emotional experience; that the spirit could keep you going long after your legs give way.

Put the approach of these two heroes together and they will show you how to run your own perfect marathon. Hundreds of thousands do so in the great mass marathons now held round the world. They know that the marathon gives them the opportunity of fulfilling a dream, to turn themselves into what they believe themselves to be, and that somehow they must endure until they get there.

Heroism may have seemed remote, rare and out of reach in 1908. But the lasting legacy of Halswelle, Hayes, Dorando and the Games of 1908 is that to endure, and never give in, can bring a touch of the hero into the lives of everyone.

APPENDIX I

Entries for the 1908 Olympic Marathon

Australasia
1 Lynch, J. M.
2 Aitken, W. V.
3 Blake, G. B.

South Africa
4 Baker, J. M.
5 Mole, A. B.
6 Stevens, C. E.
7 Vincent
8 Hefferon, C.

Greece
9 Coulcumberdos, G.
10 Coutoulakis, A.

Finland
11 Nieminen, K.

Russia
12 Lind, G.

Netherlands
13 Braams, W. T.
14 Vosbergen, A. C. H.
15 Wakker, W. W.
16 Theunissen, W. F.
17 Buff, G. J. M.

Belgium
18 Celis, F.

Italy
19 Dorando, P.
22 Cocca, A.
20 Blast, U.
21 Blasi, U. (Misprint in programme – ran under number 20)
23 Durando, P. (Misprint in programme – ran under number 19)

U.S.A.
24 Forshaw, J.
25 Hatch, S. H.

26 Hayes, J. J.
27 Lee, J. J.
28 Lorz, F.
29 Morrissey, T. P.
30 O'Mara, W.
31 Ryan, M. J.
32 Thibeau, A.
33 Tewanina, L.
34 Welton, A. R.
35 Wood, W.

Germany
36 Muller, H.
37 Reiser, F.
38 Nettlebeck, P.

Sweden
39 Tornros, G.
40 Svanberg, J. F.
41 Peterson, J. G.
42 Landquist, S. L.
43 Lindquvist, J.
44 Bergvall, J. T.
45 Lundberg, J. G. A.

Austria
46 Rath, E.
47 Kwieton, F.

Bohemia
48 Nojedky

Denmark
49 Hansen, R. C.
50 Jorgensen, J. F.

Hungary
51 Merenyi, L.

United Kingdom
52 Duncan, A.
53 Beale, J. G.
54 Lord, T.
55 Price, J.
56 Barrett, H. F.
57 Thompson, F. B.
58 Barnes, E.
59 Wyatt, A.
60 Appleby, F.
61 Jack, T.
62 Stevenson, S.
63 Clarke, W. T.

Canada
64 Simpson, F.
65 Lawson, H.
66 Goldsboro, W.
67 Goulding, G.
68 Wood, W.

69 Cotter, E.

70 Noseworthy, F.

71 Caffery, J.

72 Longboat, T.

73 Lister, G.

74 Burn, A.

75 Tait, J.

APPENDIX II

Official Result of the 1908 Olympic Marathon

Dorando, Pietri, Italy (disqualified)	2:54:46.4
1. J. J. Hayes, United States	2:55:18.4
2. C. Hefferon, South Africa	2:56:06
3. J. Forshaw, United States	2:57:10.4
4. A. R. Welton, United States	2:59:44.4
5. W. Wood, Canada	3:01:44
6. F. Simpson, Canada	3:04:28.2
7. H. Lawson, Canada	3:06:47.2
8. J. F. Svanberg, Sweden	3:07:50.8
9. L. Tewanina, United States	3:09:15
10. K. Nieminen, Finland	3:09:50.8

11. J. Caffery, Canada	3:12:46
12. W. T. Clarke, United Kingdom	3:16:08.6
13. E. Barnes, United Kingdom	3:17:30.8
14. S. H. Hatch, United States	3:17:52.4
15. F. Lord, United Kingdom	3:19:08.8
16. W. Goldsboro, Canada	3:20:07
17. J. G. Beale, United Kingdom	3:20:14
18. I. Nejedky, Bohemia	3:26:26.2
19. G. Lind, Russia	3:26:38.8
20. W. W. Wakker, Holland	3:28:49
21. G. Tornros, Sweden	3:30:20.8
22. G. Goulding, Canada	3:33:26.4
23. J. F. Jorgensen, Denmark	3:47:44
24. A. Burn, Canada	3:50:17
25. E. Rath, Austria	3:50:30.4
26. R. C. Hansen, Denmark	3:53:15
27. G. Lister, Canada	4:22:45

There were 27 finishers from 56 starters and 73 entrants (excluding the 2 double entries for Blasi and Pietri of Italy)

Diplomas of Merit for the Marathon Race were awarded to all finishers

Appendix III

Dorando Pietri's Marathon Career

1. Rome, 2 April 1906. Pre-Olympic Marathon, 42km (Porta Pia – via Salaria – Castelgiubileo – via Flaminia-Villa Umberto), start 13:43

1 Dorando Pietri (Atalanta) 2:42:06
2 Ettore Ferri (SEF Virtus, Bologna) 2:47:00
3 Antonio Tarquini (Roma) 2:49:00

2. Athens, 1 May 1906. Olympic Marathon, 41,860m, Marathon village to Panathenaikos Stadium

1 William Sherring (Can) 2:51:23.6
2 John Svanberg (Swe) 2:58:20.8

3 Frank Williams (USA) 3:00:46.8

Dorando retired at 24km with stomach pains.

3. Arona, 26 August 1906. Marathon, 41,090m – Arona – Gravellona – Pallanza then 6 laps of the track

1 Antonio De Micheli (Sempre Avanti Cavaria) 3:05:19
2 Giacinto Volpati (Post Resurgo Libertas) 3:11:50
3 Marco Cadari (Intra) 3:19:11

Dorando retired at 20km

4. Rome, 3 June 1908. Italian Championship, 40 km, through the city, finish at Piazza di Siena, 3 starters

1 Umberto Blasi (U.S. Tibertina Roma) 3:01:04
2 Augusto Cocca (S.P. Lazio) 3:10:00

Dorando retired at 33km. The previous day he had won the Italian 20km track championship in 1:10:54.6. He qualified for London by running 40km on the track in 2:38:00 (Italian Record) on 7 July in Carpi

5. London Olympic Games, 24 July 1908 (see Appendix 2)

6. New York, 25 November 1908, Madison Square Garden, vs Johnny Hayes – 42,195m on 160.93m track

1 Dorando Pietri 2: 44:20.4
2 J J Hayes 2:45:05.2

7. New York, 15 December 1908, Madison Square Garden as above, vs Tom Longboat (Can), start 14:56.

1. Longboat 2: 45:05.4

Dorando retired at 26 miles.

8. Buffalo, 2 January 1909, indoor track at 74th Regiment Armory – 25 miles, vs Tom Longboat (Can)

1 Longboat 3:03:00

Dorando retired at 19 miles, having led at 12 miles in 1:08:23.2

9. St Louis, 11 January 1909, Coliseum, vs Percy Smallwood (GB), 42,195m
1 Dorando Pietri 2:44:32.4

Smallwood retired

10. Chicago, 22 January 1909, Dexter Park, International Amphitheatre vs Albert Coray (France), 42,195m, start 21:11.

1 Dorando Pietri 2:56:00.4

Coray retired.

11. Florida, 12 February 1909, vs Smallwood (GB), 42,300m

1 Dorando Pietri 2:50:30

Smallwood retired. They had raced over 12 miles the day before in Philadelphia with a similar result

12. New York, 15 March 1909, Madison Square Garden, 42,195m, start time 21:22

1 Dorando Pietri 2:48:08
2. Johnny Hayes half a mile behind.

13. New York, 3 April 1909, open air track at the Polo Grounds, 42,195m, start time 15:00, rain, 30 000 spectators, odds quoted Longboat 8 to 5, Shrubb 2 to 1, Pietri 3 to
1, Hayes 5 to 1, Maloney 7 to 1, Saint-Yves 40 to 1

1 Henry Saint-Yves (France) 2:40:50.6 ($5000 prize money)
2 Dorando Pietri 2:45:37 ($2500)

3 Johnny Hayes 2:49:27 ($1500)
4 Matthew Maloney (USA) 2:50:29 ($1000)

Tom Longboat (Can) retired at 22 miles, Alfred Shrubb(GB) retired at 25 miles

14. New York, 8 May 1909, 42,195m, Polo Grounds track, prize money $10,000 in total, 50 000 spectators

1 Henry Saint-Yves (France) 2:44:05
2 John Svanberg (Swe) 2:50:54
3 Ted Crooks (USA) 2:52:10
4 Fred Simpson (Can) 2:54:13
5 Fred Appleby (GB) 2:56:17
6 Dorando Pietri 2:58:19
7 Edouard Cibot (France) 3:05:34

Retired: Pal White (Ireland), Louis Orphée (France), Tom Morrissey (US), Felix Carvajal (Cuba), Matthew Maloney (US), John Marsh (Can)

15. London, 18 December 1909, Royal Albert Hall, 42,195m, start time 20:15, vs Charles Gardiner (GB)

1 Charles Gardiner (GB) 2:37:01.4

Dorando Pietri retired at 23 miles, having led at the first and eleventh mile

16. San Francisco, 30 January 1919, vs Johnny Hayes, Recreation Park track, 42,195m

1 Dorando Pietri 2:41:35
2 Johnny Hayes 2:41:49

17. Buenos Aires, 24 May 1910, 42,400m, Campo Sociedad Deportiva Argentina, laps of 1060m, start time 14:30.

1 Dorando Pietri 2:38:48.2
2 Antonio Creuz (Spain) 2:45:04
3 Anibal Carraro (Argentina) 2:54:09
4 Martiniano Becerra (Chile) 3:06:15.4
5 Miguel Soto (Spain) 3:08:16

Retired: Innocenzo Bergamasco (Italy), Giachino (Arg), Lassenay (Uruguay).

Dorando Pietri disputed a total of 121 races in his career, including the 17 marathons, between 2 October 1904 and 15 October 1911. He won 87, excluding two record attempts early in his career when he was the only runner, as well as two races against a horse where only Dorando's time is given and the result is not stated.

INDEX

Afghanistan 24

Albani, Madame 139

Albert, Prince 212

Alexander I of Russia 153

Alexandra, Queen 98, 150, 180,
187, 217, 223, 232–3, 239, 241
Pietri's gift from 232, 236,
241–2, 279–80, 287

All England Club 113

All England Tennis Tournament
115

Amateur Athletic Association
(AAA) 113, 131, 146, 147, 176,
182, 201, 205

Amateur Boxing Association 176

Amateur Fencing Association 113,
114

Amateur Marathon road race,
Paris 176

Amateur Rowing Association 176

Amateur Swimming Association
176

American Athletics Federation
206–7

American Athletic Union 90

American Committee for the
Olympic Games 99

Anderson, W. D. 60

Andersson, Arne 178

Andrew, Jack 182, 183, 184,
185–6, 188, 223, 225

Appleby, Fred 213, 217, 218

Association of Athletics
Federations (IAFF) xii

Association of International
  Marathons and Distance Races
  (AIMS) xii
Atalanta Club 78
Athletic News 216
Averoff, Georgios 72

Baden-Powell, Robert xvii, 24,
  37–42, 290
Baline, Israel ('Izzy'), *see* Berlin,
  Irving
Baline, Moses 257
Bampfylde, Mayor 210
Barker, Nigel 110–11
Barrett, Harry 270
Baxter, Irving 83
Bee, Dora 272
Belakas 74
Berlin, Irving (né Israel 'Izzy'
  Baline) 257–60, 262
Birchfield Harriers 177
Blackheath Harriers 182
Blaikie, David 173–4
Blake, Arthur 73
Blasi, Umberto 129
Bloemfontein 8
Bloomingdale's 52, 63, 136, 245,
  251
Boer War xvii, xviii, 4, 7–8, 24–30,
  37–40, 290, 291, 292

Conan Doyle's history of xix,
  26, 30
Halswelle serves in 7–12, 23–30
  passim
  see also Mafeking, siege of;
  South Africa
Bologna 34
Bonheure, Emile 176–7
Bosdari, Count de 232–3
Boston Athletic Association 68
Boston Globe 48
Boston Herald 135–6
Boston Post 48
Boy Scouts xvii, 38, 40–1, 291
  blueprint for 39
Brasher, Chris 189, 270, 297, 298
Bréal, Michel 70–1
British Championships 146
British Olympic Association 109,
  114, 143, 144, 145, 186
British Olympic Committee 143,
  146, 160, 164, 243
British Olympic Council 115,
  151, 181, 240
Brownsea Island Experimental
  Camp 41
Brunetta d'Usseaux, Count 236
Bulger, Dr Michael 222, 223, 225
Bulletin 272–3

Caffery, Jack 105, 106

Caledonian meeting, Port
Elizabeth 54

Californian Peach and Fig
Growers' Association 283

Campbell, Menzies 60

Carnegie, Andrew 168

Carpenter, John 200, 201–5,
206–7, 247–8, 250

Carpi xvi, 13–21, 31, 77, 80, 277

Carr, Bill 285

Carraro, Anibal 275

Carrington, Sir William 212

Carvajal, Felix 92–3

Champion, Emile 84, 85

Channel Swimming Association 113

Chaplin, Charlie xvi

Chariots of Fire vii

Charterhouse School 3, 37–8

Chesterton, G. K. 167

Chicago Record-Herald 154

Chicago Tribune 100, 154, 155

China 151

Chinatown Gertie 258

Chris Brasher Sporting Life
Trophy 270

Churchill, Winston xvii

Cocca, Augusto 129

Coe, Seb viii

Colliers Magazine 167

Conan Doyle, Sir Arthur xvii, xix,
25–8, 29, 30, 144, 212, 284–5,
290, 292
death of 285
knighting of 30
1908 Marathon and 227–9
Pietri appeal by 249

Conan Doyle, Innes 285

Conan Doyle, Kingsley 285

Conan Doyle, Lady 249, 285

Connolly, Jim 48–50, 225–6, 245

Constantine, Crown Prince 74, 98

Conway, Patrick J. 51–2

Cooch Behar, Maharajah of 144

Cook, Theodore 114, 118, 120–3,
151, 160, 227, 247
'Mr Fair Play' sobriquet of 122
'Reply' pamphlet of 243
see also fair play

Coray, Albert 267

Coroebus of Ellis 65

Coubertin, Baron Pierre de, *see* de
Coubertin, Baron Pierre

Cox, Vera 229–30

Creuz, Antonio 275

Crystal Palace 147

Cuba 91–2

Curran, Jimmy 12, 53–6, 57,
59–61, 109, 111, 131–3, 199,
285, 291

Daily Express 197

Daily Mail xix, 144, 167, 190, 191–2, 195, 200, 217–18, 227, 228, 249, 292

Daily Mirror 277

Daily Telegraph 113, 120, 238, 271

Daily Tribune 206

Daley, Arthur 156

Dawkins, Lady Bertha 212

de Coubertin, Baron Pierre viii, xviii, xx, 63–4, 65–6, 67, 69, 81–2, 89–91, 94, 115, 147, 150, 176

   amateur status and 176

   fair play

   fair-play plea of 232

   gifts deplored by 107

   Greeks' wish to be permanent host and 81, 97–8

   internationalism as goal of 100

de Walden, Lord Howard 110, 114, 117

Derby and County 182

Desborough, Lady 145, 179, 237, 240, 241, 286

Desborough, Lord (William Grenfell) 110, 111–13, 114, 115, 117, 132–3, 144, 150, 151–2, 181, 185, 188, 208, 285–6

   commemorative medal for 241

   fair-play speech of 231–2

   Halswelle pressured by 199

   King hosted by 179–80

   at 1908 Marathon 213, 214, 218, 231

   Pietri congratulated by 237

Diack, Lamine xii

Dillon, John 29

Disley, John 189

Dodd, Lottie 239

Dondi, Teresa xvi, 35–6, 77, 78, 79–80, 107, 127, 128, 130, 221, 250, 271, 281–2

   Pietri marries 278

'Dorando' (Berlin) 260, 263

'Dorando Marathon' 146

Drayton, Jerome 299

du'Gordon, Sir Cosmo 114

Duke, Harry 159, 162, 168–9

Duncan, Alexander 183, 196, 211, 215–16

Dunne, Finlay Peter 166

Edinburgh:

   Powderhall in 53, 55, 56, 60

   Royal Patent Gymnasium in 55, 57–8

Edinburgh Harriers 54

Edward VII, King 24, 30, 98, 114,

117, 139, 149–50, 179–81, 185, 187

Games opened by 150

1908 Marathon and 212

prizegiving snubbed by 238

Elena, Queen 79

'English as Poor Losers, The' (Connolly) 245

Esher, Lord 209

Eucles 71

Euclid 246

Evans, Lucy xvii

Evening News xvi, 185, 270

Evening Post 206

Ewry, Ray 83, 138

fair play 5, 27, 113, 117–23, 167, 168, 231–3, 295, 298

see also Cook, Theodore

Fallières, President 139

Fanti, General Manfredo 18

Fascists 282

Fast, Ernest 85

Fava, Aduo 34

Field 120

Finland 153, 181

Fisher, Percy 182

Flack, Edwin ('Teddy') 73–4, 75

Flanagan, John 137, 162

Flanagan, Tom 174, 261, 263

Ford, Timmy 134

Forshaw, Joseph 196, 210, 226

Fowler, Bob 173

Fowler-Dixon, John E. 99

France 142

Racing Club of 85

see also Franco-British Exhibition; Olympic Games 1900 (Paris)

Franco-British Exhibition 139–47

Frederick William IV, King 141

Gaelic American 245

Gala Harriers 55

Gallohue 49

gambling 10

Gardiner, Charles 271

Garrels, Johnny C. 137, 152, 154

George, King (Greece) 70, 98

George, Prince 74, 106, 180

George V, King 139

George VI, King 212

Germany xviii, 41, 91, 250, 289, 293

see also World War I

Gioletti, Giovanni 113

Glasgow Herald 111

Goble, Harry 201

Gordon, Nathaniel 2

Grace, W. G. 27

Graham, Marie 151

Grand Hotel Dorando 278

Grant, Dick 87

Greek Olympic Committee 242

Grenadier Guards 239, 240

Grenfell, Gerald 286

Grenfell, Captain Julian 286

Grenfell, William 286

Grenfell, William Henry, *see*,
Desborough, Lord

Grey, Sir Edward 109

Greyhound Racing Association
146–7

Gustav IV, King 177

Hägg, Gunder 178

Halpin, Matt 98–9, 119, 138, 154

Halswelle, Gordon 2

Halswelle, Helen 2, 23–4, 30, 37

Halswelle, Keeley 2

Halswelle, Wyndham viii, 1–5,
115, 131–3, 177, 289, 291–5,
298, 300
Baden-Powell's influence on
37–8
ball-game skills of 8–10
birth and early life of 1–4
Curran's training of 54, 59–61
at Intermediate Games 98,
109–11, 113, 117

leg injury to 132

military service of 7–12, 23–30
passim, 292–5

in 1906 championships 60

1908 400 Metres and 199–208,
232, 238, 247

rematch invitation to 247–8

retirement of 248

at Sandhurst 3–4, 9, 10

in Scottish Championships
131–2

wounding and death of 294–5

see also Olympic Games 1908
(London), Marathon

Harcourt, Lewis 232

Hardie, Kier 244

Hatch, Sydney 196

Hatton, Fred 216

Hawick Common-Riding Sports
55

Hayes, Alice 45, 136

Hayes (née O'Reilly), Annie 283

Hayes, Dan 45

Hayes, Doris 283

Hayes (née O'Rourke), Ellen, 43, 46

Hayes, Harriet 45, 136

Hayes, John Joseph ('Johnny') viii,
xi, 64, 75, 133–8, 177, 250,
268–9, 272–6, 283–4, 298,
299–300

becomes full-time athlete 52

birth and early life of 43–6, 48, 49

Bloomingdale's job of 52, 63, 136, 245, 251

Boston Marathon and 68, 134, 135–6, 173, 174

coach post of 283

death of 284

House of Commons guest 244

in Ireland 244

London-bound 136–8

marriage of 283

military service of 290

1908 Marathon and 193–4, 210, 212, 213, 217, 218, 224–6, 228, 230–1, 236

Pietri contests Marathon win of 236

Pietri's marathon races with 248, 252–5, 257, 268, 273–5

post-Marathon press coverage of 244–5

post-WWI work of 283–4

at prizegiving ceremony 240, 242

recovery powers of 267–8

subway job taken by 47–8, 50–1

triumphant return to USA of 250–1

Yonkers Marathon and 135

Hayes, Michael 43, 45, 46, 244, 284

Hayes, Philip 45–6

Hayes, Willie 45, 47, 50–1, 64, 136

Head Masters' Conference 176

Hefferon, Charles 196, 213, 215, 216–17, 218, 219, 226, 231

Henderson, Lieutenant 294

Henley Royal Regatta 115

Henry, Prince 212

Herodotus 71

Hicks, Thomas 93–4

Highland Light Infantry 8

Hill, Ron 299

Hillman, Harry 110, 137

Hjertberg, Ernie 135

Hobhouse, Emily 29

Holmer, Hans 271, 283

Hoover, President Herbert C. 283

House of Temperley, The (Conan Doyle) 27, 284

'How the Yankees Beat the World' (McKenna) 245

Hudson Dispatch 283

Hudson, Inspector 186, 210

Hungary 91

Hunter, Charles Val 182

IAFF Road Race Label xii

industrialisation xvii

International Exposition, Paris 81, 82, 100

International Olympic Committee (IOC) xix, 90, 113, 114, 115, 121, 146, 176, 178

International Olympic Congress 70

International Olympic Council 236

Ireland 29, 50
Hayes's post-Marathon visit to 244
Home Rule for 151, 244
see also United States of America: Irish descendants in

Irish-American Athletic Club 135, 152, 244

Irish-Canadian Athletic Club 174

Irish Guards 239

Italian Athletic Federation 78

Italian Hotel and Restaurant Employers' Society 249

Jack the Ripper 2

Jack, Tom 215

Japan 41, 151

Jefferies, Jim 27

Jefferson, Thomas 90

Jeffries, James J. 152

John, Prince 212

Johnson, Jack 27

Kellner, Gyula 73, 74

Kemeny, Ferenc 94

Kern, Jakob 283

Kingsbury, Charles 241

Kipling, Rudyard xvii

Kiralfy, Edgar 151

Kiralfy, Imre 141, 151

Kitchener, Lord 7, 24–5, 27–8, 29, 30, 290

Klegin, Richard C. 283

Knights of Columbus 134

Kraenzlein, Alvin 83

La Patria 15, 18, 31, 80, 127, 128–30 passim

Labry, Hector 271

Laffan, Robert de Courcy 176

Langman, John 26

Langtry, Lillie 180

Lawn Tennis and Croquet Association 113

Lawn Tennis Association 176

le Grant, Millee 142

Leahy, Con 101

Lermusiaux, Albin 73

Liddell, Eric 60

Lightbody, James 111

Liverpool Courier 29

Lloyd George, David 28–9

London Athletic Club 57

London Irish Rugby Club 228

London Olympic Committee 206

Longboat, Tom 134–5, 171–6, 272

   amateur/professional status of

     174–5

   birth and early life of 172

   in Boston Marathon 173

   death of 284

   military service of 284

   1908 Marathon and 191–3,

     194, 209–10, 212, 213–14, 217

   Pietri's races with 259, 260–3,

     266–7

Lord, Fred 182, 196, 211, 215

Lorz, Fred 93, 135

Louis, Spiridon 72, 73–5, 103, 180

Luce 31, 34, 36, 126

McGough, John 60

McGowan, Mayor 250, 251

McGrath, Matt 137

McIsaac, John 60

McKenna, E. P. 245

Madison Square Garden xvi,

   252–5, 257, 260, 270

Mafeking, siege of 21, 37, 38–9

Manchester Guardian 177

Mandrio 13

Maracle, Lauretta 262

Marathon, 1908, *see* Olympic

   Games 1908 (London), Marathon

marathon races (non-Olympic)

   248, 252–5, 257, 259, 260–3,

   266–76, 298–300

   booming popularity of 269–70

   Boston 68, 93, 106, 134, 173,

     194, 299

   fading popularity of 275–6

   Great Derby 272

   Great Hampshire 270

   indoor 270, 271, 283

   London 147, 189, 270, 298

   Manchester 270

   New York City 297

   onboard 270

   Yonkers 135

   see also Hayes, John Joseph;

     Pietri, Dorando

Marathon (town) vii, 72–3, 104

   Pheidippides's legendary

     journey from 71–2

Maricar 139

Mario, Marri 127

Marsh, Lou 173, 193, 261

Mary, Princess 212

MCC 113

Melli, Pasquale 16–17, 18, 35, 36

Memories and Adventures (Conan Doyle) 228

Mercersburg Academy 285

Meredith, Ted 285

Miles, Eustace H. 58

Milo of Croton 66

Mina, Mario Luigi 78

Miselli, Ondino 125, 275, 278–9, 281, 286–7

Miselli, Tullio 125, 127, 129–30, 275, 286

Modena 19

Moore, Charles H. Jr 285

Morrisey, Tom 136, 194, 210, 213

Morse, Franklin B. 274

Murphy, Mike 57, 119, 138, 194, 201, 205, 206

Murri, Augusto 280

Mussabini, Scipio Africanus ('Sam') 58–9, 168

Napoleon I 90

National Athletic Championships 115

Nazzani sweets 16

Nenagh, Tipperary 244

New England Athletic Union 135, 174

New York Athletic Club 57, 135

New York Herald 154, 155

New York Knickerbocker Athletic Club 68

New York Mirror 283

New York Post 268–9

New York Sun 87, 154, 194, 244–5

New York Times 137–8, 156, 160, 162, 204, 246, 250, 253–4, 254–5, 261–2, 269

Newbold, Henry 42

Newton, Arthur 85–6

Newton-Robinson, Charles 114

Niagara Falls 112, 173

Northcliffe, Lord 144

Nurmi, Paavo 177–8

O'Connor, Peter 101

Olga, Queen 98, 180

Olympia 64

Olympic Athletic Club of San Francisco 154

Olympic Games:

amateur versus professional status in 171, 174–8, 195

cheating in 67

Coubertin's plans for shared hosting of 81–2

Coubertin's vision for revival of 70

early history of 65–7

Greeks' wish to be permanent
host of 81, 97
ideals versus reality in 176
Marathon first suggested for
67, 71
origins and first historical
mention of 64–5
rewards for early victors in 67,
175
royal families and 179–87
passim, 212
value and future of 245–6
see also marathon races (non-
Olympic)
Olympic Games Committee 235
Olympic Games 1896 (Athens)
48, 72–5, 100, 171
Marathon during 67, 72–5, 184
Olympic Games 1900 (Paris)
81–7, 94–5, 100, 118
Marathon during 83–7, 184
Olympic Games 1904 (St Louis)
63–4, 89–95, 101, 111, 118
anthropological days during 94
Coubertin's Chicago preference
as venue for 89
Marathon during 92–4, 135,
184
Olympic Games 1906,
Intermediate (Athens) 78,

79–80, 97–9, 101–7, 109–11,
117, 150, 180–1, 201
Marathon during 103–7, 126,
187
Olympic Games 1908 (London)
118–21, 127–8, 150–69,
297–300
American flag and 153–7, 164
Americans' conduct during
160–9, 199–200, 201–8, 238,
242 (*see also* United States of
America: competitive nature of)
'Battle of Shepherd's Bush'
sobriquet of xix, 200
construction of stadium for
145–6
Cook produces rules for 120–1
Desborough's hopes for
management of 118
400 Metres during 199–208,
232, 237, 247
Franco-British Exhibition a
godsend to 143
Irish athletes in 151
London offers to take 115
Marathon during, *see* Olympic
Games 1908 (London), Marathon
national rivalries in 151–7,
160–6
opening of 150–5

planning of 181–90

prizegiving for 238–42

public appeal launched for 144–5

'rehearsal' games precede 146

Rome's withdrawal as host of 113–14

scoring system in 163

sporting archetypes defined by xvii

tug-of-war in 159–62, 168–9

see also White City, London

Olympic Games 1908 (London), Marathon 171–2, 209–19, 221–36, 244, 247, 287

build-up to 209–14

contenders for 191–8

cyclists accompanying runners in 211

distance established at xi, xix

Pietri collapses at end of xvi, 225, 287

Pietri's formal protest over declared result of 236

Pietri's souvenir of 249

planning, distance and route of 181–90

result of 225–6

start of 214

weather forecast for 197

Olympic Games 1912 (Stockholm) 177, 189, 283, 285

Olympic Games 1920 (Antwerp) 190

Olympic Games 1948 (London) xv–xvi

Olympic Games 1952 (Helsinki) 156

Ontario 172

O'Malley, Mr 244

O'Reilly, Annie, *see* Hayes (née O'Reilly), Annie

O'Rourke, Ellen, *see* Hayes (née O'Rourke), Ellen

Orphée, Louis 272

Orwell, George 123

Our Marathon Race (Bee) 272

Oxford–Cambridge boat race 112

Pagliani, Pericle 19–21, 127, 128

Paleschi, Pietro xvii

Pall Mall Gazette 235–6

Papadiamantopoulos, Colonel 72

Paris:

Métro 82

Olympic Games in, *see* Olympic Games 1900

3km race in 78

Payne, Phil 283

Pearman, Superintendent 210

Pelham's Café 258–9, 260

Perry, Charles 145–6

Pheidippides 71–2

Pherenice of Rhodes 66

Philadelphia 136

Pietri (née Dondi), Teresa, *see*
　Dondi, Teresa

Pietri, Antonio 14–15, 16

Pietri, Desiderio 13–16, 21, 34

Pietri, Dorando viii, xi, xv–xvi,
　13–21, 75, 77–80, 115, 125–30,
　140, 142, 159, 247, 249–50,
　271–83, 286–7, 298, 299–300

　amateur status of 176–7, 249

　Arona marathon attempted by
　126–7

　in Berlin song 259–60

　birth and early life of 13–21

　Carpi fled by 282

　Carpi homecoming of 277–8

　Conan Doyle's appeal for 249

　Coray's race with 267

　craft apprenticeship of 16

　cycling and 18–19, 31–4

　death of 283

　Dondi meets 35–6

　farewell races by 286

　fastest marathon of 275

　first international success of 78

　Hayes's marathon races with

　248, 252–5, 257, 268, 273–5

　health worries of 280–1

　hoax concerning xv–xvii, xx

　hotel business of 278–81

　indoor marathon of 271–2

　at Intermediate Games 98,
　103–5, 113

　Italian record captured by 34

　knighthood of 282

　London-bound 130

　Longboat's races with 259,
　260–3, 266–7

　Marathon protest of 235–6

　marriage of 278

　military service of 36, 78–9,
　128, 281, 290–1

　1908 Marathon and 193,
　196–7, 210, 211–14, 215,
　217–19 *passim*, 221–31, 232–3,
　251–2, 287

　Pagliani beaten by 20, 128

　Pagliani beats 127

　at prizegiving ceremony 241–2

　Queen Alexandra's gift to 232,
　236, 241–2, 279–80, 287

　racing accident suffered by 32

　recovery powers of 267, 275

　report of death of 226, 235

　running taken up by 34

　shop job of 17–18

Smallwood's race with 267

solo trial marathon run by 129–30

taxi businesses of 282

training routine of 77

US marathons won by 272

wine intake boasted of 264–5

see also La Patria; Olympic Games 1908 Marathon

Pietri, Maria 13–14, 15

Pietri, Ulpiano 14–15, 18, 141, 210, 221–2, 235, 237, 247, 262–3, 265–6, 269, 275, 280–1

brother shown around London by 140

hotel business of 278–81

London move by 130

Powers contacted by 248

Pilgrim, Paul 110, 111

Pindar 65

Pisidores 66

Pius X 113

Plutarch 71

Polytechnic Harriers 181, 182, 270

Polytechnic Marathon 185

Powers, Pat 248, 252, 260, 263

Price, Jack 213, 215, 216

Queale, William 271

Queen's Westminster Rifles 292

Rampling, Charlotte 60

Rampling, Godfrey 60

Ramsden, Bob 196

Ranelagh Harriers 182

Reggio 17

Religious Tract Society 272

'Reply to Certain Criticisms, A' (Cook) 243

Retford, Ella 142

Return of Sherlock Holmes, The (Conan Doyle) 30

Revere, Paul 68

Rhea 64

Robbins, William 200, 202–4

Roberts, John 270

Roberts, Lord 24

Robertson, George Stuart 69–70, 75

Rome 79, 80, 98, 113

Roosevelt, Alice 93

Roosevelt, Theodore 50, 90, 101, 122, 164, 167, 251

Rose, Ralph 137, 152, 153–6, 162, 250

Royal Academy 2

Royal Albert Hall 271

Royal Guards 212

Royal Gymnasium grounds 55

Royal Irish Rifles 295

Royal Life Saving Society 113

Rules of Sport, The 289

Rules of War, The 289

Russia 122

Rutland, Duchess of 239

Ryan, Michael J. 194

St Bartholomew's Athletic Club 134

St James's Gazette 120

St Louis 89–90

    Olympic Games in, *see*

    Olympic Games 1904

    World Fair 90

St Louis Post Despatch 101

Saint-Mandé Athletic Club 85

St Yves, Henri 272

Salford Harriers 182, 183

San Francisco Chronicle 86

San Jose Sentinel 267–8

San Remo 282

Sandhurst Military Academy 3–4, 9, 10

Sandow, Eugene 144

Schmidt, F. A. 58

Schofield, George 182

Scottish Championships 131–2

Scouting for Boys (Baden-Powell) 41, 42

Sefton Harriers 270

Seligman, Edgar 114

Sheridan, Martin 92, 137, 152, 156–7

Sherring, Jim 105–6

Sherring, William 105–7, 126, 180

Shrubb, Alf 269, 272

Sicilia 80

Siret, J. Henri 270

Skouzes, Georgios 104

Smallwood, Percy 267

Smithson, Forrest 165

Smuts, Jan 28

Snyder, Ted 260

Socrates 65

South Africa xvii, xviii, 4, 7–8, 24–30, 37–40, 195

    Halswelle serves in 7–12, 23–30 *passim*

    see also Boer War; Mafeking, siege of

South London Harriers 183, 270

Sporting Club de Vaugirard 177

Sporting Life 181, 184, 186, 270

Sporting Spirit, The (Orwell) 123

Sportsman 154, 207–8

SS *Baron Castle* 110

SS *Branwen* 110, 114, 117, 118

Stagg, Amos Alonzo 154, 155

Standard 164

Stevenson, Sam 215

Strand Magazine 30
Sullivan, James 90–1, 101, 118, 161–2, 163, 165, 206, 243, 246
Sullivan, John L. 49
Sutherland, Duchess of 239
Svanberg, John 180
Sweden 151, 177

Talbot, Ethelbert 147
Taylor, John B. 138, 200, 202–4, 250
Temperance Bar, Birmingham xvii
Tewkesbury, J. Walter 83, 84
Thames Hare and Hounds 99
Théato, Michel 84–7
Thompson, Frederick 182
Thorpe, Jim 177
Times 119–20, 161, 165, 183, 184, 204, 241, 246, 286, 291
Tincler, G. B. 55
Toronto Globe 262
Toronto Star 173
Training of the Body, The (Schmidt, Miles) 58
Turin 36

United States of America xviii, 14, 41, 63–4
  athletes of, at 1908 Games 152
  competitive nature of 99–101,

118–19, 150, 242, 245 (*see also* Olympic Games 1908 (London): Americans' conduct during
  early marathons staged in 67–8
  flag of 151–7, 164
  Irish descendants in 43, 44, 48, 49, 51, 57, 91, 151, 153, 162 (*see also* Hayes, John Joseph)
  London Athletic Club's competition with 57
  Paris Olympics team sent by 83
  return of 1908 Games squad to 243
  track and field events won by 244
  training methods of 57
  unfairness accusations of, against British 160, 243, 245
  see also New York Athletic Club; Olympic Games 1908 (London): Americans' conduct during
United States Olympic Committee 90

Vanderbilt, Cornelius 144
Varese 104
Vasilakos, Kharilaos 74
Velouis, Demeter 93

INDEX

Venn, Harry 182
Verri, Francesco 104
Vesuvius 113–14
Victoria, Queen xvii, 289
Victoria's 286–7
'*Vitai Lampada*' (Newbold) 42
Vittorio Emanuele, King 79, 113

Wales, Prince of 139, 144, 146,
    180, 187
Wales, Princess of 98, 146, 180,
    187, 212, 214
Walker, Reggie 58–9, 168
walking races 181
war, conduct of 122, 289–90
*War in South Africa: Its Cause and
    Conduct, The* (Conan Doyle)
    26, 30
Warburton, Choppy 33–4
'Ward Marathon', Toronto 172
Wells, H. G. 289–90
Welton, Elton 195
Wembley Stadium 183
Westminster, Duchess of 240
Westmorland Gazette 215
White City, London 139–47, 183
White, Jack 57
Wigginton, Charles 177
Wilhelm II, Kaiser 250, 289
Windsor and Eton Express 183, 186,

192–3, 196, 197–8, 215, 216,
    217, 219
Windsor Castle 184
Windsor, Dean of 212
Winter, Arthur 185
Wolverhampton Express and Star 29
Woodring, Allen 285
World Championships (Leipzig)
    241
World War I 28, 87, 122, 281,
    289–95
Wyatt, Alf 196
Wyoming 270

Yaldon, J. 172